THE *Silver* TEA SERVICE

JUDY CAMPBELL

THE SILVER TEA SERVICE

A Memoir

by

JUDY CAMPBELL

© Judy Campbell 2019

First published by the kind press, 2019

The moral rights of the author have been asserted. All rights reserved. No part of this book may be reproduced, stored in a retrieval system or transmitted in any form or by any means, electronic, mechanical photocopying, recording, or otherwise, without prior written permission.

This is a work of creative nonfiction. The events are portrayed to the best of Judy Campbell's memory. While all stories in this book are true, some identifying details have been changed to protect the privacy of the people involved.

Printed in Australia, South Africa, UK, and USA.

Co-published with Story Solutions Pty Limited t/a Joanne Fedler Media
Cover and design by Ida Jansson
Cover concept by Nailia Minnebaeva
Editing by Shelley Kenigsberg
Author photo by Mark Zworestine
Cover image by Dean Ginsburg

National Library of Australia Cataloguing-in-Publication data:
ISBN 978-0-6485917-0-2 (Paperback)
ISBN 978-0-6485917-2-6 (Ebook)

*For my mother, June Campbell.
May she rest in peace.*

Contents

Author's Note   9
Prologue   11

THE SILVER TEA SERVICE   13
DOWNWARD   17
CHILDHOOD'S END   22
ONCE UPON A TIME   26
THE INSCRIPTION   31
BLIND SEARCHING   37
BURY IT   43
THE ARCHIVES DELIVER   47
THE PORTRAITS   52
HEILBRON   55
JOHAN   60
WHOSE STORY?   64
IN SERVICE OF FEAR   68
MOTHERS AND CHILDREN   78
THE GIFT OF A MAJOR CHORD   89
THE DARK YEARS   94
SURVIVAL   109
FLIGHT   121
LANDING   126
A PLACE ON THE TREE   133
MARY ANN   141
THE WAR THAT CHANGED EVERYTHING   147
FINDING ROSIE   157

ROSIE'S WAR	160
THE WAR ENDS	168
LIFE AND DEATH AFTER THE WAR	172
PRIME SUSPECT	180
THE BANK	193
SURRENDER TO THE FAMILY TREE	197
THE FALL	204
THE ROAD TO MASERU	221
MY NANNY, IDA	235
COUNTRY	246
DIFFERENT KINDS OF FAMILY	251
WHO DONE IT?	259
FINAL CHORDS	270
Epilogue	*278*
Acknowledgements	*281*
Appendix 1: Chronicles of the early Luyt Family	*285*
Appendix 2: The Presidents who entered the Boer War	*295*
Appendix 3: The curious tale of 'Captain' Weilert	*299*
About the author	*303*
Bibliography	*304*
References	*305*
Notes	*307*

Author's Note

When I started writing this book, and still thought the story was exclusively a history of the Luyt family, I assumed that doing the research would verify the accuracy of the historical characters' stories. It would just take time, care and perseverance. Over a period of eight years, I have given the project all of these things and amassed vast amounts of documentation. I've cross-checked, and in some cases corrected, genealogical information I've received from a range of sources. In addition to years at my computer screen, I've spent weeks in archives, museums and libraries, travelled twice to New Zealand and multiple times to South Africa.

Yet, still, there were small mysteries that resisted my probing. There were times when I could find no recorded evidence supporting the movement between two observable points in the story of one or other character.

I studied the broader historical, physical and emotional circumstances in which they lived, alongside the records and stories of family members. In the spirit of bringing their stories to life, and based on my understanding of them gained from research, I invented scenes and dialogue to depict how I believe they would have responded to the unfolding events of their lives.

I have, at all times, approached the writing with empathy for those concerned, and a sincere desire to describe events as accurately as possible.

If any reader has information that contradicts anything presented in these pages, I apologise for the error(s), and would be grateful to receive the correct information.

Judy Campbell
JULY 2019

PROLOGUE

You can run away from many things. In my personal flights, first from my family and then my country, I never looked back. No pillar of salt for me.

You can find relief in the distance, straighten yourself out and build a new life of substance and meaning. Then tragedy strikes and the seal on your private can of worms springs a leak. Still, you get some therapy, stuff those critters back in there and apply some chewing gum to the rim.

Then you start to write a book you think is about someone else. Next thing the squishy little buggers are creeping all over your desk and into your dreams.

THE SILVER TEA SERVICE

In 1969, we moved to Hillcrest, the too-expensive house on the hill in Camps Bay, Cape Town, with an unobstructed, 180-degree view of the magnificent sunsets over the Atlantic Ocean. A silver family relic beheld our domestic writhing from its perch in the metal fireplace, in which we never once built a fire.

My mother grumbled every week, but continued to polish the grooves and flounces on the tray, teapot, coffee pot, sugar bowl and milk jug that comprised the antique tea service. You'd expect that from an angel.

But solid silver is high maintenance near the sea. After some months, she packed the frillier items away, leaving out the large, more easily polished, tray. It bore an inscription that had something to do with some ancestor of hers. I wasn't interested, and didn't ask where the tea service came from, when it had arrived, or why she wanted to display it in our living room.

Some years before, my mother's mother, Granny Grace, had moved into my brother's room in our house-before-Hillcrest for my mother to nurse her after she'd had a stroke. He had to share my bedroom and we fought continuously, increasing my mother's stress. Ida, our nanny, was of course there to take care of us. My grandfather, who for some reason we very English children called "Oupa", (Afrikaans for grandpa), accompanied my critically ill grandmother to Cape Town.

My grandparents had lived in Durban, where we visited infrequently, making the trip from Cape Town by train. I have few memories of these visits. One is how I'd irritated my mother by washing my hands every twenty minutes in the tiny hand basin in our leather-scented sleeper compartment. Another is a table-top view, as a mesmerised four-year-old, of Granny Grace cutting pills in half with a razor blade — a scattering of white ones with red and green speckles and others of different sizes and shapes. I also recall how my brother, Mike, and I would feast in their sprawling mulberry tree until we were sick, the purple, laundry-defiant juice trickling down our chins onto our clothes.

To us, Granny Grace was a distant, intimidating woman and Mike recalls her as a "vile harridan" who took pleasure in frightening him with terrible stories.

Grace May Heering died sitting up in Mike's bed on 25 May 1964, two weeks after arriving at our house. She had another stroke between spoons of porridge, it seems, when my mother left the room for a couple of minutes to fetch a napkin from the kitchen downstairs. A small quantity of porridge from the last mouthful my mother had spooned in trickled down her chin. She was sixty-nine.

By the time Mike and I came home from school that day, all traces of her had disappeared from his bedroom. The smells of medicines, bed baths and balms that had gathered in the corners of the room were gone, eliminated by our nanny, Ida, and her arsenal of cleaning fluids, sprays and brushes. We were told that Granny had taken a bad turn early in the morning, was taken to hospital and died soon thereafter.

There was no suggestion that the children should attend any ceremony. So Granny Grace just vanished and Oupa returned to

Durban. She is buried there, so he must have taken her body back with him on the train. I assume my mother made the trip with him and attended the funeral. It's unlikely that my father accompanied her. His relentless life as a working musician and composer would have exempted him from something as banal as supporting his wife as she buried her mother. And he had a beautiful young assistant to help him endure his wife's absence.

I never saw the tea service at the old house. A few years later, Oupa moved to Cape Town, and must have brought Grace's family heirloom with him to take up its sentinel position in the centre of our troubled new home.

Oupa moved into a residential hotel — one of a very few elderly gents among lonely old ladies. His room was small, with no wardrobe space for silverware. Perhaps time had come anyway to relinquish such links to Grace and her past. As a man now in his eighties, he had to turn his attention to other priorities in his living space, like attaching carefully cut pieces of foam rubber to corners and edges to avoid sustaining injuries if he bumped into things. There seemed to be a great many such edges in his room.

Oupa was a great walker, and for years was to be seen most sunny days strolling the promenade of Sea Point beachfront with one or other lady on his arm.

Once a week my mother would bring him to spend the day at our house, where he would sit on the sofa next to the fireplace, newspaper still firmly open in his hands, his head tilted back and his mouth wide open, fast asleep. Grace's silver tray looked on.

"Hi," I'd say quietly on return from school, hoping he wouldn't wake up.

"Cor," he'd say. "Must have nodded off."

Here come the dumb, old-person questions about my important teenage life, I thought. *He'll never understand, or approve, if I answer him truthfully.*

What I'd give now for an afternoon with him.

As a child, I'd idolised my father and adored my mother. But, at age twelve, my life had started to unravel and within two years I felt all grown up. Others thought I was too. We were all wrong.

The descent into the dark years of our family accelerated during the year of 1971 and my brother's absence for compulsory military training after he completed high school. Apart from a short stretch between the army and going on the road as a musician, Mike never returned to the family home. The relationship that drawing together as siblings on the Hillcrest battlefield might have achieved, did not develop.

I moved out in early 1975, at seventeen, a few weeks after completing high school. It had been a swift, confronting adolescence and a high school career impaired by adult concerns, drugs, alcohol and deep sadness. I'd tried to be my mother's angel-assistant, to prop her up, and persuade her to leave, but had to concede that my efforts to vanquish my father's hold over her had failed. During the dark years, she and I had somehow managed to forge a deep, enduring bond, and together created memories I would always cherish, but I chose escape for my own survival.

The silver tray, polished less often now, had witnessed a great deal in our living room.

DOWNWARD

The first things to unravel were unrelated to my family.
I'd been studying music at school from an early age and had sped through two grades per year instead of one for the previous three years. My teacher had a fervent faith in my abilities. I turned in distinction after distinction; he kept pushing. By my final year in primary school I was starting Grade Eight of the Royal Schools of Music, blissfully unaware that this was the grade usually undertaken by high school students in their final, matriculation year.

One day my teacher vanished. Because I was a senior, known to be his "special" student, I was told it was because he'd been touching several of the children inappropriately and they had gradually reported the incidents to their parents. There had been cautious approaches between parents, who then formed a posse and went to the school with their justifiable raft of complaints. My teacher was gone the same day.

For me, except for a passing unease one day, which was mostly embarrassment on my part, there'd never been any other hint of impropriety. He had put a congratulatory hand on my shoulder and commented when he felt a bra strap under my school uniform. He was right — I didn't need one of those. My chest remained woefully flat as my friends sprouted wondrous bulges and the playground conversation was all about underwear.

For him to be abusive was unimaginable to me.

This incident later struck me as relatively mild in the arena of child molestation, though certainly inappropriate. His behaviour hadn't impacted me directly, but it left the first dent in the child's trust I'd had in adults.

For several weeks, all music lessons were suspended while they sought a new teacher. I knew what he'd done was wrong, but still I grieved for my lost teacher, my musical champion and his pride in me. I never saw him again.

At my first lesson, the new teacher was horrified. "This is not right," she clucked. She contacted my mother to say that she was not qualified to teach this level and I couldn't continue as her student.

My mother took me to the Music Department at Cape Town University. "This is not right." they clucked. "Find a private teacher and come back in a few years."

A private teacher was found. She lived a few streets away from the bottom of our hill and right next door to the home of another of her students, one Mark Ginsburg who would, much later, become my husband. I dragged myself to her house weekly, possibly passing my thirteen-year-old future husband in the hallway between lessons, but as the year proceeded to its end, I couldn't deny the musical spark was gone.

Other events, however, would derail my classical piano career entirely. My mother, knowing that the scoliosis that affected her might reappear in her daughter, had started watching me closely. Scoliosis tends to surface around puberty and mostly in girls. One day towards the end of 1969, and my primary school life, she had me stand in front of her and lift my shirt while she circled me.

Finally, she said, "I'd like to take you to see a back specialist."

A few weeks and many waiting rooms later, the diagnosis was confirmed: scoliosis with a 45-degree lumbar curve and a slightly smaller thoracic curve creating an S-bend. My mother was distraught that she hadn't noticed my now obviously skew hips, even though she knew the condition could emerge rapidly during growth spurts.

I didn't blame her, not then, not ever, for her genetic legacy. It would have been like blaming her for her lovely blue eyes.

My mother's own scoliosis was severe. Treatment with a simple brace during her teens hadn't persuaded her crooked skeleton to grow straight. Her main curve was thoracic and pushed her right shoulder blade out of position, resulting in a sizeable hump. Her spine was so crooked; at her full height she was twelve centimetres shorter than she should have been. The bottom of her rib cage rested on her hipbones, with her internal organs doing their best to function in the remaining reduced cavity. To add to this distress, a doctor had indicated a life expectancy of around fifty years of age, due to the challenge faced by her compromised lungs.

It was a miracle of anatomy that her head ended up centred at the top of her body.

Yet, it always amazed me how people wouldn't notice the hump at all. She made many of her own clothes and was expert at minimising it. The combination of her head being in the right spot, her sewing expertise, her great attractiveness and lovable personality meant that this significant deformity stayed in the background.

In the summer of 1969, my own body would undergo a massive process. I spent most days of my school holiday in front of X-ray machines, wrapped for hours in Plaster of Paris so technicians could craft a brace by working with a mould of my torso rather than my physical body. Even now, the smell of Plaster of Paris takes me straight back to that fitting room.

The Milwaukee brace is a type of brace sometimes recommended to slow the progression of spinal curvatures like scoliosis. They hoped this treatment would avoid the alternative: surgery to rod and fuse my spine. They said I had to wear it 23 hours a day for a year, and remove it only to shower or to swim, the only exercise I was permitted.

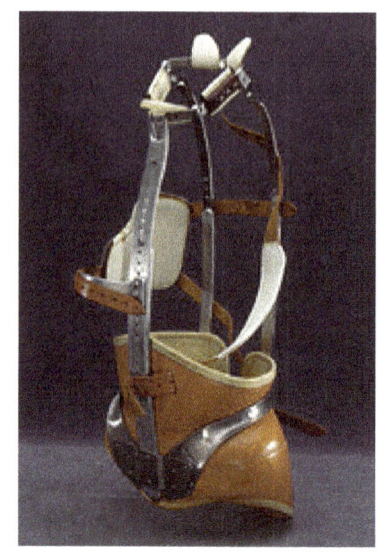

I began doing laps every day, swimming as far as I could in order to stay out of that thing for as long as possible. I slept on my back; no other way was viable. I'd started ballet at age four, but now I could no longer dance or play sport of any kind. I couldn't walk any significant distance at all; the chin piece of the neck ring rattled my teeth as it banged up against my jaw. My mother became my daily chauffeur to Camps Bay High School and to the public pool. She applied her sewing skills to make me clothes that accommodated and camouflaged the brace. It dug into my thighs at the bottom and at the top raised my chin. If I'd really been on fire about playing classical piano perhaps I would have found a way, but this new development delivered the deathblow to my piano lessons.

I started high school in the brace in 1970 and spent half of that school year standing out in the hallway. Rebellion and misbehaviour replaced the camaraderie of the sports field and dance studio as a way to find my place with other kids. I shared the hallway with other naughty ones, sent out of the classroom by frustrated teachers. This new role, so unlike my previous one of high achiever in primary school, elicited a weird kind of respect from my peers. It was better than pity.

To sit and study was uncomfortable, and with the chunks of lessons I was missing, my results plummeted. But my growth increased. It and my straightening spine meant a rapid height increase, moving my chin further away from the neck ring. Every few months, as comfort increased slightly, it would be adjusted to bring the neck ring back up to my chin to maintain the stretch on my spine.

At the end of the year I went back to the specialist having done everything they'd prescribed, and counting the hours to my liberation. He peered at the X-rays. "You've done so well and both curves are much less pronounced." Then he added, "Just another year should do it."

His words, unaccompanied by counselling or compassion, flung me right back to the beginning of the treatment, only now I knew very well what lay ahead. I'd paced myself over my thirteenth year, holding out for that moment of my release. I knew I'd earned it. For it to be ripped away as I reached for it was an unbearable betrayal by an adult. My trust sustained another dent.

I observed my mother fighting to hold back tears, and dug deeper than ever to appear stoic, to feign acceptance so as to soften her pain. In retrospect, it was one of the first steps on what would be the long path of role reversal with my mother.

A black fog gathered around my heart. From the earliest months of wearing the brace, I couldn't and didn't wish to explain to friends what it was like. I couldn't keep up with them physically, or join in the activities around which bonds of teenage friendship are forged. I spent more time with my parents and their friends. I swam, alone, further and further.

CHILDHOOD'S END

The next year, my second in high school, changed everything and hastened the premature transition into adulthood.

"I wasn't sure you'd be home," my mother said, frowning.

She was poised for departure in the hallway, wearing an avocado-green suit and holding a matching handbag.

"Come with us," she urged.

I glanced down at the jeans and T-shirt I'd been wearing for three days, likely to be harbouring vestiges of cigarette and marijuana smoke. My mother produced a smile as my dad came down the stairs patting a jangling pocket of keys.

"June, are you ready? We should go. Hi Judy."

Even if they could have waited while I showered and changed, I couldn't face spending Christmas Day with advertising executives and the other flamboyant species inhabiting my parents' world these days.

"I'll be fine," I said.

What was I expecting — roast turkey and presents? Though this was a time long before mobile phones, I could have called from a public phone to let them know my plans. But even at fourteen there was no such demand of me.

In the empty house, I made myself a scrambled egg for lunch. Even now I relive its lonely aroma.

My fourteenth year was also the year of an encounter with lesbianism. For several years there had been another person, more or less, in our family. Norina worked at my dad's studio; first as a young secretary then later as his personal assistant, becoming a central cog in the studio machine. Her knowledge and expertise spanned accounts, music and film production, client management and more. She was exotic, with perfect brown skin, huge brown eyes and long silky black hair. She was sixteen years older than me, interested and loving like a big sister, and she always looked out for my interests.

Norina lived in a flat in a nearby suburb, but was often at our house. I was often at the studio too, hanging out with my mother, helping with music copying, and I'd also started singing at recording sessions for radio jingles or soundtracks for cinema ads. She always made me feel special. At Hillcrest, my dad's music room doubled as a spare room, and Norina often stayed there over weekends.

Mike left for his compulsory military service, despite my mother's efforts to get him excused, or at least into the navy, considered to be the best of a bad spread of options. My parents were appalled to have their son serving a political system they totally opposed.

After he left, Norina would use his bedroom on weekends.

Soon, instead of just Norina at our house on weekends, there was also Tara — burly, with short, straw coloured hair and broad shoulders. She was pleasant to everyone and I had no quarrel with her. But her arrival on the scene catalysed a stream of critical events and revelations.

One day I strolled into Mike's room to ask Norina something. I knew in a millisecond that their sensual embrace was evidence of something I'd vaguely heard of. I fled, dumbstruck and embarrassed, as they looked up with dreamy faces. I'd had no idea that this was the nature of their relationship, but now thought, *Of course*, as I considered the cues I'd missed. I asked my mother who, without inviting any discussion, confirmed that they were in a lesbian relationship.

The novelty of observing this relationship pulled me, for the first time since the start of my second year in the brace, out of my state of resentful self-pity. They were less guarded now, and my senses were out on stalks, poised to detect every nuance of behaviour. Norina and Tara's sexy affection for one another fascinated me. So this was okay with my parents? *That was open-minded*, I thought. *Cool.*

But in the months that followed, in this heightened state of perception, I also noticed my father's behaviour. He hovered around Norina and Tara, his manner unnatural and forced. He sighed and brooded. And ignored me.

I had always basked in the rays of my father's love. We were fellow adventurers. At the frequent parties at Hillcrest in the pre-brace era, he would put on the "West Side Story Suite" by the Buddy Rich Band and we'd improvise a dance to it. By the big finish we'd be sweating and triumphant, surrounded by glamorous grown-ups beaming and applauding. I felt I was the most important person in his world.

Who was this sullen, uncommunicative man, and what had he done with my dad? I knew I was too grown up now for the crazy childhood games, and severely limited by the brace, but as I started my second year of high school, I missed him.

A viscous atmosphere hung in the house. I watched and waited for it to pass. Yet trouble hovered, oppressive and all around, just beyond my range of understanding. On occasion Tara would draw me to a quiet corner of the garden and conspiratorially light up a joint. By then I knew what marijuana was, but hadn't encountered it. I was afraid to refuse when she held it to my lips and looked hard into my eyes, so I puffed lightly on the roughly rolled marijuana cigarette mixed with tobacco. I coughed, which seemed to amuse her. None of it felt right, but she frightened me, so I said nothing to anyone.

I spent more time in my room, finding ways to prop up books so I could read lying down and resting, frequently fatigued by the constant traction of the brace. There was even solace to be found in homework, which at least delivered some benefits. My results improved; I even conceded that a few aspects of schoolwork were a bit interesting. I went to school, swam daily and kept my head down. My mother seemed preoccupied and distant and I couldn't summon the courage to ask, "What the hell is going on?"

After months of watching and waiting, I could no longer deny that Norina represented a new, juicier piece of fruit on my father's tree and that he was desperately jealous about her relationship with Tara.

And somehow, out of my sight, he wooed Norina away from Tara. I no longer saw them at Hillcrest. I also no longer saw much of my father.

My contemporaries at school seemed to have many siblings, cousins and other family, but we had no relatives in Cape Town except for my ancient grandfather, who was born in 1888 and seemed not to have progressed to the twentieth century. Mike was in the army and my two sets of uncles and aunts lived far away. I barely knew them at that time, and had no awareness of any family beyond them. My mother and I circled each other warily and stuck to safe topics across the dinner table. Friends my age were occupied with netball and hockey, boys, new clothes that did not have to accommodate a metal brace, and the acquisition of bigger bras.

It had taken around eighteen months for me to plummet from a successful, happy child with a unique and exciting family, to a lonely, brooding outsider tumbling in dark water while a tsunami raged overhead. It would rage for another four years, and take as many decades for me to make any sense of it.

ONCE UPON A TIME

Our family had been happier.
When I was very small my dad gave me a nickname that stuck for years: Tubby Diamond. I was a stocky toddler. The name was always used affectionately, and continued long after I'd outgrown the chubbiness. The diamond part speaks for itself. He delighted in whatever talents I displayed, and welcomed my willingness to follow the creative pathways he'd clear for me. He taught me to play one of his piano compositions when my pudgy little hands could barely hold a pencil. I was thrilled, chest puffed, though I didn't yet know the word "honoured". "You are the apple of my eye," he'd say and make up games that had us careening around the house shrieking and laughing while we looked for objects to tie to ideas. No other dads I knew played like this with their kids. His life as a musician made him more available to Mike and I during the day, and his being out at night didn't impact us too much.

My mother was fun too, a blonde bombshell who was also the ultimate "Tuckshop Mum". She volunteered every week and would always buy us something special to add to our lunch boxes, though they already contained her superior sandwiches, which were always excellent playground currency. She sewed costumes for school plays and helped us with homework.

My brother, four years older than me, already showed talent as a kid. By the time he was twelve, he played trumpet in the mostly adult Cape Town Philharmonic Orchestra. He and my dad, playing flugelhorn, conscripted me at eight to supply the bottom end of a brass trio, ostensibly so that Mike could get more practice. My dad had acquired a double B flat tuba that was almost as tall as me. They perched it across the arms of an armchair and lifted me onto the back of the chair so I could stretch my right arm over the instrument to reach the valves. The mouthpiece covered half my face and I blew as hard as I could to create the oompah bass notes. There was a lot of laughter at our rehearsals.

Mike moved from trumpet to bassoon and then to the bass guitar that would herald his entry into professional music at age fourteen. A trail of musical instruments littered our house.

Then there was our nanny, Ida. She had started work for my mother's family when she was still a teenager. She raised my mother, and when my mother married my father, Ida went to live with and work for them. She and my mother worked side-by-side in the kitchen, though Ida did most of the other domestic work. She was a second mother to us. There was no shortage of love in our household.

Nor were we short of money in those exciting early days. My father, together with a few partners, had established a recording studio in Cape Town. The symphony orchestra often recorded film scores there; a studio big band recorded a weekly radio jazz program that my dad hosted. The first money I earned, at six years old, was from preparing my dad's orchestral score sheets, obliterating — with a thick, black pen — the labels of instruments not relevant for a particular recording from each page of the hefty score pad. It might be fourth trombone, or sometimes piccolo or French horn. It helped him, he said, as he turned the pages, to see only those instruments for which he was writing. He paid me four cents a page for these patient labours. I would have done it for free, I was so proud, but the pocket money added extra sheen.

There was no stopping the studio as it grew and branched into film. At forty, my dad taught himself to use a 35mm movie camera and within two years our family swooned with pride at his first gold medal for a cinema commercial at the Cannes Film Festival. The fancy overseas family holiday to Europe came when I was nine, by which time I knew the difference between a good and a mediocre smoked salmon.

My dad had a jazz trio that performed regularly to wide acclaim. When I was eleven, he had me come and sing Gershwin's "Summertime" with them at a concert. It was the first time I sang in public and as I walked down the centre aisle of the packed hall to the stage, terror absorbed every vestige of moisture from my lips to my larynx. The performance itself has mercifully disappeared from my memory, but the surrounding excitement was heady stuff. Adults of all colours beamed at me afterwards, and the image of my father's glowing face made me smile yet again that night as I fell asleep, far later than my schoolmates would have done on a Sunday evening.

Around this time my mother, his excellent music copyist, started teaching me her skills, unaware that computers would one day render her art obsolete. We would sit at the dining table, score sheets spread out, and pen the individual parts for first, second, third violins, trumpets and flutes from the pencil scratchings on the score. Sometimes there were items we simply could not fathom. She would shake her head, and approach the source. He was usually hermetically sealed in his music room with the heater on, chain-smoking cigars as he worked. My mother would take a deep breath, nose wrinkled in anticipation of the hot tobacco-stench, and enter without enthusiasm.

She was picky and always checked my work. It wasn't acceptable if the stem of a note didn't join with the note head, or the multiple tails on groups of hemi-demi-semi-quavers were not perfectly separated.

There were occasions when my time-oblivious father ran so late that he'd have to bundle the score, the unfinished orchestra parts, my mother and I into the car and head for the studio. On those occasions, the orchestra would be recording the early sections of a score in the studio while my mother and I sat in an adjoining office, pens flying on the parts for the later sections.

I was a prefect in my senior year of primary school, first in class, had made the school netball team and was a proficient enough pianist to accompany the hymns at morning assembly. I had shifted from ballet to modern dancing and started scooping up a few trophies.

That year we moved into Hillcrest, overcoming my father's protest that it was too expensive. I had a young girl belief in his success and that there would always be plenty to fuel the shimmering fantasy of my family life. Hillcrest was a spectacular house, where my parents held all-night jazz parties populated by famous people of all shades. I never heard the words, 'It's past your bedtime'.

I didn't care that it was now much further to walk to school. It was fun to cross the Little Glen each morning and afternoon, sometimes meeting friends along the way. There was no question in those days of it being unsafe for an eleven-year-old girl to walk by herself through dense foliage, hidden from the sight of any road or house.

Film people started to join the regular crowd of jazz people in our house. When legendary film director David Lean came to Cape Town to film the beach scenes in "Ryan's Daughter", he used my dad's studio as a base for the six weeks of filming. The farewell party was at Hillcrest. I was awed at the presence of movie stars Trevor Howard and Sarah Miles in my house, but too young to be impressed by a mere film director, even if he was the maker of "Lawrence of Arabia".

On muggy summer nights, that first year at Hillcrest, we would drag the mattresses off our beds onto the huge terrace onto which our three bedrooms opened. There was not a single such night during which the chilly mist didn't creep up the hill to engulf us.

These were some of the last memories I have of a happy, functional family, retreating shivering and laughing with our mattresses into our bedrooms.

THE INSCRIPTION

In 1975, some months after I finished school and moved out of home, my parents, reduced in circumstances and resilience through the disastrous financial outcomes of a misguided feature film project, downsized to a corrugated iron bungalow on Glen Beach. Though it was still in Camps Bay, charming and right on the beach, it was a quarter the size of Hillcrest and built from demolished World War I barracks. Their new home had only an outside toilet, slanted floors and no hot water in the tiny kitchen.

During the move, the silver tea service experienced a moment of peril. Not its first, as I was to learn much later.

"What am I keeping this old thing for?" my mother asked of no one in particular. "It's just another chore, and there's nowhere to put it."

I didn't have an answer, and hadn't noticed on my infrequent-as-possible visits that it was no longer on display. I didn't know then that she had taken it to a dealer, filled with resolve to sell it. The valuation, however, was less than she'd hoped, so she wrapped it all up again, packed it into the back of another wardrobe for the next thirteen years, and its next moment of peril.

"Am I really going to take this with me?" June asked herself once again as she packed up her things at Glen Beach in 1988 to relocate to Sydney, Australia, where my husband, Mark, and I had been living since 1982.

A letter from my mother to an old friend, who gave it to me years after June's death, revealed that my mother had decided that she wanted to live wherever I was. The information caught in my throat, while a more cynical inner voice chimed in, *I'll bet she did.*

She and my father, miraculously still together, after a fashion, and solvent in spite of all, would contribute to the purchase of a "tribal home" in Lindfield. This would require something like a granny flat to accommodate my mother and also support periodic lengthy visits from my father. Our son, Dean, two years old at the time, would be raised by a mini version of a multi-generational village, inspired by traditional Africa.

With some trepidation, we agreed that Mark and I would seek a property to facilitate this arrangement. Despite my initial resistance to the suburbs, we found a patch of heaven in Lindfield in what felt like the secret recesses of a rainforest. June would have a permanent claim to the granny flat across the driveway from the house. It would be a challenge during the periods of my father's visits, but was spacious enough for June on her own.

My father still had an active film and sound studio in Cape Town, and an ongoing relationship with Norina. Each one of the strange trio agreed that my father would spend a few months at a time in each country. By then, the two women had achieved an extraordinary level of friendship, under the circumstances. Nothing about their lives was standard, and both women relished the thought of having breaks from my difficult father.

The silent silver witness arrived with my mother at the granny flat on the leafy North Shore of Sydney. Though cupboard space was limited, my mother managed to store this bulky item without my notice for another fifteen years.

A few months after my mother's death in 2002, pressure mounted to clear and renovate her flat for its next occupant: our teenage son, Dean. I still couldn't bear the pain of going through her things, hints of her favourite perfume still clinging. The kinder portion of this pain welled up as sorrow at her death at just seventy, robbing her of the years in which she had intended to enjoy her grandchildren and record the past. The darker portion seethed in the pit of my stomach at the characteristic indecisiveness that for two decades paralysed her intention to write her stories. She'd spoken about it for years, how she would change the shape of her life to make time to capture her colonial memories, and her mother's; how important they were to her. It was reminiscent of how she'd spoken during the dark years at Hillcrest about changing her life. The new failure reached back and pressed painfully on the older one.

Instead of exploring her family's past, she served *my* family in ways remembered by us all with love — elaborate birthday cakes, glittering handmade gig outfits, favourite meals, good company and countless domestic contributions. Not a word was written. It galled me now that she had missed that opportunity. And that she resisted my attempts, too late, to facilitate her writing.

An oxygen machine had supported her for a full decade before her death. She had been critically ill with respiratory failure twice during that period and on both occasions bounced back to a level of health beyond medical understanding.

"You should be dead with these oxygen readings," the nurse said, soon after my mother emerged from intensive care.

"But I feel perfectly normal," she replied.

I knew she was unlikely to reach eighty, but thought we still had time.

Her relics crossed the driveway to the house, joining the throng of old-things-that-should-be-thrown-away in the back of other wardrobes.

Two oil portraits were among the items that made the crossing. I wondered, with a flick of irritation, if the subjects of the paintings might be my mother's legendary grandparents. The patient tea service also made that crossing. It was still wrapped in the pages of the November 1975 *Cape Argus* in which it had left Hillcrest.

My father passed away six years later, dramatically, as was his way, having moved permanently to Australia the year before my mother died. His final years would feature four women, including June and Norina. The final cancer-ridden months of his life were filled with pain and angst, for him and for the rest of us.

I still hadn't been able to face going through my mother's things, but the arrival of my father's more voluminous belongings forced me to re-evaluate the items already consuming storage space in our house.

I unwrapped the tea service.

It looked valuable. The inscription on the heavy tray was a dedication to my mother's grandfather, but I didn't have my glasses on and still didn't read it properly. It was my turn to imperil the stoic family relic. Maybe it could fund the purchase of a new lounge suite. At least we'd use that.

The quote I got from the city auctioneer confirmed the set was valuable, but it wasn't enough to precipitate an immediate sale.

"I'll think about it," I told him.

I paused, as I prepared fresh tissue paper to wrap and reinstall the pieces at the back of the wardrobe.

"What're you doing?" asked Mark.

"I just thought I'd set it out before packing it away. Do you suppose people actually used this? It would have been a nightmare to keep clean."

"Maybe they kept it for special occasions."

I put on my reading glasses and looked at the inscription on the tray. Did I imagine a quiver of anticipation run through the metal surface?

PRESENTED TO
J.G. LUYT ESQ.
MEMBER OF THE
Hon.ble Volksraad O.F.State
BY THE INHABITANTS OF HEILBRON
as a token of their appreciation of his services to the Town
AS MEMBER OF THE ABOVE BODY.
ALSO
AS LORD MAYOR, 1899.

Lord Mayor was obvious, but I didn't know what the rest of it referred to, though I found the antiquity impressive. I thought the word "Volksraad" meant "Council of the People". Heilbron was a little town somewhere up in the interior of South Africa, devoid of interest, where Afrikaners lived in profusion. Nothing to do with me. Apartheid was anathema in our family, and something that existed beyond our front door. Those who supported it, never mind those responsible for it, beyond my comprehension.

This huge tray was part of my mother's story, not mine, but a tug of obligation held on. As my gaze moved over the fancy lettering, I didn't notice old patterns from our Hillcrest days slipping into my psyche. She wanted to find out more about the story, she'd said, and write about it, but she couldn't do it. I would try, at least a little, to fix this omission for her. It was her family. I knew almost nothing and had no idea where to start. Sour with resentment, perhaps mixed with a fleck of guilt, I set up a dedicated space in our spare bedroom in which to gather what I could find about this man, my mother's grandfather Johan. Who was he, and was there any truth in the sad half-story Granny Grace had told my mother of his financial ruin and early death? I resolved to try to find out before selling the tea service. No more than that.

Then life, in all its moments of phantom importance and real priorities, thundered on. Bereavement immobilises the most stalwart and any number of distractions overshadow dubious stories of ancestors in distant locations of low appeal.

"Are you ever going to do anything in there?" Mark asked about a year later. "Your parents' stuff is really cluttering up the house."

"I know, I know," I snapped.

The flame burned just enough to fuel a diversion for research during a trip with Mark and our grown-up son, Dean, to visit family in South Africa in 2011. I looked forward to putting this damn story to rest.

BLIND SEARCHING

"I don't like the idea of you driving around country roads on your own," said Mark. "Let's all just travel together."

"Okay. Thanks." I hadn't liked the idea myself. "It'll only take a few days."

It was a first, bumbling attempt to see if I could find graves, buildings, anything relevant to my mother's ancestors. Maybe, just maybe, I could put my questions to rest. But I didn't know what exactly I was looking for, or where to look for it. It was like picking with tweezers at the edges of a mountainous haystack, but I had resolved to try, and this was me trying.

I could think of three potential locations as sources of information. The first was Heilbron, the scene of Johan Godfried Luyt's long public life, and perhaps Bloemfontein, where my mother had gone to boarding school. Both of these were in the Free State, the province formerly known as The Orange Free State engraved onto the silver tray. The third was Maseru, the capital of the tiny Republic of Lesotho, an African state entirely contained within South Africa. My mother was born there in 1932, and her father in 1888. It was still a British Protectorate then, called Basutoland. I had never considered how my Granny Grace had come to live there.

Heilbron felt like a town in decay, with bits of newspaper blowing about in quiet streets filled with dilapidated buildings. We couldn't find any municipal records of a century past. Bitter local residents told us no one cares about these in the new South Africa.

But in the two days Mark, our son Dean and I had there, I did find Quarta Pretorius, the local historian who valiantly attempts to keep the story of Heilbron alive. We also found some Luyt graves in the cemetery. And graves of the Weilert family (maiden name of Johan's wife, Mary Ann). Neither Johan nor Mary Ann came to rest in the cemetery of this town that figured so largely in their lives. I wondered why.

We found the family house that Johan had built in 1884. It was on what had been the outskirts of town. Now suburban streets, homes and gardens stretched out in every direction from the grounds and outbuildings. I stood in the corridors and tried to imagine the Luyt family going about their daily business. My Granny Grace had learned to ride her bicycle in these corridors. The grand family home later became a boarding house, Craig Hall, and then a pre-school.

The school's open day was in progress the day we visited, and they had "spook-asem" on sale. Afrikaans expresses some things like no other language can — this "ghost breath" was fairy floss, the fluffy pink treat of pure sugar prized by children.

I felt no breath of ghosts. The stories of the characters who had inhabited the large house so long ago still lay waiting for me. I didn't know to visualise British soldiers camped on their lawn, or listen for the echoes of Boer War[1] gunshots in the night, a noise that would provoke permanent fear of the dark in my six-year-old grandmother. Nothing stirred in me. I didn't even take a photograph.

We made amateur mistakes, such as arriving on a Friday afternoon in Maseru when it was nearly dark and everything was closed. We'd miscalculated how long the drive from Heilbron would take, not accounting for gaping potholes on the neglected road and our having to weave between them, frequently swerving out onto the wrong side of the national highway.

The next day we found where my mother's family home had been, now an enormous block housing the South African Embassy. Some original stone houses still stood up on the hill in the British-sounding Constitution Road, but only the smallest taste of the days of British rule remained. We couldn't find a cemetery.

But a random moment was to be a turning point. We walked passed an imposing building — one of very few in Maseru. It announced itself as the Lesotho Archives. That was the first time it occurred to me I might find some information about my ancestors in archives. Back in July 2011, I might have thought, somewhere in the recesses of my mind, that there would be archives that store old stuff and somebody official must surely know how to find it. I had no awareness of the treasures, hints and clues that devoted archivists guard, with few accolades, for explorers of the past.

As I stood at the foot of the barricaded steps, a Mr Sebinane Lekoekoe stopped to ask if he could help. He was the only person to pass during the three minutes I stood there outside the closed archives, it being Saturday. He was also the senior archivist. The archives would not be open until Monday, but I had an ally.

On Sunday, Dean and I spent the day on a long drive from Maseru out to the Masite Mission, looking for traces of the origins of my nanny, Ida. It was one of the few things I'd actually planned to do while in Lesotho. Monday had been allocated to Bloemfontein, and an evening flight from there to Cape Town, but now there were the Lesotho Archives. We checked out of the hotel early on Monday morning and drove straight over there with saxophones and suitcases in the car.

"We'll just stay here and read," said Mark. "How long will you need?"

"About an hour, I suppose."

Two hours later I was appalled at having to leave. Mr Lekoekoe and his assistant Mrs Tebello Moseme had located the leather-bound catalogue of The Archives of the Basutoland Government. I'd requested a few files, but it was depressingly clear I needed a month, not an hour.

It was a challenge to find things in the boxes, as nothing was catalogued at that level, and there were no digital records. But there was information from the time before the Republic, even before the British Protectorate of Basutoland. I leafed through the boxes, pulling thin, handwritten pages up sideways from the folders. I recognised names of ancestors I never met. I was touching the very pages they signed. Not photographs or PDF files. Reverence trembled in my fingers.

I called for family reinforcements to get copies of the treasures I'd found. The photocopier in the archives was broken and they suggested going upstairs to use the one in the library. It didn't seem an issue to remove these fragile sheets from the reading room. No sign out procedures of any kind. Dean took the documents upstairs while I continued to scratch through the century-old boxes they'd exhumed from the depths of the building. Interest in the days of British rule was low, and requests for this information infrequent.

The library photocopier was out of paper. Dean, with his Australian upbringing, was astonished at the Librarian's suggestion to take the documents out of the building and go up the road to the stationery shop where they might have a copier. It was a step too far for him, and he decided to instead retrieve his professional camera from the car.

I spread the files flat on the floor of the reading room: census results, death certificates, a paper proving a longstanding myth in my mother's family that Oupa's Prussian father of the impressive moustache had been the jailer in Maseru in the late 19th century. Dean took photos as fast as I could turn the pages.

My heart was still pounding when we reached the Lesotho border. A new, very old world had opened up to me.

Another disastrous national highway doubled our drive time to Bloemfontein, and further reduced the shrinking afternoon before our evening flight to Cape Town. Everything now in haste, we visited my mother's boarding school, but it was a new campus, with no hint of old classrooms where little girls burned pages from their blotters in the fireplaces to warm their freezing hands during the Second World War.

An Internet search and GPS led us to the Orange Free State Archives. We arrived at three pm. They closed at four pm.

Mr van Wyk, the senior archivist, was helpful but shook his head at the limited time. "Estate files are often a good place to start for family information," he said as he handed me a thick catalogue.

There they were, a stream of Luyts. Not Johan, but many others. Who were these people? Surely they were connected to him in some way? I asked to see a handful of files. The system here was much more efficient. Within minutes a smiling assistant brought several enormous binders, with many files in each. The binding was a mixture of cloth and firm cardboard held together with flat, woven ribbons and as I tentatively untied the first one, a cloud of paper dust rose.

For the second time that day, I felt my heart pounding. Again, I called for help. By closing time, I was still scrambling to turn pages as Dean clicked his shutter. And I knew I would be back. Mr van Wyk had shown me the online search facilities of the National Archives of South Africa, and I would come prepared. I still didn't know if I could put my mother's story about her grandfather to rest, but the haystack had parted to reveal a door, and I had a key in my hand.

BURY IT

"I think I've found something," I told Mark, after weeks of online trawling back in Sydney.

"What's that?"

"There's a court case here. The National Bank of the Orange River Colony vs Johan Godfried Luyt. I'm not sure what the Orange River Colony is, but it's dated 1909 and it looks like a conflict involving money."

History was one of my matriculation subjects and I didn't know what the Orange River Colony was.

On our return to Sydney in July 2011, I'd plunged into the online catalogue of the National Archives of South Africa, as suggested by Mr van Wyk of the Free State Archives. The catalogue contained only titles, not images of the contents, but those titles were promising. All I'd had before then was the shred of story my mother had told me when I was younger and only half listening. I'd now set myself the task of finding out enough to bury the story. It was tedious work, and I had to constantly push aside irritation that my mother had not done this work herself. But I still hadn't discovered enough to either resolve the mystery, or lay it down feeling I'd honoured her memory by trying my best. There was no avoiding it; I would have to wade further into the past and get to know this man, my mother's grandfather.

The story, according to Granny Grace, went like this:

Her father, Johan, was a wealthy man, and the Mayor of Heilbron. Public office was an honour and privilege back then, not a paid affair, and office bearers had to find other means by which to support their large families. Many politicians were lawyers, as was Johan. As a respected and trusted public figure, Johan received funds and valuables to hold in safekeeping for members of the community. And then there came a rotten son-in-law, who somehow embezzled or otherwise caused these assets to disappear. Word got out and depositors came to reclaim their treasures, but they were gone. Johan sold everything he owned to cover the losses. This included farms on which gold deposits were later discovered. He managed to pay the townspeople back and it redeemed his honour to some extent. But it ruined him; the shame of it was unbearable, and six months later Johan Godfried Luyt was dead. He had been blameless, the victim of wrongdoing.

That was it. No names, dates, figures or other information. But the story had always intrigued my mother. She said no one wanted to talk about it, and she always had the sense that there was more to it. She let go of it only when illness had narrowed her focus to her medicines and her immediate family. Who knew to what extent the truth had bowed to personal agendas on its way down the generations? Might we have been fabulously rich?

The idea of a story featuring a villain in the family did appeal to my imagination, but I'd had no information to go on. Here was my first hard evidence of trouble. And the appearance of a bank and a court case were entirely new to the plot. It represented a smoking gun, though I couldn't yet tell who was shot, or by whom.

Towards the end of 2011, I flew to New Zealand to visit Avis, my mother's last surviving cousin. She was one of the only two cousins I remembered my mother ever mentioning, or staying in touch with. Avis' mother was Mary, the sister closest in age to my Granny Grace. I'd never thought to ask how many siblings Grace had. The relationship between these sisters was always close, I learned. They both lived in Basutoland after marrying, and their children, my mother and Avis, had grown up together in Maseru. Both families had later moved to Durban, South Africa. Had Avis heard a version of the ruin of their grandfather?

"Yes," she said, "my mother told me about it. But she said that the person with his hand in the till was an employee. I don't remember any other details."

She saw my disappointment.

"I do remember Granny Mary Ann from when I was very young," she offered. "She was so sweet. She lived in a residential hotel near the Durban beachfront and used to take me to the beach. One day in the dining room a door swung closed and hit her hard in the breast. That's where she got the cancer, you know."

The memory of a story stirred at this. My mother's Granny Mary Ann lived with them, and Grace nursed her. One day young June walked in on a bed bath and caught sight of a breast that looked like a cauliflower. It gave her nightmares. Mary Ann's death certificate supports this, stating cause of death as "Hypostatic Pneumonia; Fungating Carcinoma of right breast; Secondary Haemorrhage from mass".

So, the vile harridan could haul out the goods when occasion demanded. Who knows how willingly or otherwise she tended her mother, but tend her she did. As she was later tended by June, and June by me, though I concede that it was not easy for me to fill this role graciously. Mark was much better at it, and she wasn't even his mother. It took me months and the epiphany of composing a new song to surrender to the consuming realities of care for an unknowable period of time.

Avis' story about Johan was similar but not identical. Which was true? And her memories of Granny Mary Ann were the first insights I'd had into Johan's wife, who I hadn't considered until now. Avis' daughter Pam, my first genealogy ally, gave me some family documents and photos. They didn't mean much to me at the time.

But my curiosity had sharpened, and I contemplated a return to Bloemfontein.

THE ARCHIVES DELIVER

Diary note, January 2012:

"Birdcalls and the hum of a ceiling fan dominate the soundscape of a still summer morning that predicts a sticky day. In another hour, I'll need to close the doors and windows, draw the curtains and drop the blinds. Later still, working in my office will require the portable air conditioner; a noisy affair that doesn't work wonders but makes some difference on days like this. Will the story still be unfolding in here when it's time to close the windows and turn on the heating?

The delving reveals paths to and from Heilbron, the fateful town of Johan's making and unmaking. They traverse archival fact, family accounts and hazy memories. I follow them and try to join dots. But the paths from Heilbron have launched into their multiple futures, leaving few footprints behind. Is this quest even possible? The path to this clammy day has required more than I ever expected, has dredged the archives of my own memory, and reaches further over the horizon than I can presently see."

Six months later, in July 2012, we were in South Africa again. I excused myself from family activities in Cape Town and, a year after my initial visit to the archives, flew to Bloemfontein and checked into a nearby hotel for a week. I showed up the next frosty Free State morning with uncertain expectations and a long list of file references dredged up from online investigations.

"You have to leave your things in a locker out here," said the receptionist. I shed my beanie, gloves, scarf and backpack, and entered the reading room with a notebook, pen, laptop computer, the file references and an eager heart, free from mobile phone and other encumbrances.

Paper dust drifted in the shafts of wintry sunlight slanting into the room, which was heated to a comfortable working temperature. Three rows of wooden tables marched down the room to the front desk. Only three of the twelve tables were occupied, heads bent over documents in a thick silence punctuated by rustles of brittle paper. One head lifted with a brief smile to the new seeker here on the dark side of the moon.

"Could I please see these files," I asked the young man behind the desk.

"Certainly, Ma'am. Please take a seat."

By the time I'd removed my jacket, set up my computer at one of the tables and located the book of estate files on the shelf, the assistant returned, invisible behind a tower on wheels: enormous binders like those I'd glimpsed briefly on my first visit. They had crumbling cardboard covers, each package tied together with thick linen bows. He offloaded them onto the table adjacent to mine, three stacks of promise. I heaved the first binder onto my table. The faded cover, the cloth ribbons, the paper dust; I was really here, with days of seclusion stretching out ahead.

The very first binder delivered the mother lode. It was true: my mother's grandfather Johan had been ruined. First exhibit: a letter to "The Sherriff of the Orange River Colony or his lawful deputy" dated 23 September 1909, from "Edward VII, by the grace of God of the United Kingdom of Great Britain and Ireland and of the British dominions beyond the seas King, Defender of the Faith, Emperor of India".

"We command you," it said, "that of the goods and chattels of Johan Godfried Luyt, of Heilbron, Attorney-at-Law, hereinafter styled the DEFENDANT, you cause to be made the sum of Ten Thousand Two Hundred and Thirty-Eight Pounds Eight Shillings and Twopence of lawful Money". This was "by sentence of the High Court" made on 15 September 1909, and to be paid to the National Bank of the Orange River Colony before the court by 23 December 1909.

The documents went on and on. Johan owed the bank a staggering amount of money. A list of huge farms and town properties he'd put down as collateral in 1906 filled three pages of a legal document. What made him do that?

This was far from a homely story of townsfolk bringing Johan their belongings for safekeeping. There was no mention of pilfering by a dodgy employee or son-in-law.

There was a newspaper notice of a "Sheriff's Sale, District of Heilbron". Items of heartbreaking domesticity and pitiful value — clocks, furniture, carpets, wash stands — "will be on sale at 10 am on Saturday 23 October 1909 at the residence of the Defendant, Heilbron". No address included. Everyone knew where to go. The scandal, if anyone in Heilbron was still unaware of it, was now in plain view. The auction was scheduled for five weeks after the notice. A life was to be dismantled two days before Christmas. I felt a nip of indignation. Who did this to my great grandfather?

Over the following three days I trudged through innumerable files and found many family and civic records involving Johan. All evidence pointed to him having been a responsible, selfless and civic-minded man who cared for others in his family and in his community, just like Granny Grace had said. This humiliation and destitution seemed undeserved in the extreme.

One particularly thick file covered a legal case from 1911, more than a year after the sad, public announcements. The case, involving complainants Lotzof & Cohen, didn't seem relevant to his financial ruin, but Johan's prominent presence in the file aroused my curiosity. The many other files showed it was all over by then. But it bothered me that the period of another two years until Johan's death in 1913 didn't quite tie up with the family myth of his having died "of shame" within six months. I turned the many pages, generating more clouds of paper dust, and added another thirty or so images to my growing collection. They would have to wait several years for their moment.

On my final day at the archives, I considered possible suspects among the husbands of Johan and Mary Ann's five daughters. The only two with husbands at the time of Johan's disgrace were:

1: Rosie. Married Gideon van Rooyen in 1903.

2: Helena. Married a Mr Garner, first name and date of marriage unknown.

By chance I started with Gideon van Rooyen, Rosie's husband. I never reached Mr Garner. It took the rest of the day to sprint through the criminal cases, divorce case and related scandals that surrounded Gideon. This guy was bad news. The clincher, in a 1906 Directory, was the listing for Johan's law firm: "Gideon van Rooyen, assistant to JG Luyt". Son-in-law *and* employee, fitting both Granny Grace's and Great Aunt Mary's versions of the story.

"Can I get some of these documents photocopied?" I asked.

"Yes, Ma'am, but if you'd prefer to photograph them, there's no charge."

I left for the airport with 500 photographs uploaded to my laptop computer and my suitcase bulging with photocopies.

On the descent into Sydney I felt the usual surge of homecoming. I'd never experienced the yearnings for South Africa that other expatriates reported. The places in the Free State that meant so much to my mother's grandfather were alien to me.

Still, the archives had brought an internal shift from lukewarm enquiry to the beginnings of caring. It wasn't the closure I felt sure the contents of my suitcase would reveal, but I did feel sorry for Johan for what he went through. I had no idea of the personal journey that lay ahead.

THE PORTRAITS

I feel a sting at the thought of the six weeks that have passed since my archive discoveries in Bloemfontein. I'd resolved to start work immediately on my return. Instead, the materials teeter on my desk between books, files, mobile phone accessories, CDs, papers and chocolate bars. Suddenly I feel compelled to clear this mess. An expanse of desktop emerges. Then a sharp thought that I risk a crime of procrastination similar to my mother's sends me down the hallway to the room in which I'd intended to bring the past to life.

From the narrow space between the desk and the wall, the portraits call to me. I lay them side-by-side under the lamp, in the newly cleared space on my desk. Johan and Mary Ann, an elegant couple, captured at the time of their marriage in 1880. I know them better than I did a year ago when I last looked, half-heartedly, at these images. I now see appropriateness in the tatty edges of the canvasses, as if ripped hastily from their frames. People torn from their lives.

It's as if I have never seen the paintings before. Mary Ann looks so young; my great grandfather so noble and engaging. *Did he just say something to me?* I want to ask him so many questions about the money, the farms, the court case.

The paintings have deteriorated from more than a century in musty wardrobes, since they hung in the grand hallway of my great grandparents' home. Before the fall.

Each canvas rests on a larger piece of cardboard, a frame of sorts, on which the messy edges of the slashed canvas are clearly visible. Thick plastic seals the whole assembly, presumably intended to protect the paintings. It hasn't quite succeeded. The paint of both pictures is fissured, as if each portrait is superimposed on an image of drought-cracked land.

The portrait of Mary Ann is also punctured in half-a-dozen places — holes the size of small gauge knitting needles.

I search for any marking that might indicate an artist, date, or place. Apart from what looks like a London manufacturer's stamp on one backing, there is nothing. I wonder if there might be any clue on the back of the canvas. It seems to be stuck to the cardboard, plastic sealing the package.

The sharp cardboard cutter slices through the thick tape holding the plastic covering together. Handling the old, delicate materials with care, I pull the plastic clear of the backing, which is not stuck to the oil painting as I'd expected and lift it gently from the back of the canvas. It is not a random piece of cardboard at all. It's the original photographic portrait of Johan my New Zealand cousin Pam gave me as a digital image when I visited her and her mother, Avis. I was told it hangs in the Free State government archives. Pressure against the back of the canvas has created striations on the more than century old photograph, giving it the appearance of a charcoal drawing and I need a magnifying glass to confirm it really is a photograph.

I turn to the other portrait, extricate the plastic and lift the cardboard. Sure enough, it's a matching sepia photograph of Mary Ann, this one in good condition. I have a few photos of my great grandmother in her old age, and I have the oil portrait of her as a young woman, but nothing in between.

I look for a very long time at these huge photographs. For at least twenty-five years they've waited in my own house, brought to Australia by my mother. Perhaps they were hidden for decades before that. Did June know the damaged oil paintings concealed these treasures? Was it Mary Ann herself who packaged them in this way when she lived with her daughter, Grace? Maybe Grace didn't even know.

Days in the archives failed to explain the shadow-story passed down from these faces in fractured oil paint, but revealed enough to confirm that there is a story.

Gazing at my mother's grandmother, an eighteen-year-old embarking on a long and eventful adult life, I have a sense of crossing a threshold. I hear a portal of commitment close, already some distance behind, but barely notice the click as I feel the icy chill of Heilbron winter close around me. I hear men shouting as they try to turn a span of oxen in the muddy main street.

HEILBRON

Heilbron, "Spring of Bliss", welled into being in 1873 on the site of a perennial natural fountain ("fontein") on the farm Rietfontein. The three founders of the town collectively purchased the enormous farm for £1,800.

The fontein, bubbling fresh, clear water up from between rocky shapes far below supplied all the needs of the town for over a century, before piped water arrived. Early trekkers, a subset of the people known as the "Voortrekkers", who came from the Cape Colony in the Great Trek, had found their way to the banks of the stream by 1836, when they fought off the "impis" (armies) of Ndebele Chief Mzilikazi at nearby Vegkop.

"Here," they said, "we will stop."

In 1853, they declared this area north of the Orange River, the border between the Cape Colony and the rest of South Africa, the Republic of the Orange Free State. In 1854, Britain recognised it and guaranteed its independence.

The new republic offered the weary Calvinists a home, where

they could at last outspan their oxen and conduct their austere lives in peace. Like colonists throughout history, they viewed the land as empty, divinely theirs despite the existence of small groups who had lived along the banks of the stream for centuries. They established vast farms, and towns sprouted throughout the territory.

Immigrants from further afield found their way to the new settlements almost immediately. According to family legend, the young Christiaan "Fritz" Weilert, a sea captain from Hanover, and his English bride, Rosina Clements, arrived around 1853. They subsequently produced four daughters. The third of them was Mary Ann Christina, my mother's grandmother, born in 1863 in Heilbron.

Winston Churchill, a war correspondent with the British troops during the Boer War, described the scene as they approached the trembling town. It struck him as a "quiet, sleepy little place" with a few good buildings and pretty rose gardens, but not much else to commend it, though it had its own branch line from the main railway system. Heilbron, though insignificant to Churchill's sophisticated eye, was viewed in a different light in a description from 1907. "The town of Heilbron has been in existence about 30 years, and, previous to the war, was a thriving and go-ahead place."[2]

Johan Godfried Luyt, a dashing young lawyer recently called to the Bar in Bloemfontein, swept into town in January 1880 and set up a law practice. One of Johan's first jobs as the new attorney-at-law was to prepare the documents for the 1872 purchase of the Rietfontein farm, which had, inexplicably, never been completed. He expedited their signing and thereby, officially completed the establishment of the town.

He soon married local girl, Mary Ann Christina Weilert, and by 1882 she produced Heinrich Leopold (Leo), the first of their many children. In 1884, Johan was elected to the Volksraad (Parliament of the Republic) as the member for Heilbron, Parys and Frankfort. He held this position until the demise of the Republic in 1901, simultaneously serving as Mayor of Heilbron for many years before, during and after the Boer War. I found many testimonies paying homage to Johan for his excellent management and leadership of Heilbron, noting that its charms and prosperity were largely due to his efforts.

He was at the centre of government as war approached, and the leader of what was said to be, "an historic town with a pivotal place in Boer Settler and Boer War history".[3]

In 1899, the two barely-born Boer Republics, hands fatally clasped via a treaty guaranteeing mutual support, slid toward war against the greatest power on earth. On 18 June, the *Heilbron Herald* reported the presentation to Johan, by the inhabitants of Heilbron of a "massive solid silver tea service, each piece being suitably engraved, and a beautifully illumined address, bearing the signatures of over eighty ratepayers".[4]

> Dear Sir,
>
> In offering you this token for you personally, we wish to place on record our appreciation of your eminent services to this town as member of the Honourable Volksraad as well as in your capacity as Mayor of Heilbron.
>
> We know that in carrying out your public duties you have often done so at considerable sacrifice both of time and money, and it is your energy and perseverance that we can now boast of having the railway at our doors, as well as the promised extension to Bethlehem, connecting us with Natal.
>
> You have always carried out the wishes of the community in a praiseworthy manner, and the appearance of our town now as compared with when you first took office is in itself an eloquent tribute to the thoroughness with which you carry out the various public duties entrusted to you.
>
> In wishing you and yours every prosperity and happiness we may venture to hope that you may long be

spared to continue your efforts on behalf of the residents of this town, which have hitherto been conducted with such marked success, and caused such universal satisfaction.

We remain, dear sir,

Yours respectfully,

"Prosperity" and "happiness" were terms that hovered poignantly, to my mind, given what misfortune of as yet uncertain origin was to descend on Johan.

It was around this time in my research I was forced to accept that my ancestors must have been Afrikaners. And how stupid I'd been not to see it sooner. Johan couldn't have held his position otherwise. He must have been fluent in Dutch. To be in the government he must have worked with icons of Afrikaner history, the same history that bored me to sleep in high school. The same icons who birthed the ruling political party whose policies I opposed from as young as I could remember. It was one of the few things on which we were united in my family during the dark years of my teens.

It pained me that my mother and I discussed none of this; that we missed the chance to marvel together over the surprise of our Afrikaner heritage. Maybe once again she wouldn't have had the drive needed to pursue these discoveries on her own. I was busy and confess that I didn't care. Not really. And now the voice of regret taunted me. "There would have been so many more people still alive to ask," it said.

At least she visited Heilbron one time, in the 1980s, and saw her grandparent's house. At least she didn't sell the family tea service.

On my first, uncertain visit in 2011, I found 21st century Heilbron a sad town. It felt to be in mortal decline; despite some historical buildings and the local Afrikaner population's love for it. Yet they complained of the impossibility of getting public amenities repaired, let alone improved. There was little sign here of the new South Africa, the "Rainbow Nation". The people living in town were white, the domestic servants and council workers were not. The synagogue, which once supported a thriving Jewish immigrant population from Eastern Europe, was a museum, if you could call it that. Prayer shawls lay scattered in the pews of the desolate building as if discarded that morning, though the crying neglect swiftly negated that impression. The dusty prayer books, from another place and century, were brittle and fragile. There had been no Jews in Heilbron for decades, though many streets were named after founding Jewish citizens. They had drifted away, answering the call of opportunities in nearby Johannesburg.

The atmosphere felt better on our second visit, in 2016, but perhaps that was because the indefatigable Quarta Pretorius had supervised the restoration of the museum at the synagogue.

But maintaining a thriving town in Heilbron was no longer high on anyone's priority list. Perhaps its place in the Afrikaner heartland contributed to its contemporary neglect. The new decision makers could be forgiven for not caring that key figures in Afrikaner history came from or were prominent in the area. The only recent arrivals were, we heard, from more northern parts of Africa. They mostly resided in the un-serviced township, perilous piles of cardboard and tin, just outside the town.

And yet, the stories of old Heilbron include triumph, heartbreak, litigation, sexual exploits and catastrophes, and that's just in my family.

JOHAN

My mother's grandfather Johan left the Cape Town home of his parents in 1875 as a young man of twenty-three, precisely one century before I left my parents' home. His exit ramp was the opportunity to study law with Advocate Abraham Fischer in Bloemfontein, the capital of the young Republic of the Orange Free State, full of promise.

The census of 1875 recorded that only fifty per cent of the Cape Town population could read. Johan was educated in English, while at home the family glided between Dutch and English. These multilingual skills would serve him well. He was admitted to the Bar in 1878, moved to Heilbron in 1880 and went into practice, "at once displaying his abilities, both in professional and private life".[5]

Literacy and education would unite with Johan's natural leadership qualities and compassionate nature to raise him to public office, wealth, and the epicentre of war.

Johan's conservative mentor, Abraham Fischer, would become a key member of President Kruger's team in the Republic of South Africa, as the Transvaal was then constituted, and an important player in The Boer War. In one of many such twists of history in South Africa, Abraham's grandson, Bram Fischer would become famous as the lawyer who defended Nelson Mandela.

His oil portrait, painted at the time of his 1880 marriage in Heilbron, showed twenty-eight-year-old Johan Godfried Luyt as kindly, with soft but penetrating eyes. He had a handsome, well-proportioned face with full lips, and an ample beard that did not quite conceal his strong chin. What was visible of his build, together with his fleshy cheeks, suggested a fondness for food.

The next image of Johan was the photograph that lay concealed for at least one generation behind the oil portrait of Mary Ann. It bore no date, but Johan looked to be a man in his fifties. This placed him near the end of the 19th century, just before the terrible war between the combined Boer Republics and the British Empire, which sucked his family into a vortex of ambiguity.

The lines around his eyes and the furrows between the eyebrows reflected the demands of the years. Most striking was the change in the eyes themselves. These older eyes reflect pain and resignation. The shadows beneath them suggest sleepless nights. The road to this point had been long, and the hardest part was yet to come.

Cape Town was a thriving city when Johan Godfried Luyt was born on 26 January 1852, and baptised at the Dutch Reformed Church. His father, Gabriel Jacobus, was a blacksmith who lived in upper Wale Street on the periphery of the crowded town. The classic façade of the original house still exists, painted in the bright colours of the Malay

Quarter, which over time must have expanded to engulf some of the streets of the early European tradesmen. Areas such as Clifton and Camps Bay, these days likened to the Riviera, were empty.

Two public events in Cape Town had particular impact on the young Johan.

In 1860, when Johan was eight years old, celebrations turned the town upside down with the visit of the young Prince Alfred. Thousands lined the streets as the procession on horseback moved through town, British flags and pennants fluttering from ropes strung from building to elegant building. The prince, just fifteen himself, was there to officiate at the commencement of construction of The Alfred Basin on the new waterfront. Johan and his family were among the 20,000 who huddled against squally weather on the shoreline of the city near the Chavonnes Battery to witness a ceremony that symbolised British power at the Cape.

Sir George Grey and Prince Alfred arrived to strains of "God Save the Queen", with a retinue that included the Xhosa chief, Sandile. Formalities followed, then the young prince pulled the lever to tip the first load of stones for the new breakwater into the bay. Bands played "Rule, Brittannia", and the cannons of the Chavonnes Battery fired a royal salute. Much of that stalwart fortification, after defending the Cape for over a century, would later provide rubble for the building of Cape Town's first harbour.

The second event took place soon after.

Private contractors to the Cape Town Railway and Dock Company had imported the first steam locomotive, nicknamed "Blackie", from England. They'd had to convey the locomotive engine, a small boy's fantasy, from the ship to land in pieces. Engineers partially reassembled it on the jetty as a swarm of boys including Johan, his brothers and their friends, looked on. The reassembled engine was then housed in an iron shed built over it in Alfred's Square, a part of The Parade.

"Papa, how much longer?"

"They have to build the railway line first," explained Gabriel Luyt for what seemed the tenth time.

"But they started digging years ago."

"It may feel that way to you, but it was only a few months ago. These things take a long time, my impatient boy."

"Can we go look at the engine again?"

"Johan, it's only been a week since I took you."

The train-crazy boy had to wait another two years before he stood at the official opening of the first stretch of railway line, to Eerste Rivier (First River). He devoured every word of the official speeches, as his five older brothers grew restless and kicked at pebbles in the dust.

"Look at this boy," Gabriel said, pointing to the enraptured ten-year-old. "Why do you think he's so interested?" They shrugged and lunged simultaneously at the prize of a flat pebble they'd spotted.

Eighteen-year-old Johan was working as a clerk for a law agent and already in love with the dream of studying law when Prince Alfred, by then the Duke of Edinburgh, returned for the official opening of the new harbour. It had been a decade since he pulled the lever to release those first stones into the water. The Alfred Basin would alter the character of Cape Town's waterfront and enable it to meet the demands of the diamond, then the gold rush, and of the Boer War.

Once again, the young Johan heard words that penetrated his heart. News from the youthful northern republics, together with the speeches, ignited a vision for his future in the thrilling interior of the country where, it was said, there was a need for lawyers.

WHOSE STORY?

By 2014, I was in deep, and knew that I would do what my mother never could: write Johan's story. I'd discovered far more than she ever knew about her grandfather and his family. The voices of my newly-discovered relatives called to me from prison in Pretoria, from the tangle of trees reaching out of graves in an old Bloemfontein cemetery, from the Heilbron concentration camp, the government of the brief Republic of the Orange Free State and from exile in Bermuda during the Boer War. The questions of past centuries had started to haunt me, the injustices burn, and I'd had to face the inescapable fact that my ancestors were Afrikaners, the ethnic group that birthed the policy of apartheid, while representing only 5.2% of the population of South Africa.

The emerging story was a lot more complex than I'd expected it to be. I was starting to realise how little I knew about the Afrikaner people in general, and their early relationship to other people in South Africa. Afrikaner ancestry was appalling to me, but here it was, part of my heritage. It made me squirm, but I wanted to know more about it. I could see how ignorant I'd been as a teenager of the nuances of history and what effects they might have had on my family. I was too busy trying to stay vertical on the unsteady terrain between my parents, the characters I viewed respectively as heroine and traitor.

My family research thus far had broadened and deepened my knowledge, and aroused my curiosity. Still, I bristled with resentment, perhaps even more so now that I could perceive the magnitude of the task. It wasn't my job to solve the mystery, yet here I was, once again being the adult for my mother. I'd sworn, even when she was still alive, that I was done with all that.

Research had revealed more family, and stories about them, that related to Johan's ruin. But, to my frustration, the reason for that ruin remained hidden. I was dismayed that it had already taken years, and still with no end in sight. I suspected it would take courage, conviction and strength to write the wretched thing.

I'd had experience in writing, from poetry and essays to songs, years of business reports and technical manuals, and had co-written a musical. But this business of writing a book proved to be a great deal more challenging. I realised I needed help.

I learned of an opportunity to attend an intensive writer's course for a week in Fiji. I was nervous as hell, but I applied. I became even more nervous when I was accepted. I'd never attended anything like this, and the cost was significant. What if I didn't make the grade and had to leave in shame after two days?

That didn't happen. Instead, in a week of cloying heat, terrible coffee, and three-chord music gradually driving me insane, my mother's family tale sneakily morphed into mine. I didn't mean for that to happen, but the story of grandeur and ruin wouldn't behave itself. It unfurled tentacles into my own life, probing layers unexpectedly intertwined.

I had to answer scary questions, such as: "Why are you writing this?"

Why indeed? Because of an inscription on an old silver tray bundled for decades in a nineteen-seventies Cape Town newspaper at the back of a wardrobe? Because my mother was denied the years of life she needed to do it? That was hardly my fault. Because I was trained so early and so thoroughly to try to fix things for my mother when she was unable to do it herself? I didn't think I had been responsible for that either.

The retreat yielded no answers, but some better questions, with author Joanne Fedler leading intrepid writers into the darkness holding up a small, brave lantern. Shadows everywhere. One session left us both in tears, and me with an assignment to write about the loss of my daughter.

"But this book isn't about me," I protested.

"Is that so?" She looked out at me from under an arched eyebrow.

After Fiji, those hard questions fuelled months of thought, and the grudging recognition that I was sticking to the safety of someone else's story. That story had by then captivated me, it's true. I was elated to find records of relatives I'd never heard of, and uncover the stories of their lives. It turned out I had a big family after all, even if I didn't know them, and a spot in history. But my increasing attraction to the quest didn't explain why I was so driven to pursue this mystery.

Before Fiji, I'd viewed it as Johan's story, not mine. That was what I'd gone to Fiji to confirm I could dare to write. I'd had to draw on personal reserves of courage to get me that far. By the end of the week, I knew that still more courage was required, to review and write about the elements of my own life that might be surreptitiously driving me.

The resulting cautious, internal probing yielded the first perception of a protective thickening around my heart. I'd spent a lifetime building it, as I responded to isolation and loss. The layer created a sense of safety, but also a distance between me and other people, even Mark and Dean. It had also shut my mother out on some levels. I would have to burrow underneath the layers, and I was terrified. I hadn't allowed myself to sink fully into those waters for a long time, fearing I might drown.

But it became increasingly clear to me that this was the work needed to shift the unwanted feelings lurking in my darkest corners. How could I still carry bitterness toward this sweet, good woman, after all she'd done for me and for my family? I thought two years of therapy had unearthed and finished my business with her. Yet here I was, still grappling years later with the unspoken pieces between us, most of her relics untouchable in the wake of a complex sorrow.

IN SERVICE OF FEAR

"She was never complicated like my father," I said, gazing out the window at the traffic five floors below.

"Tell me about her," said Dr Greenbaum, turning to a blank page in his file.

I shrugged. To describe my father and the damage he inflicted was easy; blowholes all over the place, big and dramatic. But my sweet mother? There didn't seem much there that would interest a shrink. Besides, I was in that chair because of my daughter, not my parents. A surge of pain passed through me.

It was late 1990 and June had been living with us in Sydney for over two years.

"My mother is a wonderful, kind person with a great sense of humour. Absolutely selfless. Actually, she's so generous she's always seemed to live more for others than for herself." I stopped as a tongue of flame licked the edge of the mental blank page of safety on which I had positioned myself. I drew back from it.

"Yes?" asked the astute Dr Greenbaum.

"Um … she and I became great friends during my teens and had a lot of fun together, despite some difficult circumstances. Maybe because of them. She looked so young; everyone thought we were sisters. I remember thinking that was cool. She used to hang out with me and my older friends."

Another flicker scorched the rim of my safety zone.

"Older friends?"

"It's a long story."

"That's what we're here for." Dr Greenbaum leaned back in his chair.

"There was always a lot of alcohol consumed in our house, but when I was thirteen it … sort of got out of hand. My dad was out most nights, and if he did come home he'd clatter in late, sometimes pretty drunk. I started making myself scarce, not wanting to deal with him in that state. He never questioned my excuses — homework, early night. For one particular spate of his absence, my mother told me he was under a lot of stress. He and his cinematographer business partner were embarking on something bigger than they'd ever tried — a feature film in Swaziland, including a live concert in Mbabane Stadium, with the soul singer, Percy Sledge."

The weekend of filming "Soul Africa" was a study in parental neglect.

"So, who were the older friends?" asked the psychiatrist, drawing me back.

"From that second year of wearing the brace, I'd gravitated towards people older than me. My brother had always been very clear about my being his 'little' sister and he was furious at my romance first with one and then another of his friends, brace and all. But that wasn't really it. I started making my own friendships with some of my parents' friends."

Flickers grew into small flames on the curling borders. I started sweating slightly under Dr Greenbaum's scrutiny.

"When did your relationship with your mother become more 'sisterly', as you put it?"

I thought back to those winter afternoons when my mother would pick me up from school, make us cocoa, and we'd sit down near the full-length windows overlooking the sea with the sunshine streaming through.

"She and I first connected in an adult way when I asked her straight out if my dad and Norina were having an affair. I was thirteen and seeing things that I didn't want to see, noticing my dad's absences and my mum's feeble stories to explain them and this ... this grotesque, lumpy veneer of normality over everything."

I'd tried to deny it, but the more I tried, the more these thoughts consumed me. I was relieved that Tara wasn't around anymore, but now my dad was also absent most of the time, and when he was there, I was no longer the choicest apple on the tree.

"I already knew the answer, but needed to hear it from my mother."

I looked out the window again, seeking some relief from the heat.

Dr Greenbaum waited for a while, watching me closely. "How did she respond?"

"She ... crumbled. Told me a whole lot of stuff that day, not everything — that took months — about how she'd been pushed inch-by-inch, stretched and folded into tolerance of the affair. He'd manoeuvred her, like a snake, slithering up to its victim, hypnotising and then paralysing it, into a twisted sanctioning of this thing, so he could later claim that she understood, and gave it her blessing. Her blessing? She was a mess. I felt sick."

I felt myself drift away from Dr Greenbaum and his purposeful pen, and surrender to the memories I'd kept at bay for decades.

Like a cancer diagnosis that you don't quite accept until the specialist places it before you as fact, the confirmation of the affair was unexpectedly shattering. It got worse. The affair hadn't arisen from the Tara period, but had been in full swing for years before that, since I was a little girl. Norina's relationship with Tara was just a side trip, but one that eventually became intolerable to my father, who proved incapable of heeding his own self-serving lectures to my mother on the evils of jealousy. The circumstances, the emotional curiosity of a teenager and perception heightened by imprisonment in metal had combined to raise the truth to the surface. A submerged car in a murder mystery, hanging from the end of a crane, dripping mud and rotting reeds.

That night, and many nights thereafter, I lay awake burning with outrage, and with humiliation at how I had been deceived, for so long, by the significant adults in my life. Were they ever going to tell me about it? Or was I simply not a consideration in this fucked up equation?

Casualties, though I didn't think of it in these terms at the time, included:

> Childhood innocence. (I'd still had some, despite knowing about the smoked salmon.)
> The remainder of my trust in adults.
> My relationship with Norina, my "big sister".
> Faith in my own powers of perception.
> Confidence in my mother's power to protect herself, or me.

Mostly I felt profound grief at the loss of my place in the heart of some hologram I had viewed as my loving father. Yet there I was living under the same roof, financially supported by this deceiving creature with a drinking problem. Added to the pain of his betrayal and abandonment were the disgust with myself at being there at all, and bewilderment — how could life even continue between my parents?

I became an obsessive reader, sometimes reading more than one book in a day to remove myself from reality. My interest in schoolwork reignited as I buried myself in homework. I wrote poetry, and one solitary afternoon sat down at the piano for the first time in the year and a half since my encasement in the brace, and started writing the first of many tortured songs.

Everything was difficult in that brace. So, one night in the privacy of my bedroom, with my mother trapped downstairs as the silver tray reflected my father's drunken raging, I removed the brace. I sat at the haven of my grandfather's wooden desk and wrote, free from physical restrictions. Another afternoon when no one was around, I slipped it off and spent a couple of blissful hours at the piano. Again, and again, I secretly slipped out of the confines of my cure. Who the hell cared anyway?

I dipped, further and further, beneath my mother's preoccupied radar. I wasn't a blip on my father's anymore. Eventually I took the brace off when she was present, and overcame her protests.

"Swaziland was a big turning point for me," I told the doctor.

The filming was scheduled over the Easter weekend. Everyone from the studio, their partners, friends, next-door neighbours and their dogs were needed for the shoot. That included my mother, plus anyone she might have asked to stay at the house with me over the weekend.

Our beloved Basotho nanny, Ida, had, by then, retired to the mountains in Lesotho. Now, like everyone else I knew, we had a live-in Xhosa maid. She was lovely, but her connection to the family wasn't comparable to Ida's. Julia was religious and it was too much to ask her to stay at work over Easter. I was apparently too young to leave alone for four days. Ridiculous, in retrospect. On Easter Friday my mother and I flew to Johannesburg, then to Mbabane in a 4-seater plane. My father and the crew had been there for some days, setting up the shoot. Though connected to my parents' room by an inter-leading door, I had a room of my own, a new independence. I had talked my mother into letting me leave my brace at home. It was the first time in fifteen months that I had been out of its constraints for more than a few hours, even with my recent transgressions.

Transgressions proved to be the theme of the weekend, and another crash course in growing up.

"What happened in Swaziland?" asked Dr Greenbaum.

"Well, a few things." I took a deep breath.

I teamed up with a noted musician and colleague of my father's from Cape Town. He was helping with the shoot. My hands added an extra pair for his tasks and it was fun helping him. My mother was grateful. Mitch had originally consulted her about improving his music theory skills. She recruited me, given my advanced music studies. He subsequently started working at the studio; he and his girlfriend became friends of my parents, and would sometimes stay when my parents were away on a film location. They became my friends, too.

For the next three days, I saw my father only at a distance, running around with a 35mm movie camera or field recording equipment. Norina was also extremely busy and it was easy to avoid them both.

I encountered my mother only a few times during the weekend. Each time she was haggard with stress, on missions such as trying to source medication for the music director's wife, who was in violent withdrawal after the suitcase containing her drugs had gone missing. It was new to me, but my mother apparently knew about such things.

She was so busy fixing disasters that an occasional enquiry about how I was doing was all she could manage, plus one tepid complaint about my appearance on the night of the big concert.

The hot Swazi air was thick enough to slice. I wore my bikini top and hipster trousers, with much of my torso exposed. The Milwaukee brace had rendered that torso fit for viewing, the extent of the spinal curvature much reduced. I had borrowed some makeup and was quite pleased with the results, having only ever worn makeup for dance performances in the days I was still allowed to dance.

The King of Swaziland and his enormous entourage of wives and minions entered the packed stadium to pounding drums and ululations. Mitch held up "idiot boards" for the star, who to my astonishment couldn't remember the lyrics of his international hit songs. I helped Mitch, passing the next board and stashing the used ones under the stage. The role was small, but vital, saving the strutting star from fluffing his lines on camera in front of 10,000 people.

Thousands of people milled around after the show and a number of separate after-parties emerged from the chaos. I couldn't see my parents and Mitch swept me to the party in his room with other members of the crew. The atmosphere was pulsating. Wine and beer flowed and several glasses slipped down my throat, as they'd done on the previous few nights, along with cigarettes I was offered. I looked much older than thirteen and the crew had no idea. Mitch protested a couple of times, as he hung onto the last vestiges of his minder role, but then just grinned, shook his head and lit cigarettes for us both. Feeling grown up and at ease with people who had now become co-workers, I hesitated not at all when the joint moving around the circle reached me. I inhaled deeply, hoping I wouldn't cough as I'd done when puffing nervously on Tara's joints. But the recent training on Mitch's Rothmans stood me in good stead, and the marijuana without tobacco was not nearly as rough to inhale.

Mitch's arm was around me. It felt good. As the party waned and people peeled off, it seemed the most natural thing that we, like a few other couples around the darkened hotel room, should kiss. Most people left. We lay down on one of the beds. My sensory perception narrowed to the weight of his body, his gentle hands on me, my fear that this might lead somewhere I wasn't ready for, and the euphoric thrill of new sensations. He had stepped over a line, and I had welcomed him there. But no matter what erotic energy had mounted over the course of the weekend and flared up that steamy night, his affection and respect prevailed. He walked me back to my room when the light was creeping into the horizon, our relationship altered, but my maidenhood intact.

My mother shook me awake three hours later. A driver was taking me to the airport for the return journey and my parents would follow in a couple of days. I sank into a stupor on each leg and don't remember much of it. Someone must have picked me up from Cape Town airport and taken me home. I set my alarm to get up for school in the morning but only surfaced groggily at two pm. Flies buzzing in the autumn air were the only sound in the empty house.

"On the weekend in Swaziland," I told the psychiatrist, "I started smoking cigarettes and marijuana, wearing makeup, doing without parents and relating sexually to a man double my age." He hesitated, trying to glean what I'd glossed over.

"Were there any further incidents with this man?" he asked.

"No."

My Swaziland "romance" continued only in an occasional knowing glance between us, and a special, closer friendship. It was a night out with Mitch and his girlfriend when they were staying with me at Hillcrest that started a new chapter.

"Within a few months after Swaziland," I went on, "I regularly smoked, wore makeup, and had found a supplier of marijuana. I paid for it with my earnings from a weekend job at a jeans store in town, plus some income from supplying schoolmates with dope. Then at a disco one night with Mitch and his girlfriend, I met a singer friend of theirs who was twenty years old. We started dating in an innocent kind of way, after he recovered from the shock of my age. This relationship didn't last long, but through him I met three young men who would figure very largely in my life, and in my mother's."

"I'd like to hear more about them next week," said Dr Greenbaum, writing furiously, "but we have to finish soon and I need to ask you: What did you feel about your mother's acceptance of this situation with your father and Norina?" His pen hovered above yet another new page he'd placed on top of the filled sheets; he leaned forward slightly, sensing imminent progress.

"She was the victim of a great injustice," I squeezed out. "I mean, she hadn't invited this, and yet there she was covering for him to his own children, while he was out screwing his mistress at her lovely, single person apartment devoid of any domestic responsibility. How unbelievable was that? She was a saint for coping with it and being there for her family through it all. She supported my father in his work all the while, doing his music copying for recording sessions, helping out at the studio and on film locations. She was unbelievable."

"Then why are you so angry with her?"

"What?"

Dr Greenbaum's voice was even and measured. "There's a lot of anger towards your mother."

"Anger? I wasn't angry with her," I shouted. "She got this raw deal and still managed to be selfless and supportive and pleasant and maintain a sense of humour. She even got spunky and embarked on an extra-marital adventure herself. Why would I be angry with her, of all people? She was the one who suffered!"

And what the hell is the matter with me, I thought, as my pulse surged.

"Taking it from another angle then, what was your role, your experience in this family situation?"

My heart thumped against my ribs. Fire all around.

"Um … well …" *Do I really have to do this?*

"For months and years I listened to one horrible story after another. I sympathised and raged and lived it all with her. I felt privileged and grown up that my mother would share her deepest feelings and adult secrets with me. I was sometimes shocked at the content but never showed it. I tried to convince her to leave, talked for hours about how she and I could move out and find somewhere to live and leave all this shit behind. We even got as far as looking at a few places, but she wouldn't take that step." An unwelcome lump rose in my throat and acid tears welled. "I couldn't protect her. I tried so hard but I couldn't save her."

"And why did you think it was your job to protect her, to save her?"

The remaining patch on my island of safety combusted as I saw what foul lessons in disempowerment I'd learned in service to my mother's fears. "She couldn't do it for herself. She was no match for him, his charm, and his persuasiveness. Someone had to be strong for her and I was all she had. She couldn't do it." Dr Greenbaum's pen advanced across the diminishing space on his page.

My jaws clenched, trying unsuccessfully to hold back the misery of seeing. Here was another betrayal to add to the collection, this time by the woman I viewed as an angel. My flight from the family was as much because of her as my father, but I'd never before seen her as being in any way culpable for her situation, or questioned her for piling that load onto her thirteen-year-old daughter. The façade of privileged confidante, mature beyond my years, crumbled before Dr Greenbaum's intuition to expose a bile-bitter anger at the irreplaceable treasure that had been taken from me. I'd glimpsed it, but hadn't realised the full meaning of a song I wrote during one of those secret, brace-free afternoons:

> *And so I weep for innocence lost,*
> *And childhood scattered into the wind.*
> *Now it's a diamond in my hand.*

"You know you're going to have to talk to her, don't you," said Dr Greenbaum, passing me a wad of tissues.

MOTHERS AND CHILDREN

"It was a rough therapy session today."

Alarm flashed in my mother's eyes as we stood in the kitchen preparing dinner, after my revelation about her earlier that day.

"Are you okay?" she asked.

"Mum, come look, come!" yelled my five-year-old son Dean from his bedroom.

"Not really," I said, wiping my hands and gratefully heading down the hallway to admire the latest Lego extravaganza rising from the low table in Dean's bedroom.

After dinner, and the bedtime stories and songs, elongated by the artful little devil, my mother and I sat at the dining room table with mugs of tea. Mark was away on one of his many business trips, and there we were. She never managed conflict or confrontation well, an aversion my brother and I both inherited, augmented by observing my father's addiction to drama. She looked fearful.

Therapy had already revealed my need to fix the broken and make sense of the chaotic. This drive, though I didn't recognise it at the time, served me well in my work life, as I progressed from computer programmer to systems analyst to project leader to business requirements analyst. I could take findings from workers at all levels about what was broken, what didn't make sense, and convert them into a plan to make it all okay. It was intellectually satisfying work that paid well and, inadvertently, filled some of the holes in me.

The dark side of this drive, equally eluding my notice, was a neurotic need for approval. It meant innumerable capitulations in my relationships, including with Mark, rather than holding out for what I really felt. Each time I crumbled in this way, I would feel a kind of spiritual nausea. I was weak, just like my mother — couldn't stand up for myself. I would push these thoughts away and turn my attention to something easier, like preparing a system-testing plan for a national insurance company, or an organisational strategy to prevent the computer-related disasters predicted for midnight 31 December 1999 as the new century arrived.

Dr Greenbaum helped me recognise those moments of choice, forks in the road when I could either do what was asked of me but with my teeth clenched, or make a truer choice for myself, despite the risk of causing displeasure. I'd tried it a few times with Mark. It was scary for both of us, requiring a stretch of intense emotional discomfort while we waded through conflict. I didn't always make the braver choice. But when I did, the results were often, ultimately, delightful.

As we sat at the table, with my mother smiling one of her supportive but frightened smiles, I knew this was one of those moments.

To the left: Tell her something from another session that had been only a bit distressing to me and didn't involve her. She'd be relieved, and I would be left feeling nauseous and weak.

To the right: let her have it even if it would cause her pain. Scary.

Then a third option appeared.

"It seems I've harboured resentment toward you, buried deep, about loading me up with your problems back then," I said calmly.

Her eyes instantly filled but she said, "I'm not surprised. I wish I could have done better for you."

"I've always taken your side, without questioning your part in letting it all happen. It's had consequences for me. I'm working through this stuff with Dr Greenbaum at the moment. There might be times that …" and now my eyes matched hers, "it'll be difficult for me to talk to you. But I have to do this, and we'll get through it, okay?"

She nodded and we hugged, sniffling.

It didn't address the many bad choices informed by my training at her feet, but it was enough, and she wasn't demolished by the exchange. When it came to it, I didn't want to make her suffer, just to heal myself. Sometimes the real therapy happens out there in the trenches.

The depth of all we had shared had held us in a manageable equilibrium, from the dramatic days at Hillcrest to our experiences of migrating to Australia. We also shared one of the deepest losses a mother can endure.

My sister died of a blood disease when she was seven months old. I don't know how old my brother and I were when we learned of Toni-Anne's brief existence, predating our own. The subject rarely came up and it never occurred to me to ask where she was buried.

Barely a year after my mother migrated to Australia in 1988, she and I stood side-by-side in the Macquarie Cemetery in Sydney, numb and unbelieving at the fresh grave of Melissa, my stillborn baby girl. The losses of our daughters bound us together and we held each other up for fear we would fall down.

After Melissa's death-birth, my mother and I for the first time really talked about Toni-Anne. My bereavement counselling was a barren substitute for a living child, but it was an improvement on the brutal cheerfulness that greeted nineteen-year-old June when she returned empty-handed from the hospital in September of 1952. Silence gathered around the memories held in her flesh of the little fingers encircled by her own as they sat through yet another blood transfusion. My brother Mike was born the following year and people said, kindly, "There you are — it's all right now."

It would never be all right. Ida gave Mike the Sesotho name Tsidiso, meaning child of consolation, after the child that dies. It's also a name that heralds mischief, and playing with fire. "Tsidiso, Tsidiso," Ida muttered under her breath when he blew his eyebrows off playing with gunpowder emptied out of firecrackers in the concrete backyard of our house.

Our son Dean was born prematurely, three years before Melissa, delivered at thirty weeks by emergency caesarean section. He weighed 1.4 kilos. For two months, I fed an electric breast pump and spent hours every day in the neonatal intensive care unit until he was well enough to be disconnected from the machinery and come home. By then I could tell when he stopped breathing long before the monitor siren went off. He weighed two kilos at three months old. We celebrated when, at eighteen months old, he made it onto the bottom of the weight chart at the Baby Health Clinic.

The nature of Dean's arrival shocked us. We had been to all the classes and practised all the breathing. I'd been a dedicated daily squatter and pelvic floor clencher, as per the instructions. We had read the books about upright, active birthing. The reality of our experience couldn't have been more different. At least I was more or less conscious during the birth, with an epidural and sedation, though I had to fight the drugs ferociously to achieve the level of consciousness I did.

As a result of the experience with Dean, I was under scrutiny during my second pregnancy. The hospital asked me to participate in a study of what they called "high-risk mothers", which meant extra check-ups by the research team. I didn't mind. Everything was going to be fine this time. I had been on blood pressure medication since Dean was born.

But my body defied my yearning to mother many children. I threw up so often during the first trimester that it took until the four-month mark for me to regain my pre-pregnant weight. At just over five months my blood pressure blew out again and they recommended as much rest as possible. At six months, they told me to go to bed and stay there for the remainder of the pregnancy. I listened to relaxation cassette tapes, but found that the measured voice tied my stomach in knots. I read many books and played games with Dean as he kept me company. Mark moved a small TV set into our bedroom.

Three weeks passed. Our band was due to play a gig on a harbour cruise. It was the last one we had booked during the expected period of my pregnancy and I wanted to do it, despite misgivings about what the medical team might say. I rose from my bedrest and put on the baggiest performing clothes I had. It was satisfying to get out there and sing again, though I was exhausted by the end of it.

As the days crawled by, I started noticing periods of inner stillness. Then there'd be a kick or a flop and I'd berate myself for being over-anxious. But the quiet periods grew longer, the kicks fainter and my anxiety spiralled. I told Mark and my mother. We contacted the obstetrician and he asked me to come in to the Royal North Shore Hospital for an ultrasound. Waiting in the ward that evening for the orderlies to fetch me, I listened on earphones to classical pieces played by Branford Marsalis. I hoped it would block out the silence in my body.

They wheeled my bed down a never-ending outdoor corridor. I watched the corrugations of the curved roof go by overhead, with the night sky on either side, and felt the warmth of Mark's hand holding mine as he walked beside the bed. All was quiet except for the click of the wheels over the joins in the concrete. We passed no one. After the ultrasound, we repeated the process in reverse. They wouldn't say anything to us except that the obstetrician would come soon. I couldn't bear to listen to music anymore. Mark and I held hands in silence. Eventually the doctor arrived. He was kind, but couldn't soften the pitiless news. The baby was dead. We should go home and return in the morning when they would induce and he would deliver the baby.

At home, my mother, Mark and I held each other close and wept. There was nothing to say. Mark's cousin Beryl, a psychologist, happened to call at that moment to ask how we were. She put down the phone and drove straight over. She sat with us into the night and helped us deal with our situation as much as possible.

Not even the induction the next day worked. I went into labour, but bled so profusely that the obstetrician called for another emergency caesarean. I could feel my whole back submerged by the pool of blood as they sped me out of the delivery room and down the hall to the operating theatre. This time I was grateful for the drugs that spun me out of consciousness.

I don't remember much about the first few days. I do, however, remember with perfect clarity the brief encounter with our daughter immediately after I came out of the theatre. I learned later that they quickly cleaned her and somehow brought me round so that I could hold her while she was still womb-warm. She looked like Dean did when he was born. Lying on my side, I pulled her into my arms, breathed in her baby fragrance, and rubbed her velvet skin with my cheek. I don't remember them taking her away, so I must have slipped into unconsciousness again while holding her. I will always be grateful to those nurses, whose faces and names I will never know, for giving me that unrepeatable time with my baby. We saw her and held her again, as we discussed funeral arrangements, but by then her body was morgue-chilled and had started to dry out and shrivel. She felt like a doll, no longer like a real child.

I can't be sure what sustained the façade that enabled me to function after we lost Melissa. Physical recovery, the funeral and the first surge of sympathies consumed the first two weeks. I was quite ill and needed a lot of rest. Then, after another couple of weeks, our band played at a venue in Sydney. My mind flew back to those few weeks to the last time the band had played.

Did I bring about Melissa's death because I didn't do as I was told and stay in bed?

I would never be able to answer that question for certain. But the doctors decided that my body struggled to sustain pregnancy because of my compromised kidney. They said Melissa showed signs of developmental problems going much further back into the pregnancy than my day of bad judgement, though I couldn't shake the shreds of doubt and guilt. They also said it could have gone the other way, with Melissa surviving and Dean not. That shocked me, along with the information that I had at least a twenty-five per cent chance of any subsequent pregnancy ending in similar tragedy.

I could never listen to Branford Marsalis again, nor feel entirely comfortable participating in guided meditations. My hostility toward the Cape Town doctor who gave me tranquilisers instead of treating my dying kidney took on new proportions.

I started the long haul toward accepting that my only child would be Dean, the blessed three-year-old to whom I had to explain death. His little unbidden fingers appeared beside me as I grieved, and dabbed my eyes with tissues. Compassion came to him naturally, without a commensurate intellectual understanding. His heart understood, and I learned kindness from him.

Mark and I drifted in space, dealing in our separate ways with the savage sorrow.

Most of the year that followed was lost to me. It was, in retrospect, a kindness from some part of my brain that registered the total impossibility of dealing with this loss, and instead put consciousness on hold. I don't remember if I went back to computer work or did any singing during that time. I have some scrappy memories of my mother hovering over me, her eyes full of love and concern. Of not being able to hold other people's babies, and of the caring pre-school director telling me that it wasn't a problem, but just to let me know that Dean had started wetting himself. She'd seen it happen before with a trauma in the family. I also remember heaving rocks and making the garden bloom in my need to produce something living. Mark did some of this kind of heavy work too. But mostly he went to work. It felt to me like he went to work and never came back. He would have felt much more in control there than at home, I'm certain. Promotions came, and he started travelling extensively. We entered the most challenging years our marriage would face.

The fog lifted eventually. There was life after loss, but it was a different life, one that would always be accompanied by a beloved little ghost.

Many years later, in the months of my mother's final decline in 2002, sixteen-year-old Dean had the job each evening of feeding his grandmother the various colours of mush I'd made so she could swallow something nutritious. Her fading eyes twinkled as she tried to yell at Dean's antics with the spoon, echoing hers with him as a toddler. On her last night, before we left the hospital, Dean warned her not to get up to mischief with the guy in the next ward. "Piss off," she grunted with a smile. They were her last words to him. He knew they meant, "I love you, you mischievous boy."

It had become clear to me, in my mother's final months, that she would never record the story of her grandfather Johan. For the first time, I found myself thinking about it, and felt a sense of simmering desperation as I watched the possibility fade, along with her unshared memories.

"Just talk about it. I'll take notes and write them out later," I pleaded during the many hours I spent with her in those months, but her mind was receding, and she was interested only in her medications, holding family members close, and recalling her global adventures with Colin, my father, making films. I was outraged that this was what occupied her. After all she'd suffered at his hands.

June could not be left alone for more than a few minutes. Physically, she was unable to do anything for herself, and without company her spirits plummeted into a bleak valley where none could follow. My father, consumed with a new and dubious love affair, was absent from our lives, and from the round-the-clock care roster I was managing.

After his love affair crashed, my father rode back into town like a returning hero. June had by then started her final hospital sojourn. She couldn't fend for herself in the hospital environment either, and was terrified. If she dropped the call button from her bed, she was physically unable to retrieve it by herself and therefore isolated. Our private care roster continued without a pause and they set up a cot in her private ward. My father said, "I'll take the night shift, so you and Mark can get some rest". I accepted his offer without a smile. I couldn't summon the energy to voice what I was thinking. *Where has your noble magnanimity been these past six months, Dad? Don't expect me to gush with gratitude now.*

June hung on like this for two weeks until my brother and his family arrived from South Africa and she'd spent time with them. One evening we were all around her bedside — the only time every member of her immediate family had been in a room together, ever. I guess that was enough for her. Late that night, holding my father's hand, she let go of life.

The emotional and physical drain of caring for a parent at such intensity for so long sometimes leads one's gaze, guiltily, forward to the relief of grieving. But when it comes it brings a new climate of pain. I tried to navigate the toxic mess of grief and love and disappointments, punctuated with flash floods of anger at her failure to stand up for herself, at her failure to write the story about her ancestors.

I'd never been interested in them before, but suddenly felt bereft that I'd lost them along with my mother. She was going to write Johan and Mary Ann's story. Now their story was lost forever. And not only to me, but to generations of descendants I'd never known, who now rose quietly to the surface to stand sorrowfully, I imagined, around the edges of my consciousness. I blamed my mother's weakness for this loss.

These feelings subsided over time, with an occasional storm surge each time I tried to sort through my mother's relics. But it started to bother me, as I planned that first research trip in 2011, that I had no knowledge of where her immediate family members were buried. Enquiries led me to a cemetery in Durban to find a family plot. It was a double plot. On the left were Oupa, Granny Grace, and June's only sibling, Ray, who died too young.

I was shocked at the tombstone on the right. There were two names, two skeletons sharing this single grave. They were my mother's Granny Mary Ann, eighty-six, and my sister, Toni-Anne, seven months old, who died three years later.

My mother would have been at the funerals of all five people. She didn't tell me where they were buried, or that they shared this resting place. Mike and I were old enough at the times of three of the funerals, but no one suggested we attend.

The sight of these four generations collected in a place of which I'd had no knowledge sent tremors through me. I felt an eerie presence of the many family members, known and unknown to me, who might also have been at these funerals. Sadness rose at the thought that so few remained who might tell their stories. Anger and resentment reared again too, that my mother had lacked the drive to collect and record them. She was the one who had known them. Now there was no one left to do it, and I had not volunteered for the job. But guilt also pricked at me. I'd shown so little interest in the family.

As I stood at the unfamiliar family grave, these conflicting feelings crashed into one another. My sister lay there, sharing a grave with the woman who was at Johan's side through all the events I was trying to uncover. I'm not superstitious, but neither am I closed to the possible existence of mystical forces beyond my understanding. A forceful thought arose that felt like a direct message from somewhere important.

"Keep going," it said. "This quest will be meaningful in ways you cannot currently perceive."

For decades I'd held the position that families, dynasties and countries were maps of importance in other people's worlds, not mine. I would continue to be self-sufficient wherever I was, without relying on such things. Now, threads of family were starting to appear and I detected the gossamer beginnings of a map of the world on which I might just have a place. Though light and elusive, this prospect reached inside me and stirred a yearning for a place of belonging. To understand why I had denied this basic human desire, I would need to revisit more of the difficult places in my past. My heart had shut them out for so long.

THE GIFT OF A MAJOR CHORD

Why did he have to come crashing in like that? Uninvited, unwelcome, reeking of ashtrays and the day's drowned disappointments. Wasn't the closed bedroom door a clear enough message?

I wasn't sure which was worse; hearing the footsteps scrunch their way up the stairs and approach my door, or lying with a pillow over my head trying to block the outraged rise and fall of his voice floating up the stairwell. I knew so well how tedious it was for my mother, the stoic listener. Sometimes the listener would be me, if I didn't manage to dive under the covers and switch off the light by the time the footsteps reached my door.

I was fourteen and my bedroom had become a haven. With the help of Jacques, a friend who would later become my first husband, I painted the room a soothing shade of lilac. My mother made a bedspread out of the fabric I chose, a loose-woven cloth in a similar shade. She edged it with a white-tasselled trim and I stitched on sprays of white appliqué daisies here and there. A shaggy lilac carpet almost completed the cocoon, the final touch being a restored writing bureau that had belonged to my father's father; ballast to my lilac vessel as it ploughed through the heavy seas of my parents' unresolvable difficulties.

In the 1930s, when office furniture featured oak, walnut and turned legs, my father's father shipped it out from England for his office. The desk became my daily companion, enabling me to maintain some order and control with its many pigeonholes and compartments. I had a place for everything. A dedicated section for pens and pencils, for exercise books and scrap paper and for my cigarettes, and the marijuana which I would smoke in a daily ritual after school, emptying out the first inch or so of a cigarette and filling it with the leaves of relief. Having smoked it, I would immerse myself in homework. My intricate diagrams for botany and anatomy would later fetch a useful price from an incoming Standard 8 student.

That year I received the prize for overall improvement, having leapt at least ten per cent in every subject. Encouraged and supported by my much older boyfriend, I'd started finding satisfaction in the work for its own sake. My mother was proud and pleased, thinking all must be well, though she asked, with some anxiety, "When did you choose your subjects, and what did you choose?" when she discovered from another parent that all the subject choices had been made some weeks prior.

My father had no idea what grade I was in and never attended anything at school. He wasn't often home when we ate dinner. Indeed, his absences regularly stretched over several days. Since the disclosure, my mother had given up the feeble explanations for his absences. When I did hear the car pull up in the driveway, I would dash for the stairs, taking them three at a time to seek lilac refuge. It was better if he was very late, so I could pretend to be asleep, even though I lay frozen in a torment of rage and despair. Then there were nights of scrunching footsteps when I wasn't quick enough, and would be stuck with the slurred monologue, as I picked miserably at the edges of white appliqué daisies.

My parents gave me a record player of my own for my fourteenth birthday and my delight with it overcame the distaste I had by then at accepting anything from my father. It was a portable unit, the lid housing the speaker, so it became compact when closed up. I cleared a space for it on the shelf at the foot of my bed and went out to buy a couple of my favourite seven singles with the money I also hated taking, but couldn't find the courage to refuse. I resolved to find a weekend job.

Like any other fourteen-year-old I followed the progress of the pop charts — the "hit parade" — on the radio. Unlike other fourteen-year-olds I knew, I had grown up surrounded by jazz and musicians and crazy parties. But the glowing times of impromptu dances to big band records had passed. Now the parties were with ad agency men and a range of subservient wives, yawning and furtively checking their watches as the night wore on and on, and overly made up young women hanging on the utterances of the unsteady men as if they were wise. When the booze and nostalgia had flowed long enough, my dad would bring out his Louis Armstrong 78s and, as my portable was the only record player in the house that had a setting for 78s, one or other of my parents would tiptoe into my room as I pretended to sleep, unplug the record player and take it downstairs. My mother would struggle to keep the volume down, and scurry up and down the stairs into the early hours of the morning trying to placate me. She failed in all areas.

One party erupted very late, after a night at a bar with ad agency people. My father had initially been refused entry because he wasn't wearing a tie. He was always braced to meet the challenge of a maître d'hôtel looking askance at Norina's dark skin, and Norina always ready to produce the white identity card that my father and two of his partners had perjured themselves to obtain for her. But this night it was the tie. Two British sailors were also waiting to enter the hotel bar. One of them dramatically ripped off his lanyard and gave it to my father to use as a tie. The visiting sailors didn't pay for another drink all night, and were part of the group that shrieked and blustered into our house at eleven pm. I couldn't sleep, not even with pillows piled on my head. At around five am, seething, I went downstairs.

"Where is my mother?" I demanded of a woman I'd never seen before, her heavy makeup smudged unattractively beneath bleary eyes. She mumbled something about my mother taking a sailor down to the beach — he wanted to see the dawn from there. *Charming*, I thought. I wouldn't stoop to asking my father, incoherent but still in fervent conversation of a sort with one of the ad men. I retreated, stomping back up the stairs. Maybe the smudged lady got the message, because the volume of the music dropped. I cried myself to sleep. The alarm went off an hour-and-a-half later.

In my school uniform, I sat just beyond the edge of the unsteady group for whom my mother was now preparing toast and fried eggs. Still in her dressing gown, my entirely sober mother drove me to school, her abject apologies crashing uselessly against my flinty silence. That afternoon there was no evidence of the party ever having happened and my record player was back in its place on the shelf at the foot of my bed. My father was still sleeping it off and by the time he emerged that evening, my door was firmly shut. Despite my mother's efforts to thaw the frost, there was no cocoa and conversation for many days.

"We have to get out of here," I said, finally. We went as far as looking at a few rental places in a nearby suburb, but my mother was in the grip of the inexplicable paralysis that would later cause me to flee for my own survival. I could find no means by which to light a path to my father, no means by which to forgive him and no joy to share with him.

Then came the night of the major chord.

The scene was familiar: dinner with my mother, clearing away, conversation, then the car pulling up outside and the dash for the stairs. This night, however, the footsteps came immediately after me, with no time even to hide my ashtray or assume a pose of homework, far less sleep. He barged into my room, face on fire and brandished a long-playing record.

"Hi," he said conspiratorially, as if all was normal between us, and went straight over to the record player, a pungent tendril of beer following him across the room. "I have to play you something." He removed the disc from the sleeve with reverence and mounted it on the turntable. Then he sat down beside me among the white daisies.

There was a piano introduction — Oscar Peterson. I knew that Oscar Peterson and Beethoven were his two major musical heroes. I knew the song, "The Shadow of Your Smile". But then came the voices of the Singers Unlimited. I had never heard a sound like this. I hadn't yet sung in school choirs, having always been called upon to play piano for the choir at primary school. My rotten high school had no choir. I'd done a little tentative solo singing, mainly at school concerts with my brother on guitar, and was raised on Ella Fitzgerald and Billie Holiday. But this took vocal music way beyond anything I'd heard. The beautiful voices of the quintet were gentle, perfectly in tune and moved together as a single organism. I didn't have words for it then, but the sound of the complex harmonies awoke a profound musical awareness in my soul, and a love of voices in harmony that would never leave me.

For three minutes and twenty-five seconds I forgot about the pain, the hate, the love, the pretending to be asleep. A father I recognised looked at me with a light in his eyes I hadn't seen in a long time. I felt something very small shift inside me. The corners of his mouth cautiously registered the shift. Soft lanterns glowed, lighting a precarious path from the creative games of my childhood to the improvised West Side Story dances, to this moment and into a far distance I couldn't see. We smiled warily across the chasm between us. But we said nothing as the rich, close voices spread into the majesty of the final major chord.

THE DARK YEARS

As my abbreviated adolescence sped by, my friends at school, dwindling in number, seemed impressed that I was openly smoking at home and had a sparkling adult life with a ridiculous range of freedoms. That was one way of looking at it. Maybe I played up these elements; there was no possibility of sharing much else with them. It was getting harder to relate to people my own age, whom I assumed had normal families. Most families have their own brands of craziness, but I doubted any of my classmates had a home life like mine.

During my second year of high school I had started working on weekends. The jeans store in town helped me achieve some independence, in the same year the walls of the studio crashed down as a result of "Soul Africa". The film was intended to make everyone a fortune. Instead, it plunged the business into its own dark years and my parents into a new, crushing stress. They didn't notice that I no longer asked them for pocket money. In any case, it wasn't to make them feel bad, but to make me feel better.

Another film project loomed during my winter school holidays, a documentary for an explosives company supplying the mining industry.

"Come with us," said my mother.

"It'd be great to have you along as production assistant," said my father, noticing me for a moment.

My mother added, "It'll be fun and anyway, you can't stay here by yourself." I had no choice.

I always did enjoy road trips, but the subject of this film didn't sound riveting, and I didn't relish twenty hours trapped in the car with my parents and the producer, my dad's alcoholic right-hand man. I wondered why my dad needed someone like that around, laughing too loudly at everything he said, and referring to him as "Big C" or "CC" in a way that left no doubt that my father, Colin, had no closer friend or colleague. Jim was "the man", not only at the studio but also at all the parties. Amongst my parents' buffet of adult mysteries to ponder, I didn't pay him much attention.

I'd discovered the books of Ayn Rand, and used some of my recent earnings to buy *Atlas Shrugged*, a tome to last me the journey, even for the rapid reader I'd become. I didn't realise how well that book would serve me.

A couple of days before our departure, I answered the phone.

"Hi, it's Jim. Is that Judy?"

"Yes. My dad isn't home right now."

"That's okay. I hear we're going to be co-workers."

"Yes. I suppose you'll show me what my job will be?"

"Of course. Actually, I was thinking it'd be a good idea if we got together before we leave and I can tell you about it."

"Oh?" *How hard could it be?*

"There's something else I want to talk to you about too, privately." I was intrigued. "Would tonight be okay? I could come and pick you up."

"Um … um … okay."

"Great. It's something I'd rather keep just between us. You'll understand. Can you meet me down the end of your street?"

"Well, they'll be out until late, so I could just meet you outside the house."

"All right. See you at seven."

Despite my low opinion of him, I felt flattered that the producer would like to brief me on the production, and wished to confide something that even The Great CC wouldn't hear. I told our maid, Julia, that I was going over to my friend's place down the road and she didn't need to wait up for me — I had my key.

"I thought we'd go to The Clifton," he said. This was a regular haunt of most of the adults I knew, the advertising crowd and others connected to the studio, musicians, contemporaries of my parents and my brother. I'd been there many times.

From our table, we waved to a few people at the bar. I noted surprise on a few faces, seeing me there with Jim. *To hell with them, I'm all grown up now,* I thought, as I sipped my first brandy and coke. He spoke in general terms about the ins and outs of the production. It was all very pleasant and I enjoyed the adult treatment. But by my third drink I was having trouble focussing.

"What was the other thing you wanted to talk about?" I thought we'd better get to it while I could still listen half sensibly.

"You know, I feel funny talking about it here in public. My flat is right next door. I'd rather go there to talk." My curiosity level was high, as was my blood alcohol. It was only standing at his front door that an alarm bell rang in my head. *What if? No, this guy is my dad's trusted man.*

Whatever transpired between my entering that door and my re-emergence some time later, consigned itself to a place I've never been able to access. Try as I might, I have no recall other than one brief close up of an erect penis.

I do remember that I moved along the walkway to the street a sober, wax effigy, and sat frozen in the car all the way home. He touched my leg at one point, and asked, as I shrank from his touch, "Are you frigid?" I didn't answer, but the words reverberated in the vacant tin can of my brain. My only thoughts were, *I want to be home,* and *I want to be away from this man.* He dropped me at the end of my deserted street with no words and I walked the last two hundred metres, a robot in the dark.

No one was home. I was grateful. Falling into bed at last, I allowed myself to cry. *Stupid, stupid, vain girl. What on earth did you think? That he was interested in you as a person?* And, *Why did he ask me if I'm frigid? Am I?* I see now what a ridiculous self-interrogation it was for a thirteen-year-old girl who had just had a bad experience.

The next day I wasn't sore anywhere, so at least I couldn't have been raped. But I faced sharing the back seat of my parents' car for ten days and two thousand miles with a man who had sunk in my view from an unimpressive sycophant to a paedophile of unknown extent.

I was deeply ashamed, both of having been such an imbecile and of whatever might have taken place in the black hole of that evening. There was no telling my parents, or Mike or Norina, absolutely no possibility of ever speaking to Jim again beyond a small hello or goodbye, and no way to tell anyone at school. That left … no one. Another piece of youth fell by the wayside.

My parents were busy with the production and didn't notice my silence, curled into the smallest possible ball against the door of the Mercedes Benz. As we departed, around thirty-six hours after my appalling "date", I opened *Atlas Shrugged*. I remained in grateful literary captivity for ten days, apart from holding a clipboard in a few dynamite plants, hard-hatted and white coated, and making some production notes for my mother. Jim didn't once refer to our sham briefing, or ask me to help him.

The one pleasurable memory of the trip was when my father organised for me to push the old-fashioned plunger on the detonator for an explosion they were to film. The shudder of the earth was immense, then followed the thrilling sight of an enormous cliff across a quarry parting from the land on the other side. A tidal wave of dust and earth hurtled towards us. The tape recorder was still rolling and we laughed afterwards at the crunchy soundtrack of our flight, barely making it to the car before the gritty wave hit us.

Ayn Rand's novel left me with one discomfort. I couldn't help comparing her empowered heroine with my mother's disempowerment, my inability to help her and, now, my own degradation and powerlessness.

It took years — and Dr Greenbaum — for me to feel somewhat stronger. But I didn't tell him, or Mark, that story. Perhaps, having finally wept as an adult for my mother, I will exorcise the coiled fear that in the underground compartments of my soul is a gullible girl who still cannot stand up for herself. That liberation still didn't come with the news, more than a decade later, that Jim had committed suicide. I felt sorry for his family, and again shied away from the memories.

By the time Mitch, my romantic 'minder' in Swaziland, and his girlfriend came to stay during one of my parents' frequent absences, my self-esteem was at rock bottom. But it was fun to hang out with them, and there was that special connection he and I always shared. Through them I met the three young men who would change my life and that of my family.

Within a few weeks I had felt drawn to visit them multiple times in their flat in Disa Towers, the "Salt and Pepper Shakers" on the slopes of Devils Peak overlooking the city. Jacques and Ricky lived there. Another friend, Geoff, seemed to mostly live there too, sleeping on a mattress in the living room.

My brother, on leave from the army, was with my mother one evening when they dropped me off at Disa Towers and on his insistence, came up to see where I was going. He was horrified, and spent the rest of the evening lecturing our mother. "How can you let her go there? Do you know who these people are?"

I can see how it must have looked to him: shafts of feeble blue light fought through thick marijuana smoke engulfing ten or so people, somehow in conversation despite the deafening strains of James Taylor. But this was a place of refuge for me, much safer than home.

I spent a whole weekend at Disa Towers. My mother protested, but as usual, she couldn't prevail. It was heaven. That Saturday night, at the pub where no one questioned my age, there was talk about my upcoming fourteenth birthday. I hadn't felt so nurtured in a long time. A group of people in their twenties was discussing a birthday party they had conceived for me, and asking me if I'd prefer this or that. Decisions were made. I floated inside when Ricky dropped me at home, and it wasn't just the effects of the weekend's intake of illicit substances.

The night of the party was thrilling. They toasted me; we ate pizza, drank beer and smoked a lot. We listened to Carole King, Yes and Frank Zappa, with earnest discussion about everything from music to the inevitable South African politics to the nature of the universe.

As the evening wore on, Geoff stayed close to me. He was twenty-two, handsome, well spoken with a rich voice and he played guitar and sang beautifully. He'd been a major mover in planning this party. Late in the evening he nervously produced an envelope from his shirt pocket. "Don't read it now," he said.

A downside of substance abuse is that it's hard to remember all the details. I believe I slept there, among the half dozen or so fully clad sleepers on mattresses spread across the living room, innocently cuddled up between Geoff and someone else, under a mishmash of blankets and pillows. I did not comply with Geoff's instruction.

It was a birthday poem about pursuing dreams, staying strong and striving for individualism. He'd signed it at the bottom saying, "Dedicated to Judy, a far-out chick." The energy flowing from him bore no conditions, and was intoxicating. That night we shyly reached out into my first serious relationship. It would last for over two years and guide me onto a healthier path at a time when I was vulnerable.

The happiness of first love outshone the miseries of home. He was gorgeous, funny, wrote me poems, eventually discouraged me from smoking dope and encouraged me to take school seriously again. My results climbed higher.

I only wore my brace to school now, despite my mother's efforts.

There would be a price to pay. I was still growing, and gradually consumed all the gains of the first, dedicated year of brace-wearing.

Geoff's car rarely started without being pushed and, naturally, he had to be in the driver's seat. Pushing that car was the worst thing for my spine at that time, but I didn't care.

Geoff was earning very little as a junior teller at the bank, where his father had organised him a job. My income from the jeans store often paid for us to go to a movie, half-fill the tank, and have a beer at the pub.

But I was happy for the first time in a while and I loved him deeply.

My third year in high school began, Mike was in his second year in the army, and the situation took a new turn.

My dad was drinking heavily, in serious debt, and mostly absent. Building the new studio from the ruins of "Soul Africa" was daunting. Norina was back at his side after her excursion with Tara, and working hard to help him save the business. The focus, though, was film rather than music, where my mother's skills as a music copyist resided.

Geoff progressed from dropping me off at my gate to coming inside to say hello to my mother. Most often we'd find her alone. Ricky would sometimes be with us.

"Thanks for bringing Judy home. I've just made a pot of soup — would you guys like to stay for dinner?"

"That'd be great," they both said at once. And later, "She looks like your sister, not your mother."

And so the easy friendship between my mother and my friends began. I was fourteen and looked twenty; she was thirty-nine and looked twenty-five, and they were in their mid-twenties. I came to know my mother's wilder side.

With my father out of the way, and my mother getting on so well with the guys, I invited a few more of the crowd over for a swim in our pool, some food and drink. It became our summer haunt. Dope was regularly on the menu, my hash cookies now famous.

"Dad is so anti-marijuana," my mother would say, "but it's hard to knock it. You all laugh, devour milk and cookies, and then go to sleep. It seems quite wholesome compared to the nasty stuff that goes on when Dad and his cronies are drinking."

"Do you want to try it?" asked Ricky.

She giggled. "You know, I think I do."

A frontier fell. There was more to come.

I clearly wasn't watching, but Ricky had fallen in love with my mother. After recovering from the shock, I thought, *Yeah, why not. Go June.*

Later I learned that my father had encouraged it, thinking it'd keep her happy while he was pursuing happy elsewhere. He didn't account for her falling in love.

Jacques then met my mother's friend, Sharon, and the anomalous sextet was formed: Ricky and June, aged twenty-five and thirty-nine; Jacques and Sharon, aged twenty-five and thirty-three, Geoff and Judy, aged twenty-two and fourteen. It was good to feel happy, and to see my mother bloom. I knew it was weird, but happy won the day.

In my fourth year of high school, Mike returned from army service but soon left for a residency at a hotel in Pretoria. The band also engaged Jacques on bass. The atmosphere between Sharon and Jacques had strained after she'd moved in with him at the larger Disa Towers apartment to which the three young men had moved. She contributed more than she received, stocked the refrigerator and brought her decorating talents to the place. She also nagged them, with good reason, about untidiness. She wanted to know why Jacques was late from work. She wanted a ring. He left for Pretoria without her.

Ricky spoiled and romanced my mother, he rocked her softly when she needed comfort and ran errands when she needed milk and bread. He took the pressure right off me, though my mother still shared all manner of inappropriate confidences with me.

Geoff started staying over, both of us squeezed into my single bed. My mother would bring us cocoa in the morning; I'd dress for school and Geoff for work. Ricky started staying over too, in my absent brother's bedroom.

Ricky had some time off, I was on school holidays and we took a trip to visit Jacques and my brother, Mike, in Pretoria. Sharon joined us in the hope of resurrecting the passion between her and Jacques.

Ricky's car broke down after just two hours on the road. We waited three hours while the repair shop in Touwsrivier repaired it. The second, terminal breakdown happened barely thirty minutes after we were back on the road. I called home from a public phone. My mother dithered with the news while my dad took the lead. He was good at that.

"Why don't you take the Merc, pick them up and go visit Mike in Pretoria as well?"

"Um … I feel a bit nervous about driving by myself."

"Call Geoff now and see if he can get a few days off work."

She and Geoff reached us as the light leached out of the sky. She must have driven like a demon.

Sharon was pent up about the trip. The delays had sharpened the edges. She grabbed our bags from Ricky's dead car and rammed them into the boot of the Mercedes.

"Careful," I said as heavy items threatened to damage my brace.

She glared at me and carried on shoving. I glanced at my mother, who had brought the brace with her — I certainly didn't pack it — but she said nothing.

Ricky, June and Geoff took turns driving through the night. By mid-morning, we were an hour away from Pretoria.

"Can we stop soon?" I asked. "I'd like to freshen up before we get there."

"Who do you want to tart up for, your brother?" Sharon sneered.

I was shocked by her attack, hurt that my mother again didn't stand up for me, but reasoned that if I was too weak to stand up for myself, I couldn't expect anyone else to do it.

It wasn't the only time Sharon accused me, indirectly, of seductive intentions toward Jacques. She was wrong. But perhaps she intuited what neither Jacques nor I could yet foresee.

Jacques' cool greeting of her must have been tough. But she travelled with him and the band to their next residency, in Rhodesia (now Zimbabwe). There the relationship buckled under the strain of living together in a house of wild young musicians. Jacques was a few years older than them, but his heart was still in their world.

Meanwhile, my father grew aware of the unanticipated and growing threat from Ricky. Once again, one of his women had been so bold as to start really caring about someone other than him. He started spending more time at home, but this brought new bouts of drunken monologues that drifted up the stairwell and through the pillow on my head.

He took Geoff's presence well. How could he do otherwise? He was hardly modelling normality for me.

"So, I hear you'd like to be a copywriter?" he asked Geoff.

"Yes, but I don't know where to start."

"No guarantees, but I'll talk to some people in the advertising world."

Through my father's contacts Geoff got a job in Port Elizabeth, eight hours drive from Cape Town.

"Surely you know people in Cape Town?" I wailed at my dad.

"This is a great agency to start in," he said. "You'll see. This'll just be a stepping stone."

Geoff's parents were horrified at him leaving the safety of the bank and heading, as they saw it, to Mars. I went to Port Elizabeth during school holidays.

But prolonged separations, and new influences on Geoff from what I viewed as my father's world, took their toll.

Later that year, Mike and his band were in Cape Town for a few days en route from Rhodesia to an exciting job in Spain. The whole band, including Jacques, stayed at Hillcrest, and the romance between us stirred. It was unexpected, and thrilling. But it was over in a flash, and life returned to normal.

The longstanding headmaster of our terrible school had left at the start of that year and a vacuum of a year passed before a new one arrived. Nature abhors a vacuum, and during 1973 two school friends, Chris and Gordon, and myself filled it, becoming known as The Triumvirate. This was my first training ground in teamwork and leadership: being effective, and finishing projects involving many people. We started a school newspaper and spearheaded the staging of the play on our English syllabus: "Arms and the Man" by George Bernard Shaw. The production ran successfully over four nights. The party at my house, after the show on the final night, was remembered by many for the giant tube of marijuana I'd constructed, which served the entire party for a number of hours.

At the start of 1974, a new principal arrived at the school. He heard about us and called us in, keen to know about the members and initiatives of The Triumvirate. Then, cleverly, he involved the three of us in the long process towards redeeming the dreadful reputation of our school.

It was a rewarding time for me at school, but life continued strangely at home. One night, Ricky, my mother and I had spent a pleasant evening together then gone off in our separate directions. My dad came home just after I'd gone to bed. I lunged for the light switch. No one was expecting him and the rest of the house was in darkness. The footsteps came up the stairs to my closed bedroom door and kept on coming.

He sat on the side of my bed for a while, as I pretended to be asleep. Then he mumbled, "Move over."

"Hmm?" I grunted. *Go away. Please, please go away.*

"Move over … please?" He leaned over me and the fumes almost knocked me out. I moved closer to the wall without turning around. He snuggled up and was soon snoring loudly.

I extricated myself and manoeuvred to the bottom of the bed.

Nothing much was going to wake him. I went into my parents' room. No one was there. I hesitated, but need overcame discretion and I made my way down the dark corridor to what had become Ricky's room. He and my mother were in a similar state to the one in which I'd stumbled on Norina and Tara some years earlier, in the same spot.

Of course, I knew about their relationship, was glad of it, and frequently saw them being demonstrative with each other. But somehow, at that moment in the darkness of our complicated house, it was more than I could take. I burst into tears and ran to my mother's bed. They came running after me.

"I don't want to go back to my room."

"Easy, easy," said Ricky.

"Let's all just stay right here," said my mother.

If he'd woken up, my father would have seen the three of us nestled together in his king-size bed, like the bodies on the floor of the apartment at Disa Towers.

But he was still asleep in my bed when Ricky, June and I sat down for breakfast in tense silence. I looked down to see I'd smeared the tablecloth with blood. *Damn.* I recognised the risk if I tore at the flesh around my fingernail any harder but, still, I kept picking. I slid a serviette into my lap, where I tore off a corner without taking my eyes off Ricky and my mother across the table. I pressed it hard around my finger to stop the bleeding before anyone noticed.

Geoff visited from Port Elizabeth. We stayed up into the night talking, crying and eventually parting. I watched him walk to his car, lit by a harsh streetlight. I wanted this parting, but the loss of the relationship overwhelmed me. I felt alone in a whole new way, looking into an unknown future without this soulful man who had nurtured me with love and humour through what could have been a period of unrecoverable disaster. I was grateful, and I loved him still. His unique place in my heart remains. He eventually made it to Madison Avenue, New York, the mecca for writers in advertising.

As I sobbed, that night, I felt pins and needles around my mouth, and my lips puckered into a fixed position. When my fingers and wrists went rigid I freaked out. I would never have gone into my parents' bedroom when I knew my father was there, but I didn't know what was happening to me. I tried to wake my mother without disturbing him. She jumped out of bed and I led her to my room. Somehow, she knew about hyperventilation.

"I'm going to get Dad."

"No, no, don't," I pleaded. But she came back with him just a minute later.

"Stay here with her, and try to get her to stop crying. I'm going to get a paper bag."

He obeyed without hesitation, unused to her being so authoritative.

"Okay sweetie, let's see what we can think about here," he said, stroking my hair. It didn't work.

But she was back almost immediately and said, "Here, bunch up the top and breathe into it. Slowly. One, two, three, four …" They sat on either side of me, each holding a hand or arm and stroking my forehead, my shoulder, my back. My mind unclenched and I surrendered to the unfamiliar sensation of parents supporting me in a moment of need. The craziness in my face and hands subsided. I was exhausted and allowed them to help me into bed. It had been a long time since someone had sat with me and held my hand until I fell asleep.

But the golden moment passed and the levels of alcohol-fuelled drama continued to rise with the conflict between Ricky and Colin.

"Ricky wants to marry me," my mother told me.

"That's wonderful," I beamed at her.

"Oh Judy, it's not that simple."

"Why not?"

My mother chose the dramatic drunk and his fantasies for their bizarre trio.

"Why, why, why?" I yelled.

"It'd be much harder for Ricky down the track. My health could really go downhill as I get older. This way he'll make a clean start. It's agony for us both right now, but I'm doing this for him."

I was livid. And stricken with sorrow at saying goodbye to Ricky. Unable to endure my mother's concurrent proximity and predicament, he left for the UK, never to return.

The Triumvirate was a mainstay in my final year of school. We three featured in the top few academic placements. We vied amicably for those spots, with genuine joy for one another whenever some good result was achieved.

My treasured friendship with Chris quietly deepened and developed into an unofficial romance. Perhaps it would have endured. But Jacques returned from Spain and my relationship with him roared back into life. He moved into a semi-detached house in Mowbray and I spent weekends there. During the school week, I tried to study and ignore the wretched life my mother had chosen.

One night I came downstairs for dinner and my dad emerged from the kitchen, sozzled and very pleased with himself for being home so early, as if this negated the years of absences.

I hadn't heard him arrive. I stopped in the hallway, but he kept coming towards me. I realised he was going to kiss me, and dutifully presented my cheek. But he ducked off to the side and kissed me smack on the lips. Then he stuck his tongue in my mouth.

I leaped backwards, bitten by a snake. He laughed at me as I fled back upstairs.

How do you regain your footing with your father when such a line has been crossed? How do you move past this moment of violation?

I just "held still" while time lengthened after the awful kiss. I put it down to alcohol, added it to the sack of experiences I would never share with anyone, and vowed that I'd punch him if he ever did it again. He didn't mention it and it never happened again.

My parents departed on the two-month overseas shoot that would span my final high school exams. It was lonely, but Jacques and I spent the weekends together, and at least the house didn't feel like a field of razor wire.

I moved out of home at the start of 1975, giving up on my mother after years of spiralling complexity and sorrow. She continued to polish the silver tray, but it seemed that it would not shine. A puff of guilt hung around my nostrils, but I relished the prospect of no longer having to endure the daily burdens of her pain and my father's amassed crimes.

It was excruciating to say goodbye to my mother the night I left my lilac room for the last time. I took only my clothes, my grandfather's writing desk and the old piano stool with mother-of-pearl inlays on which I'd sat for the past few years while working at the writing desk. She was terrified, but I had to just leave her to it. I was seventeen-and-a-half and I'd had it with family.

I don't know how long it took my father to notice I was gone.

SURVIVAL

I moved in with Jacques, ten years older than me.

There'd been no question of my attending university or any other tertiary institution. With little parental guidance during high school, my subject choices had been guided by what would be easiest, not what would facilitate higher education. I completed high school with low marks in History, high marks in Biology, English, Afrikaans, and extremely high marks for … Typing. It was ludicrous spending two precious years of education learning to type, but I did emerge a lightning fast typist in an age before personal computers, and had no trouble getting a job as a receptionist/secretary at an office equipment company in the city.

My life guide was Jacques, a part-time musician and full-time technician for Burroughs Machines who cared deeply about me and offered stability. He suggested I do an aptitude test for computer programming.

"Me? Computers?"

"Well, you need to explore something, surely?"

I achieved an unusually high score for the test, they said, and so I started training at night school for what would be a long and successful career in information technology, before the creative clamour of my DNA became impossible to ignore.

I studied for six months at Cape Technical College while working for the office equipment company. Then a life insurance company hired me as a trainee computer programmer. It was unlike anything I'd previously encountered in my arty family and, it turned out, I was good at it. I soon bought a sewing machine, sewed curtains and duvet covers, made my own business suits and packed lunches for Jacques and I to take to work. We dreamed of relocating to Spain, where he'd worked for six months in the band with my brother. I started studying Spanish and rarely saw my parents. I was happy for a time.

In June 1976, the country exploded. By September the spillover from the Soweto riots in Johannesburg had reached Cape Town. From our fourth-floor office, we watched in fear and shock as thousands marched along the main freeway into town. Clouds of teargas rose across our range of vision, and hordes of rioters ran across the Grand Parade, police firing what we prayed were rubber bullets into the throng. The managers told us to move away from the windows, and not to leave the building all day.

I was appalled as I watched the results of this broken political system play out in the streets below. I sympathised completely with the anger of the disenfranchised. Yet my sympathy didn't stop my stomach churning at the prospect of travelling home to Mowbray, an area officially demarcated as white by the *Group Areas Act*, but that leaned toward ambiguity. Then the fifteen-minute walk with my white face from the station to our rented house in Klipfontein Road, the main bus route to the areas of Athlone, Langa and Guguletu, designated as "non-white". In such a volatile atmosphere, no one stops to enquire about your politics. I looked down at my shoes as I passed each group of black and brown people clustered around the bus stops. Powerless in the face of the opposing forces in this battle, I applied myself more diligently to my Spanish studies and what was developing into a good career in Information Technology at the insurance company.

Violent conflict continued in our city, but by then I had fresh demons to wrestle in the form of new health issues.

For nearly a year, during my frequent visits to my doctor, he had paid half-hearted attention to the pain in my back. He sent me to physiotherapy, but that made it worse. He then sent me to the back specialist I still saw occasionally for the scoliosis I had been unable to straighten during The Dark Years.

"Well," the specialist said, "with a scoliosis of this magnitude you're bound to get some pain."

My doctor eventually abandoned me. Without plumbing the as-yet-unexplored body parts known to be in the general area of the pain, this adult male, a tower of knowledge and authority, had pronounced everything okay. He prescribed tranquilisers and stronger analgesics. Even this chemical fog failed to neutralise the painful misery. And my boyfriend supported him, not me. I sat at work with hot water bottles strapped around my waist, taking the pills and lying down under my desk when the pain got too much. My parents? Well, who knew what they were doing.

My boyfriend became my fiancée during this period. He liked us to go to a local pub and though he knew I was tanked up with drugs and working full days, he felt slighted that by evening I couldn't stay awake through a conversation. I could understand how my frequent excuses of being exhausted and in pain might become tedious, so I went along with the sex during this time. It was reasonable of him to expect it, and sometimes it was the quickest path to the sleep I craved. And no, I was not frigid. But I was too ill and too focused on just getting through the day to experience much joy, or to recognise the trap of my circumstances. Perhaps also too young. Somehow, I coded computer programs to an acceptable level to keep my job, but my waking hours were like doing sidestroke through minestrone. It was a bad state in which to decide to get married, though God knows I wanted the pillar of certainty it promised.

The first collapse took place on the roadside on the highway to Gordon's Bay, about 60km from Cape Town. Mike's band, of which Jacques was still a member, was doing a gig there that night and they were given rooms to stay over at the hotel, so I went along for the ride. The whole morning I'd felt even stranger than usual — nauseous, and as if a large grapefruit had settled in my lower abdomen. Ploughing through discomfort habitually now, I noticed an odd sensation in my lower regions on more frequent than usual trips to the toilet.

"I have to pee," I said.

"We're only about fifteen minutes away. Can't you wait?"

"No. There's something weird going on."

I wasn't sure I could hold out long enough for him to pull over to the side of the national highway. Oblivious to passing traffic, I ripped down my jeans and let go. Every one of the few drops was like a razor blade. Then I noticed blood on the ground.

Of course, I should have gone directly to a doctor. But this was me back then, not now. I just lay down in the room as soon as we arrived and stayed there, apart from frequent, wrenching trips to the toilet through the night. I couldn't swallow anything but water. By the next morning I had a burning fever and it was clear to everyone that I had to see a doctor.

Yes, I went to my usual doctor, the beast that repeatedly sent me away with painkillers and tranquillisers. This time he added antibiotics and bed rest.

"And you can stop taking the tranquilisers."

No kidding.

"Thanks," I said.

I collapsed again a week after I'd finished the two courses of antibiotics. Unusually, we'd gone to a Sunday lunch with my parents at their corrugated iron bungalow at Glen Beach. This time there was no warning. Soon after arriving, nausea propelled me to the bathroom, where I threw up soundly and my roadside symptoms returned with a vengeance. Jacques was never much good at bedside manner, making me feel that I should just hunker down and wait for the trouble to pass. I writhed in pain on my parents' bed.

The raging bull that roared into life that Sunday is my first strong recollection of my father since I'd left home a couple of years before. By now I was slipping in and out of consciousness, but even so I felt the sweet glow of "applehood" again, as the hero of my childhood briefly reappeared. I later heard that he had hauled my doctor off the golf course, deploying language he'd no doubt refined through his extensive experience in bars, and demanded that he send an ambulance. The good doctor didn't think the circumstances called for such drama, at which point my father told him to fuck off and that he would take care of me himself.

They carried me to the car and drove me to emergency. I was in a ward within minutes, stethoscopes flying and drips plunging into blood vessels as I sank into grateful oblivion. There followed a week in hospital, visits to a urologist and four thousand different kinds of X-rays. I was booked in for major kidney surgery, with antibiotics holding matters at bay. A "Pelvo-Uretary-Junction (PUJ) Obstruction" they called it.

It wasn't clear whether it was a constriction from without or a blockage from within, but a tube connecting kidney to bladder was allowing only the tiniest amount of fluid to pass. This caused extreme trouble in the kidney, now enlarged to more than double its correct size, and resulted in the rampant infection that finally burst its banks and could no longer be ignored, not even by my doctor. No one seemed to have any idea of the impact this neglected kidney would have on my dreams of procreation later on. If they did, they didn't say.

"Why don't you postpone the wedding until you're over all this?" my mother suggested weakly. Pretty reasonable idea, really. But no, I was only on painkillers and antibiotics now, it being obvious to any passing stranger that tranquilisers were not indicated, and feeling great compared to the previous twelve months. This wedding was something

I had some control over.

Apart from the historic stone church in the charming cobbled square, it wasn't a formal affair. I made my own wedding dress out of patterned cheesecloth and my mother and a couple of friends organised the party at a sports club. They ordered in lasagne and salad, and there was plenty of alcohol. Jacques and I went home afterwards to our house in Klipfontein Road, where it took my liver and one functioning kidney three days to get through the hangover. Two weeks after the wedding, in April 1977, I went into hospital with my new surname.

These events appeared to remind my parents that I was still just nineteen, and that maybe I could use some parental presence. My defences had no chink through which to allow influence or actual guidance, my parents having long since forfeited that right. I'd charted my own course, however badly, for years already. But they were there when I went into surgery, and they were there for me afterwards.

The night of the surgery I was still in the operating theatre two hours after they'd said I'd be through, when a picture randomly fell off the wall in my parents' beachside bungalow. It spooked my dad, who called the hospital demanding to know what was going on. They told him I'd haemorrhaged after they'd sewn me up. They'd had to open it all up again to stop the bleeding, and replace a large proportion of my blood via transfusion. The surgery left me with one rib fewer, 200 internal stitches, who knows how many external stitches on the fifteen-centimetre wound, and two drains which would replace the function of the kidney for the first couple of weeks of my month in hospital. From a long way off, I heard someone calling me, "Mrs De Villiers … Mrs De Villiers … Can you hear me?" *Who was that*, I wondered.

My parents insisted that I stay with them for the first month after discharge from hospital. I'd shrunk dramatically and was very weak, needing special feeding, bed baths and a pillow between my knees to separate the unpadded bones knocking against one another at night. Jacques was grateful. He was working full time and frankly didn't know quite what to do with me. It was a month of healing on multiple levels. For the first time in years I risked allowing my mother to mother me; she did it brilliantly and my father even diverted his gaze from himself for a while.

I eventually returned home and gradually to work, but was unprepared for the change in my new husband's attitude. Having been a fairly normal partner, if a tad unfeeling at times, he seemed to have different ideas about what was appropriate behaviour now that I was a wife. He made statements about tradition and expectation that would have been far better articulated before going through a marriage ceremony. I didn't see it coming. In my defence, I couldn't discern much of anything in the months leading up to the nuptials.

Still, just the absence of searing pain was liberating. I never, ever went back to that doctor, who after failing me, had felt compelled to visit me nearly every day in hospital. I never greeted him warmly.

A musical change came next. When I felt strong enough, I joined the band, largely at the urging of my brother's wife, the lead singer. My brother allowed me to sing only backing vocals, and glared at me with special big brotherness if I made a mistake, but I was thrilled to be inside the magic circle now. We also took home two gig fees rather than one. But suddenly the fun of hanging out after the gig, often the best part, sparked a series of ferocious fights. Nothing had changed as far as I was concerned, but now that Jacques had his wife with him, it had to be straight home afterwards. No partying.

What?

There were surprises on the financial front too, now that we were married. He earned much more than I did, as he would repeatedly remind me, and that meant he had more clout in our now joined lives.

"But I'm just starting out," I protested. "There's no possibility of my earning as much as you do, even though I work just as many hours. And actually, my salary is really good for someone my age," I pointed out. "Plus, I do nearly all the domestic work. Don't you think my working hours count as much as yours?"

"No."

I seethed. But life and country had trained me to put up with injustices.

I turned twenty; he turned thirty. He wanted to put his feet up at the fire and have me bring him his slippers. I guess our life together thus far had set up expectations of a pliant, subdued woman who sewed and cooked, went to bed early to sleep for ten hours, and was grateful to be allowed to sing backing vocals.

"Don't complain," he would say when I mused about the possibility of one day being allowed to sing a solo. "You're not that good." I assumed he should know. But I yearned all the same.

Neither of us faced up to the realities of our altered situation. I hadn't signed up for the role of a traditional wife, and he hadn't signed up for the emergence of a rambunctious young woman, starving for life. Healthy and clearheaded for the first time in years, I was ready to boogie. I loved singing in the band, no matter how small the part, and then additionally in a new vocal trio "Suzy" with my sister-in-law and her sister. We did cabaret shows, and then some TV shows. High cringe, looking back, the three of us dressed in matching sequinned outfits that looked great on my two buxom colleagues but dismally highlighted my lack of womanly accoutrements. Some outfits were downright perilous. The sequinned boob tube, for example. With nothing to hold it up, there were many times when a dance move had me certain that all was about to be revealed on public television. A surreptitious "hoiking up" of the elasticised top can be seen in several shots. Embarrassing, but the alternative was even less appealing. The straight line of the garment across my chest unhappily mirrored my square shoulders, like my father's, known in his navy days as "The Campbell Coat hangers". In the infancy of TV in South Africa, despite these challenges, it was the most exciting thing ever to be part of it.

"Suzy" recorded an album for the South African Broadcasting Company, with my brother as musical director. Then another. On the second one, my brother asked me to write the vocal arrangements for two of the disco songs and, at the same time, translate them into Afrikaans. That was the deal for these albums: a portion of the music had to be in Afrikaans. I glowed with little-sisterly pleasure and worked hard on the vocal score, which he used with almost no alterations. It was my first taste of vocal arranging and it tasted good.

At my day job, they gave me increased responsibility and a series of raises. I learned that I could do systems analysis and lead a small team of people, all older than me. My brain was capable of working out stuff that my family of acclaimed jazz musicians found incomprehensible. I liked that, small and untalented as I felt beside them. Though I hankered for music, this unexpected world of computers was satisfying and lucrative, with the added bonus that my husband was proud of me at last. He could talk binary to me over drinks at the local and I no longer fell asleep.

Still, I found myself constrained by a new brace of emotions and expectations; incarcerated in its virtual framework and trying to hold onto the thought of the good it was supposedly doing me.

A few months after the wedding, the surgery and the slow recovery, I drifted into an affair with a gorgeous man at work, a man with a wife and two children. He was caring, and funny, with a furry voice that did strange things to me at close range to my ear. He had sensual lips and dark eyes a mile deep.

I knew my husband would find this development one hundred per cent unacceptable, but that knowledge failed to outweigh the compulsion. Exposed from an early age to people doing such things, the concept of having an affair didn't, of itself, strike me as wrong, just likely to be unpopular. The irony that I was following in their footsteps didn't strike me at all. And I'd learned early to keep my mouth shut.

Politics, always a greedy consumer of conversation in South Africa, were of special concern to my lover and me. One day, as we once again walked together to the train station after work, I felt fire rising in my belly. "No," I said as we approached the separate entrances to the train station. His eyebrows shot up. Instead of parting company as usual, I threaded a defiant arm into his and we walked together under the sign "Non-White Entrance".

His skin was a luscious brown and he was classified as "Coloured". The only place we could go for a beer after work was an outrageously expensive hotel in town with "international" regulations. I started working overtime. There was no shortage of venues for sex in an office building emptied by a weekend. Like the tiny room, really a large broom cupboard, out the back of the computer department. It barely accommodated a chair and an old desk on which perched the hand punch we programmers would use sometimes. We're talking about the days before personal computers, before computer screens of any kind, when operators would capture our coded computer program instructions from handwritten sheets and punch them onto stiff cards to be loaded into a huge mainframe card reader. If just one or two cards needed correcting, then rather than resubmitting coding sheets, we'd just go and use the clunky hand punch.

Avoiding the mops, buckets and brooms, and balancing across the desk and chair so as to avoid impalement on the hand punch, we joyously vanquished the *Immorality Act*, that hated piece of legislation that made sex across the colour bar illegal. It wasn't that I needed the sex. There was plenty of that at home. It was the absence of expectation, and how much he seemed to enjoy just being with me. We fell in love.

It was also illegal for us to share a park bench while we ate our sandwiches, so we found a patch of city lawn. We rode the train home together as far as my stop on the "grey fringe" of town, leaving him on the train to continue on to the Cape Flats. It drew some looks, but nothing compared to the certain eviction if he'd tried to ride a white carriage with me. "Coloured" could range from absolutely black to absolutely white, but the faintest tinge of swarthiness in a white train carriage was unworkable. I wondered if a rail inspector had ever demanded an ID card from a particularly dark-complexioned Greek or Spaniard.

It played out over an intense, wonderful few months, during

which my indignation against apartheid rose alongside my repeated experience from the other side. The affair was marvellous; it rescued a portion of my battered self-esteem, but there was nowhere for it to go in apartheid South Africa, not to mention the fact we were both married.

I couldn't bear to look anymore into those dark, deep pools, and in between the warmth and the pleasure to see flickers of pain and disempowerment. They mirrored my own, and the sight of them whispered despair. It was heartbreaking to take leave of the backroom where the relationship between our bodies and souls had bloomed. But it was time. I emerged from the affair with a deeper gloom for the future of my country.

A representative from the blood bank came to our office. Good opportunity, I thought, to give back just a small part of the pints of blood I'd received to keep me alive during the operation. A few of us went to donate at lunchtime. I couldn't say whether it was the psychological effect of having a tube in my arm again, or the clotting they said was still in evidence, but within a few minutes the room started heaving around me and the attending medico ripped out the tube, calling for reinforcements.

When the walls steadied, a young man was standing beside the bed, holding a cup of tea with a couple of biscuits on the saucer.

"Hi, I'm Mark." He smiled and sat down. They must have told him to keep me talking, because he asked questions relentlessly. In less than five minutes these questions determined that we knew a great many of the same people. He was a musician, a saxophone player who was doing a chemistry and biochemistry degree, and working at the blood bank during the university break. He knew my brother.

Fast-forward another twelve months to 1980. My brother invited Mark to come and sit in with our band at our three-night a week gig. Delighted to renew our acquaintance, I learned that Mark was now working part-time building systems on the technologically dazzling new personal computers — prehistoric by today's standards — at his family's insurance business. The building was adjacent to mine in the city.

"We should have tea sometime," he said.

We did. At age twenty-four, in 1982, my five years of experience in computer programming provided an exit ramp from South Africa, not to Spain with Jacques, but to Australia with my second husband, Mark.

FLIGHT

In my adopted country, the Aboriginal people define "Country" to encompass the physical — landforms, flora and fauna, air and waters. Country also takes in knowledge, stories, songs, art and people past, present and future. People have a responsibility to care for their Country in every way. It's beautiful to connect to one's land and significant people so deeply.

But what is one to do when the anchors of life come adrift? Growing up in South Africa, the ruinous politics of what should have been Country appalled me. I saw no hope of peaceful resolution and felt, strangely, little resonance with African cultures, despite my family's history. I was powerless in the face of my parents' troubles, not close to my brother, barely knew my few immediate relatives and had no awareness of the larger circle beyond. No part of the country held my heart, with the exception of Camps Bay, where I grew up watching the setting sun scatter diamonds across the Atlantic Ocean.

In the pumping adrenalin of the early 1980s in South Africa, I chose flight.

That said, our orderly departure in 1982 could hardly be described as fleeing. Nor did it feel like it at the time. It was much later, long after the inevitable couple of years to overcome the pangs of displacement, that I recognised my departure from South Africa as personal flight.

It's true, I didn't want to live in a country racked with intractable problems, where the daily newspapers made you weep and politics dominated every dinner table. I didn't want to raise my hypothetical children in the socio-political system in which I'd grown up, nor in the midst of a bloodbath. I couldn't see a pathway between these two potential futures. Turns out I was wrong, and Nelson Mandela opened up just such a path. But by the heady years of his release and rise to leader of the country, there was no going back for us.

In 1981, Mark and I decided to emigrate. We were committed to one another, but not big on formalities. We got married to create a single unit for our immigration application.

I spent one harrowing day in court securing my divorce from Jacques, and then booked the wedding, such as it was. No doubt my mother-in-law felt unsatisfied with the brief visit to the office at the Magistrate's Court with the sign outside that said, "Marriages, Rehabilitations and Mental Patients". Our four parents and Mark's three brothers were in attendance. Afterwards Mark and I went to the pub with my parents and that was that. But the news I'd given Mark's parents earlier that day compensated for any shortcomings in the ceremony.

The morning of this less-than-high-society happening I had announced my decision to convert to Judaism. They had always been warm and welcoming, and didn't raise the idea until we told them of our marriage plans.

"Just think of your future children," they said.

"No way am I going to have this pressure on Judy," was Mark's quick retort.

"We're not making a big issue here. We expected this news, are very happy about it, and are just asking that you give it some thought."

"I don't want to hear any more about it," said Mark.

But it stayed with me. They knew we aimed to leave. Mark's father had longstanding, serious health issues and couldn't travel. We had few resources; who knew when we'd be in a position to come back and visit. Mark's parents were saying all the right things to encourage us, but they must have dreaded our departure.

There was also the reality that I was joining an Orthodox Jewish family and, despite having grown up in an area with so many Jews that the government school I attended all but shut down on Jewish holidays, I didn't know much beyond Friday night dinners at friends' houses. I needed some education.

My family was heathen. No religious denunciation required there.

All they'd asked is that I think about it. I didn't discuss it with Mark. It had to be my decision.

The day of our strange wedding, eyes shone and I knew I'd made a good choice.

Soon after our marriage we started preparing. Our aim was to leave South Africa, and we couldn't afford to go anywhere first to take a look. We were drawn to the USA, but it was hard to obtain permanent residence. We wanted to travel there, and suspected that if we were refused a weightier visa, then applied for a tourist visa, the consulate staff would laugh at us. We'd never been to Australia, but one of Mark's many cousins lived there, and was willing to sponsor us. Five years as a mainframe computer programmer put me on the desirables list for Australia. This collection of realities made the path clear.

We assumed there'd be a long wait once we'd done the interviews, medicals and fingerprinting. But the papers arrived an alarming two months later, saying we had twelve months to get to our new country of residence, Australia. That timeframe would have to include our planned six-month odyssey across the United States.

We moved into the downstairs rooms of my parents-in-law's home to save on rent. I quit my job and devoted myself full time to the studies in rituals, history, Halachah (Jewish Law) and Hebrew required for conversion.

"Something feels good to me about this," my father said. "You know my mother was Jewish."

"Really?"

We only realised the implications of this information when my studies revealed that his mother being Jewish qualified him for membership of the tribe, even though he didn't have a Barmitzvah or religious instruction of any kind. Not for me though. I continued my studies, but this discovered thread of belonging lit up my efforts.

Those last few months were, unexpectedly, the happiest with my parents since my early childhood. Mark and I spent time with them, enjoying sundowners on the veranda of their Glen Beach bungalow, sailing and camping together, planning to add Sydney onto their filming travel plans. It was the polar opposite of the excruciating farewell to Mark's parents, largely due to his father's illness. We discussed postponing our departure, but he wouldn't hear of it.

Mark's father died one week after we left.

I couldn't hear the details of the murmured three am conversation, but the cardboard walls of the house couldn't blanket the sound of pain, and I sat bolt upright on the mattress in the living room of our friend's house in New Jersey, our first stop in the US.

"He's gone," Mark croaked, ripped apart, even though the threat posed by his father's critical health had hung over him his whole life.

"There's nothing you could do if you came back," his eldest brother had said. "You've barely left, you said goodbye knowing this was likely. What's the point?"

He was wrong. I'm not sure that Mark ever got over not being at his father's funeral. We found a synagogue where he could say Kaddish, the Jewish mourner's prayer, and then we got into our campervan and kept going. We floundered in our relationship on our travels, with no community or family to hold us, and no experience of dealing with grief.

Gradually we clawed our way back to firmer ground, and took

pleasure in the people and wonders we encountered. My mother joined us in Arizona, we bought a small tent for us, and she, gamely, slept in the van. She spent two months on the road with us.

My dad joined us for a while in California before he and my mother returned to South Africa. He could be so charming, clever and entertaining. After the normal-feeling family time we'd had before Mark and I left, then the break of several months, I saw his charm in a less reptilian light. Was charm in itself such a terrible thing?

The end of the odyssey across the United States found us in Hawaii on Yom Kippur, the Day of Atonement. I experienced a small turning that day, and a sense of appreciation for the occasion, though it would take a few more years to feel a full connection to the tribe I had chosen.

In the introspective spirit of the day, and the softness of the eternal equatorial summer, I thought about what we had left behind, our journey, and the unknowable future awaiting us in just a few more days. As we sat on the shore, I thought about Mark's father, my brother, my complicated parents and the treacherous terrain of my feelings about them.

"It wasn't all my dad's fault you know."

"Hmm?" said Mark, drowsy with Maui sun.

"People have choices, and if they make bad ones, they can't always blame someone else," I murmured to the gentle ocean, starting a bold and scary letter to my father in my head as my toes wiggled in the fine, white sand.

LANDING

We arrived in Australia as permanent residents in 1982, having never set foot in the place. The only person I knew was one of my brother's school friends, whose sister had been my ballet partner before the scoliosis put an end to my dancing career. Barry, an accountant, immediately helped us get a credit card, even though we were such poor financial prospects. More than thirty years later, Barry is still our accountant and friend.

Even Mark, always better connected than me, knew only a handful of ex-South Africans. His cousin and family generously housed and fed us for a few weeks while we bobbed around in our new environment.

The meagre proceeds from the sale of the campervan represented the full extent of our stash to start a new life in Sydney. It bought us a machine resembling a car, the rental bond and one month's rent on a dilapidated house in Naremburn — long before it became the trendy Sydney suburb it is today — and a set of clothes in which to go to job interviews.

I went directly from the store to my first interview. The sales assistant cut the labels off the new garments and, with some distaste, put my tatty jeans and sandals into a shopping bag. We found jobs as computer programmers immediately, but had to wait a couple of weeks to start work.

We signed up for the dole, anticipating — correctly — that this would be the only time in our lives that we would request it. *God bless Australia,* we thought as we banked our dole cheques. We joined the Musicians' Union and did a few gigs that yielded a little income.

Even with these infusions, after we'd bought a few basics at garage sales, and filled the tank of the bomb that was our car, there was no money left for food.

It was a scary few weeks. We knew to not rack up too much debt on our credit cards, as that eagerly anticipated first pay cheque had to cover so much. We cautiously bought food on credit at Grace Bros department store, but ate bread and jam for dinner more than once during those long weeks. From our third pay we could breathe more easily, and deregistered from the dole.

We both took a drop in status from our jobs in South Africa, but we were grateful for the work. We missed small things about South Africa; foods and other familiar items, but discovered new ones we liked just as much. We hung out with Mark's South African friends and became a warm little family for one another. We made lifelong Australian friends at work. Everything was just fine. On the surface.

Mark didn't land comfortably in his brief first job or, his still briefer, second one. He was somewhat unlucky in these work situations. He also struggled to make the transition from youngest of four brothers in the Cape Town family business, afforded all manner of privileges, to being just like everyone else. My life had given me lower expectations, and better training in fending for myself than he had.

Mark also had to make the transition from being quite the star on the jazz scene in Cape Town to being an unknown new arrival in a much larger place. I didn't have *that* problem either, never having been more than a lowly working singer in party bands and a girlie vocal trio.

We soldiered on. My job was going well. A benefit was access to low interest staff home loans. In a gesture of kindness that I found hard to accept, but even harder to refuse, my parents gifted us a deposit and we bought our first home. A two-bedroom apartment in a leafy area, convenient to work and some friends, with a lower monthly loan repayment than our rent had been. Low interest employee loans had been available at the insurance company I worked for in Cape Town too, but only for men. "God Bless Australia," I reiterated.

Still, there was something that didn't gel for me. It wasn't anything specifically wrong with Australia. And I never once yearned to go back to South Africa. It was a relief not to look back. But we loved America and talked many times about trying to settle there. I started quietly looking at job ads.

I wrote the letter to my father that I had been musing on for so long. I wrote it several times, weeping over it and unsure I could ever summon the courage to send it.

But I did, two months after arriving in Sydney. My father claimed until he could no longer speak that receiving that letter was a turning point in his life. I described all the hurt and bitterness, anger at his heartlessness to those he claimed to love. But I also expressed a new understanding of his flaws and oddities, and that not every wound in our family was exclusively his fault. It ended with this:

> "You drive me absolutely crazy at times and I doubt that I could live under the same roof as you. However, in distance and time I've come to realise that I do love you very much. I admire your talents and abilities and I'm proud of your achievements. I'm proud of your head too. It's a treat to be able to communicate with one's father on this level, considering the uptight relationships that so often prevail, preventing family members getting to know one another as people. I hope you'll share your feelings with me. There must be a lot of things you've never had the right space to express — well I'm tuned in to your frequency and ready to receive."

His reply arrived as quickly as it was physically possible pre-email for my letter and his to cross the skies. He said, in his over-the-top dramatic way, that he'd been waiting for years for someone to listen, and he was thrilled. Thus began a new era of communication between us.

I was glad to have opened a braver conversation with at least one of my parents, but continued to proceed with shield and spear in hand.

My parents started visiting us within months of our arrival in Sydney.

"Brace yourself," I warned Mark.

As predicted, drama accompanied every visit and turned the full attention of the household onto my father. Sometimes it concerned the inevitable calamities of the current movie he was making. It often revolved around money. The crash of 1987 set the scene for a tumultuous visit.

One day my heart went squishy at the sight of my father with eight-month old Dean nestled in the curve of his shoulder, both fast asleep. The next I was plunged back to picking at white appliqué daisies as my father sobbed, drunk, on my shoulder over the money he'd lost, my mother hovering helplessly behind. One letter didn't miraculously make everything okay.

My parents were still travelling extensively, filming lavish cinema commercials for the biggest booze-and-cigarette company in South Africa. The ethics of all this seemed questionable only later; in the 1980s it wasn't considered life threatening and certainly not uncool, to smoke.

The future of South Africa was uncertain and monetary regulations forbade movement of cash into safer havens. Some emigrants, desperate to "export" as much capital as they could, packed newly acquired Kruger Rands into the legs of dining tables to ship to Australia and Canada.

For my father, not yet officially emigrating with his household goods, the international film productions afforded a range of creative possibilities for moving capital. We referred to this period as my father's "James Bond phase".

As a film maker using unexposed 35mm film stock, he was given an exemption from having the stock X-rayed, as the process would ruin it. In a heavy black bag designed for handling unexposed film, he hand-wound a roll of film onto an empty spindle he had filled with Kruger Rands. He loaded the newly wound roll into a silver film can that would resist the light outside of the bag, and filled the now empty spindle with more of the golden hope for the future. The coins fitted perfectly into the plastic cylinder — there would be not the slightest rattle to disclose the presence of contraband at the heart of each roll of film. He placed another can of unexposed film into the bag, and repeated the process again and again.

Safety deposit boxes in multiple American cities grew heavier. Still, he obsessed about his future security, that of his family and his various women. He could never be accused of being a fly-by-night lover.

Almost two years after we migrated to Australia, I received a tentative offer for a job as systems analyst from a company in Washington DC. "We would like to interview you in our offices," they said. My brother was soon to graduate with a Bachelor of Music in Jazz from North Texas State University. My parents planned to be there, so instead of travelling on to visit us in Sydney, they flew us to the United States so the family could be together at Mike's graduation.

I booked the extra flights from Dallas and started to get excited.

Mike, who had barely scraped through high school, had enrolled at twenty-seven as a mature age student in Texas. He spent four years in Denton, Texas, with his wife, Diane, and at last achieved to his potential. Our small family stood together and watched him graduate *cum laude*, proud and happy, despite the unresolved currents of the past between us all.

In DC, the sight of the building dampened my excitement. The area wasn't one in which I'd expected to find a company requiring a systems analyst. Semi-industrial yards shared the streetscape with houses and apartments in varying stages of decay. Mark waited downstairs.

The "office" was a poorly lit, dingy apartment. I don't remember much about the work side of the conversation — the issue of the visa took centre stage. Perhaps I had misunderstood; perhaps they'd painted a rosier picture than the truth. The upshot was that they offered me the job but couldn't guarantee a Green Card.

"It'll be a mere formality once you've been here for a year," they assured me. The memory of the migration to Australia was still fresh, and the thought of doing it again not once but twice should their information also prove dingy, was unbearable. I thanked them and said brightly that I'd think it over, but by the time I reached the car my shoulders had sagged.

Then on the return flight, I felt a shift. We came into Sydney from the north on a shining blue morning. The calm water sparkled and the Opera House shone through the girders of the Harbour Bridge. In the midst of the visual feast my thoughts flew to our attractive apartment, our two fluffy cats, my good job near the harbour, dear work colleagues and friends who had become like family … our life in Australia, far from the tentacles of the past. I was home.

My mother migrated from South Africa with her silver tea service when our son Dean was two, and came to live with us. This brought diminished privacy as a result, but our lives were unquestionably blessed by her presence.

"What's it like having your grandma living with you?" asked someone of ten-year-old Dean. I eavesdropped shamelessly.

"It's like having three parents," he replied after a long pause.

Dean and "Ma" as he, then everyone, called her, were fiercely allied co-conspirators. He inherited her wicked sense of humour, which accompanied him through his childhood escapades and the many tender afternoons with his grandma.

Ever complicated, my father planned to alternate between Sydney and Cape Town for a few months at a time. His film business still operated to some extent, with Norina's help, and he wasn't ready to retire. When in Sydney, he would live with my mother in "the cabin", as it became known.

Mark travelled a lot for work during Dean's childhood. Still having two "parents" at home made it viable. I was often working full time in Information Technology. It was Ma who took on the role of parental representative and won the Canteen Volunteer of the Year at Lindfield Primary School, three years running. She was still helping years later, even when her health was fading. Dean would look forward to his free sandwich from the Killara High School canteen on the days Ma volunteered there. He would sneak out to meet her at the car, offload her portable oxygen machine and wheel it to the kitchen door. She'd organise the plugs and tubes and settle down to a couple of hours of chopping and smearing before recess. I was grateful. I could always provide a party band at school fundraisers, but I just wasn't school tuckshop material. A surprising giant of domesticity given the presence of servants throughout her earlier life, Ma would pick up as primary parent when I'd head off for six weeks at a time to sing in the cocktail lounge at a 5-star hotel on the Great Barrier Reef. And that was after she'd run up a couple of shimmering new dresses for me and driven me to the airport.

This is the woman everyone remembers. I remember her too.

But it's another woman with whom I need to reconcile. Not even a woman. I need to understand the fearful child who shared that beleaguered little body with the heroine, and inflicted so much damage.

A PLACE ON THE TREE

In the 1990s my mother received a copy of the Luyt family tree that covered most of a wall in our living room.

"Look at this," she shrieked.

While I looked at it with some amazement, I wasn't riveted. Mike and I were there, squashed onto the very edge of the upper right-hand corner of the chart, but the rest was an incomprehensible jungle of names and dates connected by lines.

Two members of this expanse of ancestral foliage: the famous dancer Lionel Luyt, and Gwen Craig, unknown to me, had assembled the massive family tree. They completed it in 1970, in an age with no email, Google or even fax machines. They had also created a book that included a little information about some of the ancestors. Years would pass before I became aware of that.

When, in 2011, I took out the gigantic chart and started looking for trails through the jungle, I remembered how much I'd enjoyed the way, in Gabriel Garcia Marquez' novel *One Hundred Years of Solitude*, he brought out the humour in the endless repetitions of the names "Aureliano" and "Arcadio" in the Buendia family. At every turn of my family there was a Gabriel Jacobus, a Daniel Coenraad and a Johan Godfried. There were profusions of Marys, Johannas, Jacobas, Wilhelminas, Christinas and Hendrinas in a range of permutations. Could they not think of any other names? Or was it customary to repeat the same names in *every* generation, and in *every* branch of the expanding family, even in the same generation? They confound the novice researcher probing online archives and genealogy web sites. I failed to find the Marquez humour as I spent hours down one rabbit hole after another before realising I was in the wrong hole.

Still, there was a system to it, I learned, with children being named for paternal and maternal grandparents, parents and so on. There were some good points to this approach, like an easy ride in picking names for the first few children in a family. But it's a headache for baby genealogists trying to connect individuals to their proper family unit, especially when the many children in one generation bled into the next and various individuals with the same name were close enough in age to create major confusion. Add a fair amount of marriage between cousins, and renaming of new children for others that have previously died, and you have a daunting maze.

In the gentler years of his later life, my father expressed the view that we humans are like ants scurrying across the planet, stopping on occasion to communicate briefly with others. Some of us carry loads, some journey in purposeful, bidirectional lines, some in random reconnaissance groups, and others wander alone, looking a bit lost.

I think he had a point.

Unlike ants, however, we have this terrible habit of arriving in new places and imposing our value systems and beliefs on those we encounter there.

In South Africa, at least for white people, the ant trails started with 17th century Dutch interests pursuing the fragrant riches of the East Indies. They had stretched their supply lines beyond the maritime capabilities of the day, and needed a refuge somewhere between Europe and Batavia. Actually, the ships could have made it all the way. It was the humans, with their annoying limitations, that were not up to the task. The spice barons had little concern for the humans in question, but sailors dying of scurvy left insufficient crew for manning the ship.

In 1652, the Dutch East India Company (VOC - Vereenigde Oostindische Compagnie) claimed this corner of Africa. They built a fort to protect the garrison, and a garden to grow fresh food for their ships passing around what was known, for good reason, as The Cape of Storms.

The outpost started expanding almost immediately, as some employees were released as "free burghers" and given farms to increase the volume of produce. Within six years of the Dutch arrival, 360 people, consisting of soldiers, freemen, slaves and a small number of women and children, had settled at the Cape.

Until the Cape became British in 1806, the population and political clout were predominantly Dutch, with Dutch the lingua franca. Germany didn't yet exist as such, but immigrants known as "Germans", and also French Huguenots, were significant minorities, I learned.

Friederich Leitt, a twenty-two-year-old master carpenter, was one of the approximately 4,000 "Germans", almost all male, who migrated to the Cape. He sailed in 1735 on the Petronella Alida from the Baltic seaport of Königsberg in East Prussia (later Kaliningrad in Russia), nestled between Poland and Lithuania, as a soldier for the VOC.

I couldn't verify a claim in the family that Friederich was a Jew but found evidence of many VOC employees from Europe being Jewish. Company rules required all settlers to be Protestant and some converted before sailing for the Cape; others after arriving. Many are said to have shown up at the VOC offices, put their hands on their hearts and said, "Sure, I'm a Protestant".

Friederich became a free burgher with a land grant in fertile Stellenbosch, fifty kilometres to the east of the Cape.

Many German immigrants shed the original spellings of their names in favour of a Dutch version. Friederich became Frederik and

Leitt became Luyt, and sometimes Luijt, or Luit. The family henceforth described itself as Dutch, though there were still to be at least as many French, German and British entries to the family tree, plus a few, more exotic additions along the way.

In 1748, Frederik married the German-Dutch Hendrina Steenbrugge who gave birth to seven children.

From here the vast Luyt family of South Africa set forth in multi-directional ant trails, reconnaissance parties and as lone explorers. Some reached great heights and some became a bit lost along the way. Some did both. Luyts or descendants with different surnames are found in almost every part of South African life and in other countries too, having migrated all over the world. All trace their roots back to Frederik and Hendrina.

One century after Frederik's arrival at the Cape, Johan's father Gabriel married Helena Gertruida Barendina Berning. Like their forbears, their seven children grew up to the sounds of hammers on anvils and the crackling of a blacksmith's furnace. I discovered that Helena descended from French nobility, and generations of Spanish nobility before that. To my astonishment, her genealogical trail led to the discovery that my 91st great-grandfather was King David, the Sweet Singer of Israel. The Jewish strands of my DNA quivered as I noted King Solomon and generations of Judean kings in my heritage.

"An appropriate level of deference will henceforth be required of you in our interactions," I advised Mark.

"Not gonna happen, Your Highness."

I had become captivated by this genealogy thing. Alongside my reading about South African history, it brought a sense of order to the past, despite the chaos of many individual stories. I gained a glimpse of why families had moved from place to place; how they splintered and the fragments lost touch. The picture that emerged suggested that my view of Afrikaners had been uninformed and narrow. It didn't change my feelings about the regime they had ushered in, but I realised I'd made assumptions about history without realising I'd made them. My reading and digging into the family history intensified.

The Luyt family had cut a wide swathe into the face of the early Cape. Their stories included murder, marriages between first cousins, marriages into Jewish families, and unions with slaves.

I was thrilled to discover, even further back than Frederik, the slave Anna of Bengal in Johan's mother's bloodline. It balanced, and added an ironic touch to the Afrikaner part of my family, the realisation of which had so pained my liberal soul. Her owner emancipated her and her children in 1712, but Johan's great-great grandfather was born a slave.

"Hmmm. Does this mean we have to renegotiate our marriage contract?" Mark asked.

"Well, exactly. There's another one back here too, a 'Mulatto', from Java. And a Dorothe from Angola."

Many years before Mark and I married in 1982, along with the creation of *The Immorality Act, The Marriage Act* had been amended to make interracial marriage illegal. It was also illegal to have white and "non-white" musicians playing together on a bandstand. At the venue where we performed in the months before departing from South Africa, management had apoplexy when we invited a singer, the late Donald Tshomelo, to appear with us. "We could lose our liquor licence," they wailed. Mark and I glanced at each other with our familiar, "I can't wait to get out of here" look.

Did my Afrikaner ancestors of the white purist years know about this duskier background, that turns out to have been common in Afrikaner families? Many of the wives on our vast family tree had names dating back to the era of slavery in the Cape, with more ancestors of colour possible, even probable, given the statistics. Gazing at a map of the Bay of Bengal I could feel my own connections on planet Earth broadening; hear the ropes creak on the 17th century wooden ship sailing out of Java, bound for the Cape of Good Hope. I imagined Anna's stomach heaving with fear at the oncoming, impenetrable unknown, as an officer barked instructions at her in a language she didn't yet understand.

In the early years at the Cape, the few hundred white men far outnumbered the women. Many slaves who arrived were women sold to officials of the VOC, from around the Bay of Bengal, incorporating the modern coastlines of Sri Lanka, India, Bangladesh, Myanmar (Burma), and a slice of Thailand. Some of these officials relocated to the Cape. For others, the Cape was the last stop on their way home to the Netherlands, where slavery was outlawed; a perfect opportunity to discard the goods they couldn't take home with them, like bins in which to dump fruit at Australian airports before officially entering the country.

What happened next was hardly surprising. These women, together with darker African slaves infused a range of "dark blood" into the ancestors of hundreds of people who would later establish the Afrikaner race. How did they sneak that one past the 1950 Office for Race Classification? Feelings ran high as recently as 1985, when some of the many Afrikaner families that historian and author, Hans Heese, traced through archival records back to Asian and African slave ancestors, tried to sue him for libel. Descendants included several conservative politicians. One, a Pretoria City Councilman, was so outraged at another Council member for noting his family's presence in Heese's book, that he hit him twice on the jaw.[6]

My complexion has always been described as "olive". At least two distant relatives I know have a dark complexion. I checked the definition under the 1950 *Population Registration Act* of South Africa. It classified each inhabitant into a race group: White, Bantu — black Africans, Coloured — mixed race, and Asian — Indian and Pakistani. The legislation could classify a child differently from a parent or sibling, and subject them to different rules about where they could live or go to school.

The Office for Race Classification defined a white person as one who "in appearance is obviously a white person who is generally not accepted as a coloured person; or is generally accepted as a white person and is not in appearance obviously not a white person". Apart from being an almost unintelligible sentence, it was not what I was expecting. I thought the rules were similar to those governing Jews in Nazi Germany. I checked, in case I got that wrong too.

In Germany, according to the Nuremburg Laws passed in 1935, anyone married to a Jewish person or who had one Jewish parent was legally a Jew. I scored on both counts.

But dark ancestors six or seven generations ago put us on the right side of the law in 1982, despite my complexion. "We're good," I told Mark.

But what about Johan at the dawn of the Afrikaner nation? Even though four generations behind him, would it not have delivered a blow to his political career to drop that titbit over dinner?

I found a clanging oversimplification online.[7] "White South African" is a term which refers to people from South Africa who are of European descent and who do not regard themselves, or are not regarded as, being part of another racial group (for example, as Coloured). In linguistic, cultural and historical terms, they are generally divided into the Afrikaans-speaking descendants of the Dutch East India Company's original settlers, known as Afrikaners, and the Anglophone descendants of predominantly British colonists."

The story of South Africa was much more complex, the ethnic pathways much more diverse, including the many British colonists who sided with and ultimately became Afrikaners, and descendants of the settlers of Dutch, German and French origin who became as English as fish and chips. It's a national history filled with fascinating stories influencing characters to make flawed decisions that seemed good to them at the time. I could almost start to care about a country with such a rich and nuanced past, as opposed to the one-dimensional version I learned at school.

After all the fuss of the apartheid years, most people I encountered now doing research on their early slave heritage seemed to consider it a badge of honour, or at least interest. I certainly did. I loved revisiting

South African history from fresh angles, rather than the one that bored me to distraction at school, to find that it was … well, really quite interesting. I loved discovering places in Cape Town that somehow eluded me during the years in which I lived there. Visitors to the tourist attraction "The Waterfront" might know of the Chavonnes Battery but few locals I asked had any idea of the riveting museum situated beneath the shopfronts and restaurants, nor the ruins and relics it contains of a time when mid-town Strand Street (Cape Town CBD's main thoroughfare) was at the beach.

I lived in Cape Town for twenty-three years and never saw the stunning edifice of the beautiful National Library at the foot of The Gardens. Construction commenced the year that Johan was born, a few blocks away.

I mourn my mother's loss of her family history. I don't believe she knew much of it … the slaves, the house where Johan was born, her ancient Jewish strand, her Afrikaner heritage or how that turned out to be more complicated than one might have expected. I wondered how the combination of these forces had made as good a woman as my mother so strong and so weak at the same time?

I was drawn again and again to the family chart, as if its dense foliage harboured secrets that would make my damaged love for her whole.

MARY ANN

June was a teenager when her grandmother went to live with them. Old enough to remember Mary Ann clearly. Yet she never said much about her. Perhaps she was too busy in her teens falling in love with my charming, dangerous young father.

I don't remember my mother ever showing me the portraits of her grandparents. Or was I too caught up in my own life for the images to stick? As I penetrated deeper into the story of the family, I wanted to know more about Mary Ann than my mother's recollection of her cauliflower breast, and that she had delivered the tea service into the hands of my Granny Grace. I considered the portrait again, and what I could deduce from the family chart on my wall.

At the time of her marriage to Johan, Mary Ann was quite a beauty. Apart from an impressive Roman nose, her face was all soft curves, her skin dewy and flawless. Her damaged portrait in cracked oils revealed a strong chin gracefully followed the slope of the lace collar reaching up to her jawline and a delicate ear bearing a subtle earring. The blue eyes, my mother's eyes, contrasted strikingly with the dark hair piled into a woven arrangement held with a clasp.

The whole impression was dark and conservative, with the exception of the rim of white lace and a pink rose adorning the heavy velvet dress. No ostentation there.

At just eighteen, and having lived a sheltered life in a small town several days by ox-wagon to the nearest town, how did she feel about her imminent marriage to a man ten years her senior? Was her slightly vacant look a protective veil concealing both apprehension and excitement? Marriage was the first of the two major female aspirations of the era, the second being to raise many children. Johan would have been the catch of the year, possibly the decade. Her parents would have been thrilled at the match. Johan and Mary Ann certainly wasted no time, marrying at the Dutch Reformed Church ten months after Johan's arrival in town. Her expectations of life must have soared on her wedding day. Both public achievement and tragedy lay in wait.

Mary Ann's background was very different from Johan's. I'd known almost nothing about her, but now discovered she was born in Heilbron, the third daughter of Christiaan Weilert from Hanover, and Rosina Clements from Colchester, England.

Her youngest sister, Wilhelmina (Winnie) would marry Johan's nephew Coenie, becoming both Johan's sister-in-law and his niece by marriage. Families were large and complicated, and the white population from which to select marriage partners, small. Winnie was destined to die young in the concentration camps of the Boer War, according to the family records assembled by her and Coenie's grandson Lionel Luyt, now a vital source in my research.

A photo of Mary Ann's from around 1882, inscribed "Dad, Mum & Winnie" suggested literacy, but the handwriting is appalling. It looks like the scrawl of a small child, not a young woman of nineteen about to bear her first child, Heinrich Leopold — "Leo".

The Luyt children after Leo came thick and fast, some barely a year apart. There would be eleven in total, three of whom would die as infants. I knew this was common in those days, but imagined the loss of a baby or small child would still have affected them all deeply. In Heilbron I had seen the tiny grave of one of the lost children, who had died at two years of age. I couldn't find records of the other two, but presumed they must have occurred during the larger gaps between the surviving children. I noted that one of those gaps was when my Granny Grace was a small child, and wondered if Mary Ann had needed to explain the concept of death to her, as I'd done to Dean after Melissa's stillbirth.

    1884 — Rosina ("Rosie")
    1885 — Helena ("Lenie")
    1890 — Edith Cora
    1892 — Mary (Avis' mother)
    1894 — Grace (my grandmother)
    1900 — Johan Godfried ("Obie")
    1904 — Frederick James Luyt ("Fritz")

I found a photograph showing Mary, Grace and Lenie in Bloemfontein, circa 1897. Grandly dressed little girls, in the family's heyday, before the fall. It drew my mind back to my discovery of Anna, four or five generations before these girls. Put little Lenie into a sari and she could indeed be Bengali.

"Such lovely skin. She could be a little Indian baby," I imagine their Basotho servant, Puleng, observing as she swaddled baby Lenie and brought her to Mary Ann to feed.

"Hush Puleng … what a thing to say."

Mary Ann's later photo, concealed behind Johan's portrait, showed a confident woman with no fear, vacancy or concealment in her demeanour. This was a woman in her prime, someone to be reckoned with. I had to look hard to pick out threads of grey at her temples. Her skin remained flawless, except for a few tiny wrinkles beneath her eyes.

The light blue of her eyes was not visible in this image, but the eyes were striking for a different reason: they look engaged, and harder. Though much more was to come, her life experiences had by then included birthing nine of her eleven children, three of whom she had buried. She had lost her father, and become the "First Lady" of Heilbron as her husband swiftly rose to become a member of the Volksraad for the district, and also Mayor of Heilbron.

I imagined the late 1890s, as dark clouds gathered over the Luyt family. The frenzy of diamonds and gold in the interior of South Africa had dramatically altered the physical and political landscape, and was about to unleash a war that would change everything.

Mary Ann could not sleep at night, consumed by what would become of her English mother, Rosina, who now lived with them, and how Johan would walk the fine lines of allegiances facing him. His extended family spanned many parts of the British Cape Colony and the Orange Free State. It was the latter he served, and its largely Dutch descended "Africander" population — the term "Afrikaner" did not yet exist.

But in June 1899, before the storm broke over the Republic to which Johan had devoted nearly twenty years, a ray of sun penetrated the gloom.

"I told you you'd do us proud," said Mary Ann, smiling at her reflection in the gleaming silver tray.

"What?" asked Johan, trying to tame the corners of his mouth.

"Don't be coy with me, you public personage, you. Gracie, don't touch it with those grubby fingers."

Grace withdrew her hand and contented herself with standing on tiptoes, also trying to see her reflection, but no matter how hard she stretched, all she could see was the top of her head reflected in silver. She had just turned five, and didn't understand what was going on, though she could see that her father was at the centre of it and her mother couldn't stop smiling. Grace had enjoyed the attention of the many visitors, including Uncle Coenie and Aunt Winnie from Frankfort, who had brought her birthday presents.

"I'm sorry we weren't here for your actual birthday, Gracie," said Auntie Winnie, bending down to kiss her, "but it was too far to make the trip twice in two weeks with Baby Willie". Tragedy lay in store for Willie, but on this happy day such losses were unknowable.

Coenie and Winnie's eldest was named Daniel Coenraad, like many on the family tree, but called Tuli. He had teased Grace and her sister, Mary, in the annoying way of boys, but cousin Dorothea had been fun. The highlight was unquestionably the impressive expanse of cakes and sweets spread across the table in the parlour, vestiges of which still clung to Grace's hands.

"You're right my dear, as usual," Johan conceded, allowing his satisfaction to overcome the natural modesty restraining his lips. "This acknowledgement is not unpleasing."

From time to time I took the tray out from the back of the cupboard in my house in Sydney and beheld my face and my office reflected in dull silver. I imagined Mary Ann doing the same with this final surviving evidence of moneyed times, and perhaps persuading my Granny Grace to serve tea on it for special occasions when members of the family were together. Did that ever happen?

I assumed my mother must have had connections with her wider family. But she'd mentioned so few of them. I'd met even fewer of them, mostly when I was less than five years old, and remembered almost nothing. June's old address books might have held information, but I wouldn't have recognised the names of her aunts, uncles and cousins, apart from Avis and her daughter, Pam, in New Zealand. Mary Ann and Johan had so many other children besides Grace. I knew the names in that generation now, and was especially interested in the eldest daughter, Rosie, and her husband Gideon of the many criminal charges, but who were their descendants, and could they help me with information about our common ancestor's story?

THE WAR THAT CHANGED EVERYTHING

In this, the last "gentleman's war", commanders on both sides sent notes of sympathy to the other when their leaders fell in battle. It was the last British war fought largely without mechanisation, where men and horses ruled. It saw the birth of guerrilla warfare in South Africa, as Boer commandos recognised the futility of engaging British battalions, and took to the hills to continue fighting for nearly two years after Lord Roberts, Commander-in-Chief of the British forces in South Africa, announced the war was "practically over".

This was the war that put the phenomenon of the concentration camp in the public eye, complete with the suffering and ensuing bitterness this institution fomented.

The Boer War had been in the curriculum at school, yet I had emerged with no real awareness of the events and outcomes of this conflict.

Through two senior years of history in high school I'd managed to learn about European history, but South African? No chance.

Our pale grey textbook had tiny print and almost no illustrations or photographs. The sections on the Great Trek and the Boer War held lists, endless names, places, dates and casualty statistics that I found impossible to memorise. Nothing hooked them to my brain, or my heart. It was the history of a people (not mine) whose ideology I despised, in whose country I happened to be born. I barely scraped through the subject.

The night before the final exam a rare event took place at a local jazz venue, a legendary African American band visiting South Africa. I couldn't miss that, but made the concessions of no alcohol and of leaving immediately after the gig. Both parents were overseas on film locations for two months, covering the critical period before and during the exams. I stayed alone in the house with our maid Julia, the second domestic servant who worked for our family after Ida retired to Lesotho in her old age. She provided meals and occasional company. My skewed perceptions did not register the timing of this parental absence as inappropriate.

After the gig, I took caffeine pills and crammed until about three am, hoping that some of the stultifying detail might stick until the exam, just a few hours away. I got up again at six am, took more pills and crammed for a last, desperate hour before the final exam of my school life.

As soon as I read the history exam paper I knew it was not going to go well. Afterwards, trembling with caffeine-strangeness, I returned to an empty house and repeated my scrambled egg experience of a few years earlier, tears dripping onto my plate.

The whole topic of South African history covered events irrelevant to my life, or the lives of anyone I might know, and held little of human interest for me. Told through the lens of the prevailing order at the time, all the juicy stuff had been stripped away. It must have taken real talent to render this human saga, full of dilemma and paradox, so boring.

Nowadays, history is taught differently, providing students with ways to examine the same material through different lenses. The lens in Southern Africa today is tinted with the deeper shade of a new prevailing order. I found many "white records" swept away in places like Heilbron and Maseru.

Not so for the Boer War, a focal point of Afrikaner bitterness that fuelled a delusional ideology that would one day contribute to driving me from my country of birth. A massive body of information exists in archives and resources all over South Africa recording the heroism, suffering, greed and brutality of this conflict. The paper it's printed on could probably cover a three-lane highway around the planet. Thousands of stories of the black peoples caught in the crossfire are, now, part of the historical legacy. These were not to be found in my grey textbook, nor were stories about the mess made of families with members on both sides of the divide.

But the Boer War turns out to be part of my history after all.

Both sides endured shocking hardship and suffering. For the people of the Boer Republics the horrors included having the British burn their farms and ship prisoners of war in their thousands to camps in Bermuda, Ceylon and St Helena.

Mary Ann failed to hold back the tears as she told her children that their Uncle Coenie had been captured and sent to Darrell's Island, Bermuda.

"Uncle Coenie?" the Luyt children clamoured around her. "When will he come back?"

"I don't know, but everyone says the war won't go on for long, so let's be hopeful."

Coenie, Johan's nephew who had married Mary Ann's young sister Winnie, was gone for nearly two years. While latter day Bermuda conjures resorts and beach towels; those images utterly belie the conditions for the men held there in suspended animation during the Boer War. They hovered, powerless, desperate for the sporadic news from home. Many spent their days crafting toys and trinkets from driftwood, like scrimshaw that whalers would carve on the bones and teeth from whales to help pass the months at sea. Coenie, a lawyer like his brother-in-law-and-uncle, Johan, spent *his* time acting as legal representative to the other men.

Johan fretted as he followed the news of prisoners of war in the *Heilbron Herald*. "That boy is like a son to me."

"He's a grown man, Johan," said Mary Ann. "You have to trust him to look after himself. And at least Winnie and the children are safe." One of Johan's older brothers had settled in Ceres, in the Cape, and Johan had sent Coenie's two older children there.

The Boer War had been a long time coming.

The migration known as The Great Trek was sparked, at least in part, by Britain taking over rule of the Cape Colony from the Dutch in 1806. Within thirty years many of the original Dutch, French and German families, now merged under the Dutch banner, hitched wagons and went into the interior in search of freedom. The irascible groups of trekkers couldn't agree on much, and established tiny republics where they pursued their austere way of life. London politicians had no stomach for attempting to control these vast, sparsely populated lands of no value, inhabited by such troublesome people.

Leaders of note did eventually emerge, and united the trekkers into what became known as the Boer Republics, the Transvaal in 1852, then the Orange Free State in 1854.

Then, in 1870, Kimberley and environs yielded their sparkling treasures. After the diamonds came the discovery of gold in the Transvaal, which unleashed a scramble of fortune hunters from around the world, and turned the gaze of the British Government to the interior of South Africa.

The OFS quietly got on with the business of dreaming their country into being. The newly constructed train lines of the later 1800s had brought educated young gentlemen in search of opportunity. As I read of these times, I could see what might have caused my great grandfather to leave the relative refinement of Cape Town.

It was an adventure of a different kind; an exciting time for lawyers, like Johan, who often became the leaders. Men who would become famous facilitated Johan's immersion in Afrikanerdom. There was Francis Reitz, the father of the Boer War hero, Deneys Reitz, a friend of the Luyt family. And Johan's mentor, the legendary politician Abraham Fischer, who was elected to the OFS Volksraad the year that Johan qualified under his tutelage as an attorney. Then Marthinus Steyn, in whose cabinet Johan would serve in the Boer War. These names were central to every book, article and website I read on the subject of the Boer War. My high school history teacher would have been astonished at the intensity of my interest, and the rate at which I devoured the information. But neither of us knew, back then, of Johan's story, or that these names were among those that would appear on the legal documents punctuating his demise.

The first Anglo-Boer war had broken out in December 1880. Despite efforts from the Transvaal to drag her neighbour republic into the fray, the Orange Free State managed to stay out of it. With my history knowledge as poor as it was, I hadn't known that there were *two* such wars.

"Very worrying, what's going on up north," said Johan to Mary Ann, his bride of barely a month, standing before an array of fabrics in their new home in Heilbron. Four years were still to pass before the completion of the fine house that would swell with children and relatives for the twenty-four eventful years before the fall of the family.

"I suppose so, if *you're* worried about it," she replied, turning back to the fabrics. "Do you think the blue or the yellow for the parlour curtains?"

The defeat of the British was unexpected and swift. But the discovery of gold on the Witwatersrand, and Britain's slimy grab for the republic would soon change everything.

"Now here's a thing," said Johan. "Abraham has been encouraging me to nominate for Parliament. With this trouble over, I wonder if I should express some interest. Public office would be good for business, if I can get the votes … I think I could make a contribution."

"You'd do a wonderful job." Mary Ann held out two hands to take his. "I'm sure everyone would vote for you. I'd be very proud of you."

Johan joined the Volksraad in 1885 where he would serve for sixteen years alongside future presidents Fischer, Reitz and Steyn. I was impressed by the connections Johan had with these leaders, and the part he played in their successive governments. Newspaper cuttings showed that Johan was a force on the Volksraad, even challenging President Steyn on constitutional matters at times. He worked hard to prevent war, alongside these men of big futures, including Christiaan de Wet, another Boer War hero-in-waiting, as all their paths converged on the OFS Volksraad. In the meantime, Johan brought the railway line to Heilbron, and endeared himself to all in his communal life.

But the ideologies of British imperialism and Boer republicanism were on a collision course. And now there was the matter of all that gold down there.

In my research, I read many publications about the issues and the war itself. None mentioned Johan, yet his story ran closely alongside the stories of the main players. One newspaper article in a family scrapbook confirmed that he was one of six men comprising the Special Commission that drafted the resolution to pursue peace, not war, and presented it to the rest of the Volksraad. It passed unanimously. I'd been unaware of attempts by the Boers to avert this famous war.

In June 1899, Johan attended a conference in Bloemfontein, led by President Steyn, between the key leaders in a last, desperate attempt. It failed.

Johan leaped onto the platform before the train from Bloemfontein had come to a stop.

"What's the rush?" asked Mary Ann, who had brought little Mary and Grace on an outing in their Cape cart to meet him at the station. Their servant Khubane supervised the horse while Puleng tried to keep the eager girls amused next to the carriage.

Johan placed a swift kiss on her cheek. "I must call a meeting of our Town Council immediately."

"The conference didn't go well?" She tried to keep up with his large strides.

He stopped while still out of earshot of his daughters and met her eyes for the first time since stepping off the train. "We must brace ourselves for war. I will need your help in contacting all members of the family. I'm not quite sure where some of the Luyts in the Cape will be forced to place their allegiances."

"What about *our* allegiances, Johan?"

"We'll speak with your mother tonight. And you will need to be in communication with your sisters. There is no question about our allegiances."

On 9 Oct 1899, Francis Reitz, by then Secretary of State of the South African Republic, handed an ultimatum to the British Agent in Pretoria. War broke out two days later.

Despite successes in the initial six months, the Boer commandos couldn't hold back the much larger British forces. In May 1900, President Steyn and General Christiaan de Wet moved the capital to Kroonstad, while the British uneventfully occupied Bloemfontein.

The Free Staters fought on, led by President Steyn, General Christiaan de Wet and his brother, General Piet de Wet. But soon the Boer Government had to retreat again. Johan was the sitting Chairman of the Volksraad and the last to leave on the day he closed its doors in Kroonstad. President Steyn retreated with secretaries and councillors, "bringing the 'seat of Government' with them in a Cape cart"[8] to the Luyt's home in Heilbron.

For many Britons, the Anglo–Boer War came to be seen as almost quaint, with few remembering clearly why it was fought, how it was fought, and what consequences followed. Facts may have dissolved into myths, and all who took part are long gone, but the resulting fears, hopes, attitudes and prejudices reverberated through the Afrikaner people and South African Government for decades.

My research revealed two items among those to have caused the most misery.

One was the furious schism between "*hensoppers*" (hands uppers) and "*bittereinders*" (bitter enders). This conflict became increasingly relevant, as I drilled into a national story intertwined, unexpectedly, with my own.

From relatively early in the war, as Britain's troops advanced, they offered a kind of armistice to those who would surrender, and sign an Oath of Allegiance to the British Government. Many Boers saw no hope of overcoming this enormous army, surrendered, and signed the oath in the interests of bringing the war to an end. They were called "*hensoppers*" (hands uppers), by those Boers who swore to never give up, but to fight "to the bitter end". They were known as "*bittereinders*" (bitter enders).

I'd never heard of this before. But I now found articles and papers by many academics who had compared the heroic *bittereinder* camp to the fearful *hensopper* camp. Arguments emerged on each side that they were acting in the best interests of their people, though heroism came across as the more compelling quality to me. The famous stoush between the brothers Christiaan and Piet de Wet, both generals in the OFS commandos, epitomised it. Maybe the grey history book mentioned this, but if it did, it didn't stick.

Piet, after fighting and winning battles for the Boers, in 1900 came to the decision that the Boers would be better served by joining the British. He took on the leadership of the Orange River Colony Volunteers, who, under British command, tried to persuade Boers to lay down their arms and even serve with British units.

His brother, Christiaan, fighting together with three of his sixteen children, was the quintessential *bittereinder*. He vowed, speaking of Piet, "If I see him again I will shoot him like a dog."

Tens of thousands died, their farms destroyed, after the efforts of the *hensoppers* failed to persuade the Boer leaders that surrender would be the best way forward. But in Afrikaner circles, the stain of traitor clung to *hensoppers* for decades.

Another major source of bitterness was the phenomenon of the concentration camps, where over 26,000 women and children died from typhoid, measles and dysentery. And that was just the white people. The black peoples of the land served on both sides, and also died by the thousands through battle and internment in concentration camps. But they were "*just kaffirs*" (this was the terminology of the time, used on both sides of the conflict, before the term became utterly unpalatable) and the numbers were not recorded.

The camps have been viewed as a British plot to herd Afrikaner women and children into detention and subject them to degradation, suffering and ultimately death. This provided the Afrikaner nation with a bottomless well of bitterness from which to draw. There are awful photographs of starving children and anguish. For those whose relatives suffered thus, it must be difficult to see it in any other light.

In Elizabeth van Heyningen's book, *Concentration Camps of the Anglo-Boer War,* I discovered, however, that like most complex situations, it wasn't a simple case of heroes and villains.

Many Afrikaners called it a euphemism, but the camps were indeed established as "refugee camps", and the British did view it as their responsibility to provide shelter and sustenance for the destitute families of Boers on commando, or held as prisoners of war. The scorched earth policy only came later, with the rounding up of Boer families as a strategy to eliminate support for the guerrilla fighters.

The British were woefully unprepared for the consequences of their strategy. Their incompetence in the face of disease, and unexpected numbers of people, fanned the underlying intent into a massive humanitarian tragedy. The ignorance of many Boer women didn't help. They were apparently so suspicious of camp doctors that they rejected attempts to introduce sanitation. Typhoid, spread in faeces, was unstoppable.

Doctors moved many children from their families into camp hospitals to control their diet, as the disease ripped at their digestive systems. But some women believed the British doctors to be starving their children to death and sneaked in "proper food", in many cases killing them.

Johan had served for years on the Volksraad with both de Wet brothers. Yet, his wife's mother was English, and that was the language they spoke at home. Their son, Leo, served in President Steyn's personal guard.

Piet de Wet ran the Orange River Colony Volunteers out of Heilbron. His brother Christiaan and his strapping sons were legendary *bittereinder* heroes in the Heilbron Commando. Johan was the Mayor of Heilbron throughout this period. Such were the complexities that faced those less famous folks on the B-side of history.

The wartime role of Rosie, Johan's eldest daughter, added to the complexity. She already interested me because I believed she would lead me to her miscreant husband, Gideon, the son-in-law who was also Johan's employee, and who's recorded misdeeds I had discovered that electrifying day in the Bloemfontein Archives, near the start of my search. I had subsequently learned that Rosie was a spy for the Boers.

FINDING ROSIE

Ten years after my mother's death, I found myself online and in the archives, even grinding through the South African telephone directory, in search of any descendant of the children of Rosie and Gideon. I had no initial success.

I'd learned, however, that an unexpected morsel might arrive in an email, or fall from a side detail on an archive record. I listed hundreds of archive files of possible interest, visited archives in Cape Town, Bloemfontein and Pretoria, and took hundreds more photographs of documents. I lacked context at the time, and nothing monumental leaped from the pages.

But it pays to reread documents that previously yielded nothing. Revisiting brings insights, liberated by other knowledge acquired in the interim. A name heard twice will make one stop and pay attention. I assembled multiple, concurrent jigsaws from what I could glean of the stories of the van Rooyen children. From time-to-time some dots joined up, and a sleeping document's moment arrived. These are rousing episodes in the dogged quest of the genealogist.

One day, I again entered the confounding world of Geni, an online genealogical tool that had become indispensable, and noticed new entries and a new name. Records for some of the van Rooyen children had been entered by one Rory Kroon, resident in South Africa. I wrote to him and received a reply within a couple of days. He identified himself as the nephew of the husband of one of Rosie and Gideon's daughters. It was a stretch. But he was interested to continue the exploration so I sent him a few titbits. A rush of correspondence and suddenly I was in excited contact with Daphne Hollis, a granddaughter of Rosie and Gideon.

I'd searched for Daphne online, in Pretoria, in the archives and phone books, but I was looking in the wrong country. I found her in Sydney, thirty minutes' drive from my house. She had lived for twenty years in the suburb adjacent to mine. We'd probably passed each other in the aisles of the local supermarket. I could have wept at how my mother, also living right there, had missed the chance to meet her cousin.

It struck me that Daphne might not want to know the damning minutiae of her grandfather's life. From our telephone conversations, it was clear she knew less about him than I did. She knew that he did time, was blamed by the family for the downfall in Heilbron and that it had something to do with embezzling money from clients. She also told me that he delivered Rosie and the children into dire poverty and no one wanted anything to do with him.

Daphne had stories. She showed me a breadbasket saved from the Luyt's house in Heilbron, and an initialled jewel box that belonged to her grandmother Rosie.

Daphne's mother was named "Cissy" because she was The Big Sister who had to be a little mother to the other five van Rooyen children. Daphne gave me a copy of Cissy's memoirs, just two typewritten pages. She related how when her father, Gideon, was away in prison or in the war, her mother Rosie took in sewing to earn money. Rosie also went out at night to play piano at the cinema and for dances in Parys, the town to which the Luyts had retreated after the fall of the family.

Cissy, all of twelve years old, would have to stay up to look after the baby and to let her mother in when she returned. She recalls, "One of the highlights of my life was when she played the piano to us with the lights off and around the fire. She could play from memory for three hours without repeating herself once."

Cissy told her daughter Daphne that Gideon deserted the family in Pretoria. Perhaps they had moved there from Parys after his release from Pretoria Central Prison. The children gathered in Rosie's camp, and why wouldn't they? They never spoke of Gideon.

Always compassionate, Rosie took Gideon back into their family home in Pretoria in the late 1930s when illness rendered him helpless. The children still at home helped nurse their errant father until his death.

How did Rosie, the feisty Boer War spy, succumb to the charming but dangerous Gideon van Rooyen, I wondered?

ROSIE'S WAR

Rosie was exhausted. She had spent the night sitting bolt upright with her hand on the lock of the door handle of her compartment. It looked rather flimsy to her capable eye. Twice she could have sworn she felt an attempt to open it. She was seventeen, the only woman on an overnight troop train from Heilbron to Bloemfontein, and she wasn't leaving it to chance.

The night had passed without assault, thankfully, and now she stood, reeling with fatigue but still defiant, before a major of the British army.

"I do not shake hands with Englishmen," she said in perfectly enunciated English, ignoring the major's attempt to retract his outstretched hand without loss of dignity.

"Young lady, if you had been fighting any other nation but the British, you'd have been put up against the wall and shot," he said in a misguided attempt to improve the frosty conditions in his tent.

"I would only like to shake the hand of a very brave woman," he continued, annoyed, waving the spurned hand in the air.

Rosie had been arrested in Heilbron as a Boer spy and sent to detention in Bloemfontein. She had been running dispatches for the Boers for twelve months since the surrender of Heilbron in June 1900.

Those were the heady days of her romance with Willie Steyn, son of the dear lady who gave the talented Luyt girls piano lessons, and played the organ in church on Sundays. When Rosie was fourteen, a visiting German Professor heard her play and told Johan that if he could take her to Germany he would make a world-renowned performer of her.

"It would never do to have a young lady travel to Europe on such a venture," said her father, exchanging surprised looks with Mary Ann, as four-year-old Grace peered eye-level at the beckoning piano keys and wondered what it was that a world-renowned performer did.

Did Rosie's father ever learn of her secret engagement to Willie Steyn? This dashing young relative of President Steyn served in the Heilbron Commando under the famous *bittereinder* General Christiaan de Wet. News of each encounter with the Brits crackled into town like the latest chapter in an action novel.

After the Volksraad retreated from Kroonstad, the Government Secretary Piet Blignaut packed up the government archives. They now sat in piles in the home of the Luyts in Heilbron, the latest site of the government of the Republic of the Orange Free State. Rosie, then sixteen, eavesdropped on her father Johan's discussions with the elegant visitors who had taken over the parlour for the past week, by helping her pregnant mother ferry refreshments into the room on the large silver tray bearing the inscription to her father.

"Thank you," Government Secretary Blignaut smiled at Rosie as he accepted a cup of coffee, then turned back to the men. "Do you think General de Wet will be able to hold them?"

"I fear not, from dispatches, but I pray so," Rosie's father replied. "They gather at Lindley as we speak. General de Wet will be in town any day now, and I look forward to hearing an update from him."

Rosie swooned with anticipation that her heroic sweetheart Willie would soon be back in town with de Wet's commando.

Intense discussion continued in the parlour. "Mr President, I see no way to avoid further retreat," they said. "The forces march in great numbers."

President Steyn looked down for some time. "Gentlemen," he said finally, "we lose another battle but we have not lost the war." Murmurs of "hear, hear" went around the room.

"Johan, we will take care of your boy," said President Steyn as the entourage withdrew once more, this time to Frankfort. It was Sunday evening.

"The idea is for him to take care of *you*, Sir, but thank you," said Johan, concealing his fears for his son Leo, serving in the personal guard of President Steyn.

All of Monday the town held its breath.

War correspondent Winston Churchill's account of the next day describes how, just after sunrise, Christiaan de Wet appeared with "sixty wagons, five guns, and a thousand burghers". They were worn out from trekking all night, and grateful for rest and refreshment. They had just outspanned their exhausted oxen and settled down for coffee when the leading patrols of a formidable British army appeared on the hills to the south of the town. It was a terrifying sight. The Boers frantically resaddled their horses, inspanned their hungry oxen cheated of their well-earned food and rest, and the commando sped out of Heilbron to the north.

"Never give up, my Rosie!" Willie called to his sweetheart, his eyes pulled backward toward her until his horse was in a full gallop.

"I'll be here," sobbed Rosie. No tired, hungry ox felt more cheated than she.

Churchill describes the agonisingly slow process of seeking formal surrender of the town. The customs of war dictated that the white flag must proceed at a walk from a distance of over a mile toward the enemy line. Time passed while the parties discussed the terms. The return journey was faster, but the whole exercise took almost an hour while officials from both sides strained to follow the distant figures.

Johan felt the swell of their next child against his abdomen as he hugged a rigid Mary Ann in the hallway of their Heilbron home. The freezing June wind cut him as he walked out with his tumultuous feelings to meet the fluttering white flag.

Rosie's secret fiancée Willie Steyn was captured in battle and sent to Ceylon where he, and four others from Heilbron, made a dramatic escape that became the subject of his book *Die Vyf Swemmers* (The Five Swimmers).

But in mid-1900, the British forces were still pushing towards Pretoria, thinking the war would be over soon. They left forces peppered across their "conquered lands". The Luyts' house, the largest in Heilbron, was commandeered by the British for their officers.

"Talk to *me*," said Rosie, standing tall. "My mother is indisposed."

There was no doubt that the eldest daughter would not yield, and to insist otherwise, as it was clear that the lady of the house was pregnant, would seem boorish.

"You can take the rooms out the back," Rosie said.

She called to my grandmother Grace, six, and Avis' mother Mary, eight. "Girls, it's not safe outside, but why don't you take your bicycles and ride them in the passage?" Four small eyebrows shot up. "Yes," Rosie responded. "I'm positive. It's fine."

A British Major soon emerged, complaining about the noise. "And the worst," he muttered, "is that it's in English."

As the birth of the baby drew near, Mary Ann became less interested in the activities of the house and town, and relied on her older daughters to keep the household running. The air was frequently thick with crisis, as Heilbron filled with English regiments, then Boer commandos, then English again, in pursuit of the eternally elusive General de Wet and President Steyn. Railway lines were repeatedly blown up. It pained Johan, who had been so instrumental in building them in the first place.

Rosie became embroiled in espionage. Her daughter Cissy's memoirs relate stories her mother told her. One night, for example,

Rosie was almost found by patrolling British soldiers as she tried to send secret messages on the transmitting machine in the darkened post office. She melted away into the night just in time, the machine concealed beneath her cloak.

On another night, British soldiers arrived to search for books they believed to contain records relevant to the resistance. They left empty-handed. Family friend Deneys Reitz, son of ex-President Reitz, was visiting. To his surprise, Rosie ran to a chest in the back of the house, dived in and cleared the items she'd piled on top of the incriminating books. Within minutes of starting to incinerate the evidence in their kitchen hearth, there was another knock at the front door. Deneys looked at Rosie, who leaped to her feet.

"What's all the smoke about then?" asked the recently departed British soldier, his eyes narrow as he pointed to the chimney.

"We're making cocoa, it's so cold tonight," she chirped. "Would you like some?"

The young and friendly girl, looked up at the soldier and moved her eyes across his broad shoulders and chest. She took in the shiny buttons and manifestations of rank and smiled. He hesitated, but she knew she'd won.

"Thank you, Miss. You enjoy your cocoa and I'll be on my way."

Cissy's account of Rosie's arrest said she was "betrayed by her own". I never did find out what that meant precisely.

Did Johan know about Rosie's covert activities? In August 1901, after she'd been held for five weeks, he wrote a letter to the British authorities, saying there must be some misunderstanding. He was bewildered they should suspect her; that Rosie was just a child. "She assured us that she has done nothing for which she deserves being severed from her people and home," he wrote.

Either he was surprisingly unobservant, playing a double game, away a lot, or a combination of all of the above. And what of Mary Ann? Johan's letter read, "She is in delicate health, cannot bear the strain and worry much longer, and she is naturally anxious to have her child back under her own roof."

And then …

"As I have taken the Oath of Allegiance, I naturally feel that any serious charge against my daughter, a minor in my house, might reflect upon me also."

He signed the Oath of Allegiance to the British. My mother's grandfather was a *hensopper*.

I felt absurdly disappointed to discover that Johan was a *hensopper*. It was an interesting response as I'd never identified with the Afrikaner cause in any way. But I had now read heroic tales in books and letters, learned of the complexities and challenges of the conflict, had built a real respect for the resourcefulness of the Boers and realised that the English/Afrikaner divide didn't exist before the Boer War in the way I assumed it always had.

What did the Boer spy Rosie, with her boyfriend Willie in *bittereinder* De Wet's commando, think of that? Did she know?

Johan's letter goes on to describe his various roles in high office for the annexed Republic and, since surrendering Heilbron, his efforts to persuade others to surrender their arms and take the oath.

The war had pushed some members of the Luyt family into British regiments, and some into Boer commandos. Did the Luyt family in the Cape Colony feel allegiance to the British? What did Johan's immediate relatives in prisoner of war camps think of his taking the oath? What did Mary Ann think, and his children at home? His son Leo, in President Steyn's guard?

Johan's petition failed, and Rosie would remain in detention as a "matter of security". But Johan was still influential, a man of means. It's not clear how he managed it, but Rosie was released, though she had to remain under surveillance in Bloemfontein. She resided for a while at Polley's Hotel. Polley's was also the establishment of choice for men such as Conan Doyle and other war correspondents. As it was not seemly for a young woman of marriageable age to live unsupervised in such a place, Rosie soon moved into the home of Mrs Cecilia Blignaut, sister of President Steyn and wife of Government Secretary Piet Blignaut, who had brought the government's records to Heilbron.

Cecilia was a Boer legend, who started the Ladies Relief Committee who worked so hard to ease suffering in the Bloemfontein concentration camp.

She recruited Rosie for the Committee. Rosie can be seen second from the left in the front row of the photograph.

Rosie would have been well supervised at the home of the Blignauts. But she was a feisty girl with a taste for wild young men.

Bloemfontein was also the home of Gideon van Rooyen, a rakish young man of twenty-three. Gideon never bore arms or served a Boer commando, unusual at that time, and in March 1902 took the Oath of Allegiance so despised by the Boers. By what means did Gideon sufficiently impress the young "Mata Hari" of the Orange Free State, who at sixteen years of age had personally trained horses for Boer commandos, that she would give up her secret fiancé, the hero Willie Steyn? Rosie's daughter Cissy said that Rosie and Gideon met at "The Theatricals". It struck me as a light recreation for an able-bodied young man in such a dark time.

It took Willie Steyn until just after the end of the war, after his famous escape from Ceylon, to journey back to Heilbron via Russia, Amsterdam and the emptiness of German West Africa, as Namibia was then known. When he reached Heilbron after his long odyssey, he found that his mother, Rosie's kind piano teacher, was one of the 602 who had perished in the Heilbron concentration camp. By then the news of Rosie's engagement would have been public. She had returned to Heilbron from Bloemfontein in June 1902.

In his book, Willie wrote:

"June 1902: Heilbron had changed so much that I found life there almost impossible".

He stayed only twelve days, then left for the Cape Colony.

Rosie married Gideon van Rooyen in Heilbron in January 1903. To my surprise, Willie Steyn was one of the two witnesses on the marriage certificate. I'll bet Rosie later wished she'd hung on for him.

THE WAR ENDS

In my extensive reading about this period, it puzzled me to find no mention of Johan, immediate ex-chairman of the Volksraad and Mayor of Heilbron. His town was a centre of activity and meeting for commandos, as well as the Orange River Colony Volunteers, led for the British by Piet de Wet. How these two forces both used the town as headquarters is baffling, given the intensity of emotions involved, and the movements of Christiaan de Wet's commando back and forth through Heilbron.

The family felt the pressure as the fighting dragged on. One morning, in a manner uncharacteristic of her, Mary Ann barged into Johan's office.

"Johan, Piet's boy Gabriel has been taken, at Sandfontein," she exclaimed.

"I heard. These papers here are an attempt to house his family in the town instead of the camp."

"Some of the houses they're using for prisoners have all their doors and windows blown out. How can a family find shelter in such a house?"

"They want us to call them refugees, not prisoners."

"Ask *them*. They'll tell you what they are."

"Please don't make my life even more difficult than it already is."

"I'm sorry, Johan," she said, softening. "Just try to secure adequate housing. There's nothing we can do for your captured nephews, but we can surely help their families."

"I am doing everything in my power, believe me," said Johan.

Mary Ann hovered at the door until Johan looked up at her again. "What?"

"Johan, you know I try to be calm and avoid gossip, but I heard that typhoid has broken out in the Heilbron camp and even among some of the families held in town. Is it true?"

He turned his head away, and nodded as she advanced on his desk.

"Our little ones. And the baby, he's not even two months old."

"I know, I know. I wasn't going to frighten you with this just yet. But you should not accompany me to take supplies into the camp anymore. Make sure Puleng prepares our food to the strictest standards of cleanliness. And I'll see if I can find any extra meat for us."

"Not if it means that others get less than they need."

He stood, walked around the desk and put his arms around her.

"You can be sure that no one will get as much as they need, including us. As soon as it's safe for a few days, I'll take Motsumi out to look for game, though the veld is stripped bare."

The signing of the Treaty of Vereeniging on 31 May 1902 officially ended the war. Even Christiaan de Wet, the ultimate *bittereinder*, had to concede that the bitter end had arrived.

The Boer Presidents set up a meeting at Vereeniging where each Republic brought thirty delegates to vote on the agreement. They wrangled for days. The leaders wrangled on in Pretoria. The wrangling at Vereeniging resumed.

"It has been said that we must fight 'to the bitter end,'" said General Botha, "but no one tells us where that bitter end is. Is it there where everyone lies in his grave or is banished? Is the bitter end not there, where the people have struggled till they can struggle no more?"

He continued, "Then there are also some of our own people, who have taken up arms against us, and if matters go on as at present there will shortly be more Africanders fighting against us than for us. The question now is, what must we do?"

The vote on surrender was fifty-four in favour, six against. When this resolution passed, there were not many tearless eyes in the tent. Christiaan de Wet, like many others, would return to a ruined farm.

Acting Transvaal President SW Burger concluded, "We must also be inclined to forgive and to forget when we meet our brothers. We may not cast off that portion of our people who were unfaithful."

Family mythology maintained that Johan was one of the signatories to the treaty. But there is no evidence of it. The four Orange Free Staters who signed the Treaty included Christiaan de Wet (in spite of his having thundered against it), but not Johan.

I would have expected someone of Johan's stature in the defeated government to be a part of this historic event, over which generations of Afrikaners would shake their heads, but he is not on the list of the OFS representatives.[9] Neither is Piet de Wet. Had any of the men on the list taken the Oath? I suspect not. I read commentaries holding that, in omitting them from the discussion in favour of only the *bittereinders*, the British prejudiced the future of the very people who had co-operated with them.

"You should have been at Vereeniging," fumed Mary Ann. "Did you hear what General Botha said? It's just what you said two years ago."

"It did contain some echoes, I'll admit. But they only selected men still serving."

"There's more than one way to serve your country," she continued bitterly. "Think of how many thousands of lives would have been saved if they'd followed your lead."

"Nothing to be done about it now."

"But they called those who took the oath 'unfaithful'. That is unbearable. You are a man of the highest honour, Johan."

"Botha also suggested that everyone put these differences behind them and focus on what now needs to be done. I agree with him. The work of restoring Heilbron will take years, not to mention achieving self-government. For now, let's look forward to Rosie's return. Her young man is charming, and the first marriage among our children seems imminent," he said, trying to lighten Mary Ann's thunderous mood.

LIFE AND DEATH AFTER THE WAR

"Would you like a big wedding? Or money to buy furniture?" Johan had asked Rosie.

"We'll be happy with the furniture Papa, and just a small wedding."

"Could we manage both for the first marriage in the family?" Mary Ann whispered into Johan's ear as he lay in the embrace of his beloved wife that night, the orange glow of an early spring fire still dancing gently in the bedroom hearth.

The wedding was a big affair. Johan also gave Rosie and Gideon a house and the furniture in it.

You'd think that Gideon would be the one seated beside Rosie, but I'm not sure. He looks older than twenty-four. And I expected Gideon to look more devilish, like the young man standing behind Rosie. Could it have been common back then, for the groom to stand behind the bride? Leo, the eldest brother who served in President Steyn's commando, is there. He is the only one smiling in this dismal wedding photo. Rosie's sisters are there too, and cousin Carlie, recently returned from Ceylon, where he was a prisoner of war. The famous escapee from Ceylon, Willie Steyn, looking stoic, made it into the family inner circle too.

My grandmother, "Gracie", and her sister Mary are in the front row and, like the other flower girls, look about ready to pass out. I wondered for how long they had to hold still for a photograph in 1903.

Rosie lost her first baby, a boy, due to pre-eclampsia, which I learned runs in the family. She also nearly lost her life.

"More ice," shouted Lenie. Puleng ran to the kitchen for another sack of ice to tip into the bath where Rosie lay delirious, while the doctor monitored her pulse.

"We'll have to keep up these ice baths," he said to Mary Ann. "Do you have a good supply of ice?"

"Mr Luyt has already gone to find more."

How he procured ice at short notice in the summer of 1904 in Heilbron is baffling. But family mythology holds that Rosie's life was saved by immersion in ice baths.

In a 1999 survey of Americans, the refrigerator — often taken for granted and rarely celebrated — was voted the appliance they could least do without. Would a survey today place the refrigerator ahead of the smart phone? I'd vote for it. Back in the early 1900s, affluent households had iceboxes kept filled by the ice harvesting trade from freezing climates. Ice-making businesses operated in some cities.

I paused in gratitude for the advances in medical science that delivered our son, Dean, born ten weeks early due to my pre-eclampsia, from the harmful clutches of my genetic heritage. Perhaps Melissa would have survived too, if she had been born a hundred years later. Maybe in a century to come, they will speak of the late 20th century perils of infancy.

Post-war life in Heilbron and environs was a time of realignments and war compensations. The Boer Republics acknowledged British Sovereignty. The British Government paid three million pounds compensation to rebuild farms and, of course, rehabilitate the gold-mining industry, which the war had all but halted.

In 1901, Johan submitted a significant claim of £976 to the British for buildings, equipment and fruit trees destroyed, and livestock taken from his farms.

An official response recommended that he be compensated. "Mr Luyt, although very much against us at first, advocated peace immediately Pretoria was captured, and has since run very straight. He is a solicitor and very well-educated man, broad views, and has in many ways rendered willing and valuable assistance. He is well deserved for compensation."

But after the war he withdrew his claim, saying, "Sir, referring to our conversation of yesterday, I wish to state that it has been my intention to give to the needy whatever amount I would have received on my claim. In the hopes that the poor and destitute may benefit by my action, I hereby beg to withdraw my claim. I have the honour to be Your Obedient Servant, JG Luyt."

The men of the Luyt family directed their energies towards the surge of development and colony building; the women prepared for weddings and produced babies. Mary Ann and her daughter Rosie could pick up breastfeeding any of their babies at any given moment, if needed.

"Oh, just pass him over. I'll take care of him."

"Thanks, Rosie. He's so fussy this morning. And I've got to get this tea service polished in time for this afternoon. Puleng, please bring the silver polish."

Puleng appeared in the doorway holding up the polish in one hand and a bundle of cloths in the other. She asked in Sesotho, the language into which the multilingual family effortlessly glided, from English or Dutch: "Madam, ha u sa battle hore ke etse seo?"

"Thank you Puleng, but this time I want to do it myself."

"It'll be lovely to see Oom Abraham again," said Rosie. "He'll have stories to tell about Europe, I'm sure. I hope there won't be any difficulty between him and Papa."

"I hope so too; it'd be such a shame after everything they've been through. Ach, this business of pointing fingers makes me mad. English, Africander … We're all bilingual, we fought, we lost, now we must make life good again."

After Abraham Fischer's return from Europe, where he had attempted to build support for the Boers, his political career continued to soar. Like Deneys Reitz, he remained unwavering in his loyalty to the Boers during the war. And, like Deneys, he threw his talents into building a new country after the war. In 1906, together with Christiaan de Wet, Abraham would found the "Orangia-Unie", which became the ruling party when the colony received self-government. "Oom Abraham" would be the first and only Prime Minister of the Colony before Union was declared in 1910. Christiaan de Wet would be his Minister for Agriculture.

But the paths of Johan's high-profile colleagues still lay in the future when the Luyt family, like so many others, had to face the immediate, tricky consequences of the war. Johan's nephew Coenie and several other relatives had to effect what would have been an emotionally charged re-entry into their communities, after lengthy periods as prisoners of war in far-flung locations. Some had experienced concentration camps.

Johan had endured immense stress, first in a government attempting to preserve the Republic, then navigating between his new English masters, the needs of his town, and the hostility of some former colleagues. Soon after the war, though only still in his early fifties and still fathering children, he suffered a stroke. He recovered, but never quite to his former strength.

In June 1904, Mary Ann's sister, Wilhelmina, died at Frankfort. She was only thirty-six.

"Auntie Winnie?" cried the girls.

Mary Ann fought the waves of shock and tried without success to draw a deep breath.

"Why?" asked little Johan Jnr, too young to understand, but old enough to feel the emotional voltage forking through his family.

"Mama," said ten-year-old Grace, feeling guilty about all the times she'd shrieked at her cousin Tuli for teasing her, "What will Uncle Coenie do?"

"I have to feed baby Fred," she said in a voice the children didn't recognise. "Johan …" She fled from the room, leaving her husband to deal with the tear-streaked faces of Grace, Mary, Cora and Lenie.

"You know how Auntie Winnie and Wilhelm had to go to the camp when Uncle Coenie was taken prisoner during the war?"

They nodded. Coenie had only returned from the Bermuda prisoner of war camp near the end of 1902, and they were aware of the struggle he'd had since then to restore normality to his family. Johan Jnr was too young to remember, but he nodded with his sisters.

"And you know how sick they were by the time we were able to move them to Heilbron?"

Nodding again.

"Well, Auntie Winnie and Wilhelm haven't been well ever since then. The doctors have been trying to help, but they couldn't save Auntie Winnie."

Wilhelm, the youngest of Coenie and Winnie's three children, didn't survive long after his mother's death.

Three months later, Johan and Mary Ann's eldest child, Leo, married Gideon's sister, Cornelia, and started farming on "Zandfontein", one of Johan's farms near Parys. Babies followed.

By the end of 1906, life in Heilbron was more stable, even as news arrived of conflicts raging in nearby Johannesburg, with Mohandas Gandhi, not yet Mahatma, leading protests by Indian-born workers.

Johan, having clawed back some of his health, was again the Mayor, and serving on multiple community committees. He was also attorney for the National Bank and was appointed by the Sheriff of the Orange River Colony as Government Appraiser for the district of Heilbron. The *Bloemfontein Friend* dated 4 Oct 1906 reported people from the town and district:

> "thronging" to a meeting about the new Education Ordinance, the furore over Dutch or English as the language of tuition being the subject of intense debate at the time: "Mr JG Luyt, the worthy Mayor of the town and vice-president of the School Committee presided."

The *Heilbron Herald* reports on an event of the Heilbron Gymkhana Club:

> "… a very successful concert was held in the Town Hall and during the interval the prizes were presented to the various winners by the popular better half of the worthy President of the Club, Mr J.G. Luyt. Speeches were given by Messrs J.G. Luyt, …" Etc.

Technological developments enticing Heilbron into the 20th century also raised the spirits of the townsfolk.

"Mr Mayor?" invited the engineer.

"I would like Mrs Luyt to have the honour," said Johan, as he motioned to Mary Ann to flick the switch and illuminate the streets of Heilbron with electric light for the first time. The darkening main street was filled with local families. Cheers went up and the excitement of modern progress glowed on every face.

"Responsible Government," reported the 1907 *Braby Directory of the Orange River Colony*, "has been awaited with much eagerness by many, and with some anxiety by others. Before 1907 has passed there is very little doubt that the Colony will be self-governing; and then the next step will be for a United South Africa."

In 1907, Mary Ann's mother died. She had lived with the family for many years, and helped through the births of the many children. Grace remembered her grandmother's presence in their house.

In late 1907, despite unreliable health, Johan was elected the Member for "Northern Towns" in the Legislative Assembly of the self-governing Orange River Colony. His public image had withstood the signing of the oath sufficiently to deliver him to this august body along with *bittereinder* Christiaan de Wet and Abraham Fischer. Family mythology claimed Johan received a medal from King George V for his service in 1910, but I could find no evidence of this, far less the medal itself. By then a medal wouldn't have compensated anyway — it would be all over for Johan in Heilbron.

But at the end of 1906 everything was still buoyant. In 1906, Rosie gave birth to their third child, another Edith Cora, my cousin Daphne's mother who would be known as "Cissy". Gideon was the secretary of the Cricket Club. Ever interested in theatre, he also held the position of Hon Secretary and Treasurer of the Amateur Dramatic Society.

In the rush of excitement over my finds regarding Rosie's husband, Gideon, I still hadn't investigated "Mr Garner", husband of olive-skinned Helena (Lenie) Luyt. I tried again, but found nothing. The trail of the researcher is a delicate one; it takes only one small error or omission on a family tree chart to derail the effort. I was to find several errors.

I returned to the salacious trail of Gideon van Rooyen, and tried again to locate his and Rosie's descendants. His penchant for theatre was soon to surface in real life.

PRIME SUSPECT

I wondered at what point in his life Gideon Pieter van Rooyen started to go bad. Some records stated he had come from the town of Brandfort, sixty kilometres northeast of Bloemfontein. One can't be sure, as other records state Ladybrand as his place of birth. He was always slippery.

Born in 1880, Gideon's childhood would, most likely, have been a comfortable one; his father was said to be the Mayor of Brandfort. But I found no records of this part of his life. The earliest record I found was an affidavit from Johan, on behalf of Gideon soon after his marriage to Rosie, claiming compensation for a bicycle the British had commandeered from him in Kroonstad during the war. Gideon claimed to have bought the bicycle in order to surrender in nearby Lindley. He subsequently lived in Bloemfontein until after the peace in 1902. It was during that time that he met and wooed the detained Rosie — and signed the Oath of Allegiance.

The first legal proceedings against Gideon were dated May 1912, barely two years since his appointment as a legal practitioner, trained and vouched for by his father-in-law.

A Ben Naar had provided bail for his brother, being defended by Gideon, and charged the latter for withholding the repayment of the bail money.

The Resident Magistrate said, "Even supposing the Court accepts the statement that the delay was due to carelessness only, then the conclusion must be that such carelessness in the handling of trust monies amounts to misconduct … The case is one that calls for a disciplinary order being made against Mr van Rooyen of seven days suspension, the Court realising that the period of suspension is of small account in comparison with the fact in itself that an order of this character is made."

Prophetic words, as the cases started to stack up against Gideon.

Rosie appeared in Ben Naar's evidence. He reported going in desperation to the attorney's home to reclaim his money, efforts at the office having failed.

"At the house," he said, "I saw Mrs van Rooyen, who told me that Mr van Rooyen was sleeping". It was two pm. Ben Naar had already lost one day's much needed pay by having to come in person to seek his money, and was trying, in vain as it turned out, to avoid losing a second day's pay.

Three weeks after Gideon's sentence, he was back in court before the same Magistrate; this time it was more serious. The new complainants charged that he withheld a much larger sum from them, for the purchase of a property in which he had been their legal agent. Gideon requested two days to make good on the debt before sentencing. Deneys Reitz, the attorney of the complainants, recommended that Gideon's request be granted. Was Deneys' generosity fuelled by a memory of burning Boer evidence with Rosie in the hearth of the Luyt's kitchen, I wondered?

Four days later, the Magistrate said:

"Mr van Rooyen has practised in this Court ever since I have been connected with the Heilbron district and I cannot but feel sorry for his present position. For some time past, complaints have (as he knows) reached me regarding the difficulty certain people have had in connection with money paid to him, but no definite complaint of misconduct was preferred until May, when a Native Ben Naar charged him with misconduct regarding a sum of sixteen pounds. On that occasion I took the most lenient view possible and strained a point to accept Mr van Rooyen's statement that the delay was due to nothing more than carelessness, but even then carelessness could only be regarded as culpable and, accordingly, I ordered Mr van Rooyen to be suspended for a period of seven days."

"I presume the publication of this order caused other people to examine their position, with the result that the present complainants, Mr Goodman and Messrs Lotzof & Cohen preferred definite charges, but Mr van Rooyen knows that other delinquencies of a very grave character have been brought to my notice, and admitted by him to exist. It was my earnest hope that he would have been able to carry out all the adjustments he promised. Had he done so it could not have obliterated the misconduct, but it would have given some ground on which to base a judgement that would not have precluded him altogether from hope of practising as a legal practitioner at some future date. But he has failed in this respect. This fact, coupled with the knowledge Mr van Rooyen is well aware I possess, compels me to regard the case against him in its most serious light, and I have therefore no alternative but to issue an order removing his name from the roll of Admitted Agents."

Gideon's pattern of partial confession, contrition, undertakings to make things right, and failing to do so, was to emerge repeatedly.

Taking all I'd found into account, I was sure I'd found the culprit, the man who ruined Johan. But none of the verbose records of his crimes confirmed this. The names "Lotzof & Cohen" were familiar to me. I revisited the cases against Gideon, but couldn't find them anywhere.

Johan had slunk away to Parys by 1910, but news between the towns took only eight hours by the daily mail wagon — faster than the current Sydney postal service.

Mary Ann jumped to her feet in their modest living room. "It's nearly 5 o'clock. The mail will be at the post office."

"Please don't. I don't want to hear any news today. It just gets worse and worse. Help me up, will you? I need to lie down." The cane on which Johan now relied curved visibly under the pressure, and Mary Ann braced against his weight on the other side. "It's barely two years since I commended that boy to the Conveyancing Examiners. Simply intolerable that he should degenerate like this. This is the father of my grandchildren. Shame upon shame."

"Do stop, Johan. It's not good for you to work yourself up. There now, I won't go to the post office today. Or get tomorrow's newspaper."

Worse was to come.

Gideon was arrested less than a month after being struck from the roll, on two charges of "Theft by means of Conversion to use", i.e. repurposing trust money held by him. He was released from Heilbron Prison on £300 bail until the next circuit court in Heilbron. I couldn't determine who paid such an amount to cover Gideon's bail. Whole farms belonging to Johan sold for less.

He pleaded guilty, as usual, so there would be no trial, and once again stipulated, "I do not wish any witnesses to be called," apparently to save the crown further expense, but I was suspicious … once again he was containing public damage and trying to ingratiate himself with the magistrate. Or was he delusional and couldn't bear to hear the realities of his own actions? How could he have expected to get away with this indefinitely, telling blatant lies to stave off exposure that was inevitable?

"I take into consideration your attempts at restitution," said Judge Maasdorp at the September sentencing, "but your professional position as legal adviser to people coming to you for advice, makes your crime a serious matter. The least sentence I can inflict upon you is six months on each count — in all, one year's imprisonment with hard labour."

At that point Rosie had five children under eight years old, the youngest a six-month-old baby, and no income. What does a woman do in such a situation? Rosie moved to Parys to join her parents and her four siblings still at home.

"Children everywhere! Grace, help," shouted Johan.

My young Granny Grace and her beleaguered sister Rosie exchanged a look. It was good to see their father smile. Though Rosie was ten years older than Grace, she relied heavily on her eighteen-year-old sister, particularly as both felt the aching gap where their sister Cora used to be.

"Stop teasing the little ones." Johan tried to feign sternness to his two youngest sons, as they chased Rosie's shrieking children around the sofa on which he was seated.

Rosie rocked the latest baby. Nearly a year old, she was already squirming to join the spectacle.

"Seriously, Grace. Do something."

"I'm coming to get you," growled Grace, dropping onto all fours in an uncharacteristic moment of lightness. The shrieking went up a notch.

"That's not helping," he shouted. "Mary, where are you?"

Mary Ann appeared in the doorway, wiping white, floury hands on her apron. She burst out laughing at the mayhem in the living room, but it pained Johan every time he confronted the reality of their reduced circumstances. He'd wanted her to live like a queen forever, not to have to roll her own dough for the family's dinner.

"That's enough," Johan waved his cane. "Everybody out … and leave me in peace. And is anyone ever going to take down that Christmas tree? We're well into January."

Grace supervised her young brothers in the removal of decorations, while Rosie shooed her children out into the garden. Mary Ann followed her.

"What are you going to do, Rosie?"

"I don't know. If Gideon's appeal works, we'll find somewhere else to live, but there's no money. I saw an advertisement outside the cinema for a pianist. Would you be able to take care of the children tomorrow while I go to enquire?"

"Dear God, a pianist at the cinema. We should rather have sent you off with that German fellow. Yes, I can mind the children."

Gideon's appeal for early release was approved in February 1913; he could join them soon in Parys. Rosie was too busy to think about what would happen after that. She had secured the job as accompanist for silent movies but, there being no piano in the Luyt home anymore, had to find time to go to the theatre to practise. When she did go, it was Grace who looked after the children. Her blank expression unnerved Rosie as she left.

A black hole follows in the family records, until Gideon's next conviction, a year later. Verifiable events within that black hole are:

1. Johan died "at his home" in Zastron Street, Bloemfontein, on 31 May 1913, after six days of illness with "Thrombosis and Haemophlegia". Mary Ann was at his bedside and signed the death certificate.
2. Gideon was in Parys for a time, and Rosie fell pregnant again.
3. Gideon later claimed he had a number of jobs, but was dismissed each time his criminal record emerged.

I found no further information about Johan's final illness, when or why they moved from Parys to Bloemfontein, how they paid for the move, or whose house they moved into. Did they give their house in Parys to Rosie and Gideon? Perhaps Johan found it intolerable to live there after Gideon's release. Records listed no Luyts resident in Bloemfontein at that time. But there they were, with no formal welcome or announcement of the arrival of this esteemed family.

When I imagined the scene, I saw just the priest, Mary Ann, Grace, the two young brothers and, perhaps, some of the older children at the graveside in the approaching winter chill, with two respectful gravediggers standing by to complete their job.

On my first visit to Bloemfontein in 2011 we looked for the house. At that address, we found a car hire company and Zastron Street, considered to be on the outskirts of town in 1913, was a multi-lane road thronging with traffic in central Bloemfontein.

We looked for the grave.

"The guy at the archives said the cemetery isn't safe," Mark cautioned.

"There are three of us," I said.

"It's going to be dark soon," added Dean, "and our flight is at six."

"The guy said the cemetery is especially not safe after dark," said Mark.

"I know, I know. Just this last thing … please."

The cemetery was deserted, the office closed, sky darkening.

"None of these numbers tie up with the form," said Dean as we crawled at five kilometres an hour around the perimeter.

"What's out there? Are those graves?" asked Mark.

At the far end of the cemetery, a tangle of rotting vegetation rose from a swamp. Scraggly trees grew — double the height of a man — out of graves with crumbling headstones just visible in the darkness between the twisted trunks. This is the fate of the untended dead.

"I'll come back one day and find it," I said in a small voice between the cemetery and the airport. I meant it at the time.

In March 1914, Gideon was charged with "forgery and uttering" in Cape Town, where he had bought a car and paid for it with a forged cheque. He claimed to have been drunk, and to have returned the car as soon as he sobered up. He received a relatively light sentence of four months with hard labour. After serving his four-month sentence, Gideon did everyone a favour and enlisted for military service. Their sixth child was born that December in Parys, in his absence.

But his criminality continued after his return, committing offences, pleading guilty with declarations of regret, and trying to slime out of the consequences in dramatic letters to officials.

On 26 September 1917, Gideon was arrested in possession of a sack of jewellery, and detained at Kroonstad Prison. The next day, he claimed to have been "under the influence of liquor" and tried to garner some sympathy. But the testimony of the witnesses, including the shop owner contemplating the smashed window of her shop, was damning. He was committed for trial for "Shopbreaking with intent to Steal and Theft".

Gideon immediately wrote a letter to the Attorney General in Bloemfontein.

> "For myself I ask nothing — but beg and pray for my wife's sake. I have had thirty-two months service military in German West and East, character on discharge in each case 'very good'. Drinks, assisted by a very weakened malaria system were the cause of my downfall. I have had two attacks of cerebral malaria."

I gave Gideon the benefit of a minute's doubt and looked up cerebral malaria.

1. High-grade fever alone can produce impairment of consciousness and psychosis.
2. Malarial psychosis: Occasionally patients with malaria may present with organic brain syndrome. More often it can develop due to drugs like chloroquine and mefloquine. Malaria can also exacerbate pre-existing psychiatric illness. Patients can manifest with depression, paranoia, delusions and personality changes.

3. Antimalarial drugs like chloroquine, quinine, mefloquine and halofantrine also can cause altered behaviour, convulsions, hallucinations and even psychosis.

During the court case, Gideon also wrote an impassioned, sympathy-seeking letter to the judge. He recounted his enlistment in The Duke of Edinburgh Rifles, a Cape Town regiment for service in German West Africa, listed his various roles there and in German East Africa (Tanzania), and how "enormous sums of money and other property passed through my hands."

He had been on his way to Cape Town to join the Native Labour Contingent, and was changing trains when the crime in Kroonstad took place in 1917.

"The parting with my wife and infant children after thirty-two months' absence was a painful and distressing one. My system, weak from fever, nineteen attacks, including two of cerebral malaria — and from quinine and morphine injections — could ill stand the strain. Like all fools I sought relief in liquor of which I had a supply of brandy. I was drunk when I landed at Kroonstad. I drank more and later in the evening about 9.30 pm I committed this grave offence. I do not remember much about it and I was arrested at the railway station after being awakened from a deep drunken sleep. From the time of my arrest till waking up in the cell all is a blank. I found then that I had spent seventeen shillings, sixpence on liquor alone. I tried to commit suicide by secreting a bottle of spirits of salt and again a razor but which attempts were fortunately frustrated by the attentiveness of the gaoler."

"At Parys," he continued, "I had a bad attack of cerebral malaria and wanted to kill my wife and children. I was placed in the gaol hospital for three days for observation. This was in May 1917. I was sent to another hospital. Had another attack there and hit a nurse and two orderlies. This was in July 1917. I am confident that this awful crime I committed was under an attack aggravated by alcohol. I am deeply grateful that all the property was found and that no loss has resulted to the lady. I have a wife and six infant children now absolutely without means of existence."

"May it please Your Lordship to pass such a sentence that hope shall not be killed. I can stand all, but the punishment falls hardest on my innocent dependents whom I have so cruelly wronged. Give me a chance to get out of South Africa and to start life afresh in a new country and I shall make good. I am still a young man and a trained soldier and am prepared to go to Europe for service and not to return to South Africa. … Duty to the state as a soldier is better service than as a convict."

Maybe he did suffer bouts of malaria, even cerebral, but I couldn't trust him. Even the judge, in passing a sentence of eighteen months imprisonment with hard labour commented that none of the "facts" claimed by Gideon were verifiable. On 11 March 1918, Convict 8163 wrote another letter, from the Pretoria Central Prison, asking for remission of sentence. It was denied.

It was only out of consideration for my fellow researchers in the hushed reading room at the Bloemfontein Archives that I didn't cheer out loud when I found the divorce file.

It was 23 May 1918 and she'd finally done it. "I, Rosina …" She had no shortage of grounds for divorce to choose from, but was claiming, "A Decree of Divorce on the grounds of adultery."

Extraordinary that they'd managed to produce six children by then, in between his prison terms, a supposed absence of two years serving in World War I, his afternoon naps and his self-confessed adultery with upwards of fifty different women. Even if perpetrated over time, that was a lot of women to keep happy. What man would have the energy when he came home at night? But there it was, in writing.

"In the month of October 1917, the defendant has admitted to the plaintiff in writing that he has committed adultery on innumerable occasions with more than fifty persons during a period extending from the date of the marriage to the present time."

Could he have made his first conquest at the wedding reception?

"The defendant further committed adultery with one Mrs Willet in or about the year 1911. The adultery took place on the occasion of the fancy dress ball held at the Heilbron Town Hall and one JA van Niekerk, then a Lance-Corporal in the South African Police, caught the defendant in the act of the said adultery."

That Mrs Willet had always been a wild one. She'd been in to Gideon's office a few times on minor legal business and on every occasion the air between them had crackled. Was she just a tease, he wondered?

The night of the fancy dress ball at the Town Hall the guests were in high spirits, tipsy with champagne and anonymity. Gideon was additionally intoxicated by a recent string of successful cases, some against opposing celebrity lawyer, Deneys Reitz. It was an aphrodisiac like none other. Rosie had attended the ball for an hour, but went home early; there were babies to tend.

As a cloaked magician, masked and dashing, Gideon wandered through the crowd, trying to identify Mrs Willet. She recognised him first. As the exotic Cleopatra approached him, there was no doubt in either mind that there would be sex tonight.

"You are spectacular," he told her.

"I know," she purred, licking her lips.

Gideon steered her through the throng, his mind racing to locate a private room upstairs at the Town Hall. He felt the strain against the zipper of his magician's pants.

"Up those stairs," he said. There was a conference room he'd used a number of times for meetings larger than his offices could accommodate.

It was locked, but the smaller room down the hall was not. Lit by moonlight pouring through the high window, they made for the sturdy table in the centre of the room. Gideon's mouth was on her neck as his hands manoeuvred her silky Egyptian robe up, up. He ripped off his mask as he entered her.

"Oh yes …" she murmured.

At that moment the door opened and Lance-Corporal van Niekerk, on special patrol duty that night due to the ball, entered the room.

"Liewe God!" he shouted.

Officially, no one knew of this latest indiscretion, but of course everyone in a town the size of Heilbron knew. Rosie, still reeling from the shock of her father's recent change of fortune, remained stoic and silent.

Percy Fischer, son of the illustrious Oom Abraham and father of South Africa's famous lawyer and Afrikaner radical, Bram Fischer, was Rosie's divorce lawyer.

On his death in 1940 in Pretoria, aged sixty, Gideon left no immovable property, no estate and no will. But, incredibly, the death certificate showed that Rosie was present at his deathbed, still his wife.

I was horrified, and scurried back to check the divorce case. The file held pages and pages of records, but no certificate of divorce. I'd assumed it. Whatever else he might have lacked, Gideon van Rooyen seems to have been a magician of charm.

What would I tell their granddaughter Daphne? Would I show her documents from all the criminal cases resulting in Gideon's prison sentences? Would she want to see the handwritten letter in which her grandfather says he tried to kill his family in Parys in a fit of madness that he claims was due to malaria?

She never did ask to see them; I didn't push it.

It was clear that Gideon was the disaster he'd seemed when I first skimmed those criminal cases. But the demonstrable facts didn't tie in with the stories remembered by my mother or her cousin Avis in New Zealand. His crimes and misdemeanours came long after Johan borrowed that astounding amount from the National Bank of the Orange River Colony in 1906. I had found no dramatic family event, and no interjection of history that explained the need for the money.

If Gideon was to blame for the financial ruin of the family, why did Johan continue to employ him between 1906 and the fall in 1910? Gideon was still practising law in Heilbron after Johan had left his beloved town in shame.

The bank ceased to exist in 1910, after a brief life of eight years between British annexation and the establishment of the Union of South Africa.

It seemed unlikely that I'd find anything, but I typed in "National Bank of the Orange River Colony" just in case. To my astonishment, something came up. The First National Bank of South Africa had an archive in Johannesburg, which included, down a jagged ladder of mergers and acquisitions spanning more than a century, the archives of the National Bank of the Orange River Colony. There was an address in Johannesburg and there, further down, an email address and phone number. I was set.

THE BANK

The path of research requires an iron constitution, a readiness to bat aside disappointments and to never, ever give up.

The archivist's email address on the web page for the First National Bank Archives returns as undeliverable. I call the number and get the disconnected message. No one in the four departments who pass me around at head office has any idea what I'm talking about. Mark's brother, a high-end financial advisor who knows people at the bank, tries to find out. He encounters the same response: "We have an archive?"

After more research, I find out that the Rand Foundation owns the bank. I call them, repeat my story several times and finally reach someone who suggests I call the Marketing Department. This sounds promising. My hopes rise further when I notice that it's not one of the phone numbers, all disconnected, that appear on their website. I call and ask for Marketing. Voicemail. I leave a message with my email address and ask that she contact me. Weeks pass. I call again, this time from Australia. Voicemail again; I leave another message. Months pass.

I try again and a human answers, the same one as on the voicemail message. I resist the temptation to carp about her not responding to previous messages. She doesn't know about the archive herself, but thinks she knows who might. This is the strongest glimmer so far, assuming the archive still exists. I am abjectly appreciative as I leave my email address with her, and wonder how many more months will pass before the next contact. But within twenty-four hours she copies me on her email to Masego Masilela, asking her to please help me out.

After eighteen months of pursuit-by-email, during which people have told me, "you're wasting your time, you'll never find anything", I go through a security process that makes Heathrow Airport look slack and am finally standing with Masego in a vault in the basement of an unmarked building in the middle of Johannesburg. There is no archivist, no catalogue, just rack upon metal rack of boxes labelled with the names of the many banks that have been subsumed by this titan. Masego thinks the older records are, "somewhere down there on the right."

"This is not my real job, you know. I just look after the key for the vault."

A young bank employee is stationed with me. It's unclear whether she's there to help me or to make sure I don't abscond with this information so vital that almost no one on the bank payroll knows it exists.

I have an hour-and-a-half before meeting Mark at the spot where he left me, to catch our flight to Cape Town from Johannesburg's Oliver Tambo airport. I am now several blocks away, having followed Masego without taking much notice of the route as we stepped over piles of street merchandise and drooping vegetables, avoiding potholes frothing with unsavoury liquid. My stern instructions from Mark are to not, under any circumstances, be late. He's been around this research carousel a few times now.

It takes an agonising twenty minutes to find a cabinet down the back with records dating back to 1906. Another precious twenty minutes to reach the dispirited conclusion that these are not the records I want. But wait … what's in this closed timber cabinet?

It's hard to describe the thrill of discovering in that cabinet not one, but half-a-dozen massive, five-centimetre-thick ledgers, ornate covers disintegrating at the edges. I am holding the minutes of the board of the National Bank of the Orange River Colony from 1904 to 1910. My yelps of excitement bring the assistant running. She is very sweet and gets caught up in the vortex of energy now swirling around. Only forty-five minutes remain before I must gather my things and sprint back to the meeting point.

The front of each book contains an index. My finger runs down, down, and there he is. Next to "Luyt" there must be twenty-five or more page references. I turn to the first one and the neat handwriting records figures, reasons, comments and background I've been dreaming of. Some of the names of the men present at the meetings are familiar to me. I recognise some other names in the index. I have no chance of reading this alluring content now, so with the assistant holding the pages flat, I photograph and photograph. Eventually Masego, who returns to see how it's going, helps too. I move on to the next book. There are even more entries for Luyt. They are all about Johan's tragic bank loan.

But time is heartless and there are too many pages to photograph in what's left of it. I have to abandon the task, cursing, but now possessing the certain knowledge of the existence and whereabouts of these records. I thank the assistant profusely, grab my things and stride after Masego back to the meeting spot. She is now also quite lit up with my find and gives me a hug as I say goodbye. I wonder when she last had a demented person doing cartwheels down the vault aisles, over a crumbling, forgotten ledger.

Back in Sydney, I transcribe the entries I photographed. They confirm that there was dire financial activity going on, but they don't make sense without the entries that came before and after.

I find and engage a local researcher to continue the bank mission. It will be months before he manages to gain entry to the vault, take the hundreds more photographs of records pertaining to Johan's debt, and send them to me in digital form. Still more months will follow before I spend the ten days it will take to transcribe the contents of the florid handwritten entries.

I turn my attention to finding descendants who might have more information, more relics.

SURRENDER TO THE FAMILY TREE

Diary note, August 2012:

"Here I sit in my winter woollies with the heating on, way down the rabbit hole and no end in sight. I see that this could take years. It would be completely impossible without the family tree chart."

The chart was the skeleton of the quest. The years of research and writing added muscle and sinew to create an incarnate body from this expanse of cold data. I mined and drilled with no suspicion of how many winters would pass in my search for the heart of the story of my mother's grandparents.

"Why?" asked Mark.

"Each discovery opens up more questions," I said. But it wasn't really an answer.

Growing up I had little sense of family beyond my parents and brother, and our few immediate relatives, including my lone first cousin. I was shocked when I learned that Mark had over one hundred first cousins. Okay, that's excessive. But an undeniable mist of isolation settled around me as I stood at the bustling family celebration a few months after Mark and my wedding-of-sorts, with my contingent — two parents, and a third cousin I barely knew. I had no knowledge then of my vast family.

The moment came in 2012, long after my mother's death, when I knew I had to locate that chart, unfold it and submit to the jungle. It was dark and overwhelming in there. It would be years before the lives and fortunes of these strangers, the Luyt family, became recognisable among the lines, dates and names.

I had a giant copy made of the chart and cut out relevant sections so I could stick them up on the wall next to my computer.

Mark squinted at the expanse. "I thought you weren't going to go so deep."

"I'm not. It's just easier than spreading it out and putting it away every time I need to consult it."

But actually, I liked the feeling of those seven generations gazing down on my efforts. They maintained their vigil during the long fallow periods as other commitments clamoured for attention. But I was starting to learn about these ancestors, and details about their lives. I received or found an occasional treasure in the form of an old letter, memoir or photograph, which put flesh over the muscles and sinews. Some emerged from periodic revisitations to my mother's papers, leaving me incredulous that I'd not seen this or that item before, or not recognised its significance. Others emerged from my ongoing efforts to find the descendants of Johan and Mary Ann.

Seven of their eleven children survived long enough to have children of their own, a gnarled branch for each on the chart. One was my grandmother. Another was her nearest sister, Mary, whose daughter Avis and her family had moved to New Zealand. Avis' daughter Pam was the only fellow great grandchild of Johan and Mary Ann I'd known until I found Rosie's granddaughter, Daphne, just around the corner in

Sydney. Pam had developed a passion for genealogy long before me. The materials about our shared great grandfather she'd given me on my first visit were starting to mean something, now that I'd been on his trail for a few years.

I visited them in New Zealand again to talk with Avis, in her nineties, and to exchange materials with Pam. She gave me precious letters from my mother. One of the letters mentioned that it took thirty-one years to assemble the family tree. I resolved to stop bleating about my few years' research thus far.

In 2015, an unexpected morsel arrived in the form of a website link from cousin Pam.

"It lists a few Luyts," she said.

It was an unwieldy site, but I half-heartedly persevered. The other half of my heart leapt to attention at the sight of an entry for "Heinrich Leopold Luyt (Leo)", with an address and phone number in Washington State, USA, current as at 2008. This had to be a descendant of Johan's eldest son, Heinrich Leopold, known as Leo. Could they still be there seven years later?

They were. Leo's wife answered the phone and confirmed that he was my third fellow great-grandchild. They put me in touch with his sister Elena, still resident in Pretoria. Their mother, Marta, was also still living there, aged ninety-five. She was the widow of one of the original Leo's sons.

Less than twenty-four hours after flying into Johannesburg, I was sitting with Elena in Marta's living room in Pretoria, hearing her speak warmly of her father-in-law, Leo, Heinrich Leopold. I was riveted. Here was a woman who with her own ears heard Leo talking about his father, Johan.

"My father-in-law was a real gentleman," Marta said. "He said he learned to be a gentleman from his father, Johan. He was the complete opposite of my mother-in-law, Cornelia." I was hungry for any insights Cornelia, Gideon's sister, might have shared with her daughter-in-law.

Marta told me wonderful stories about the family; how Leo, with his English education, was known as "die Engelse Boer" (the English Boer) and was fluent in both languages.

"He told me that his father, Johan, had worked with the Brits," she said, "to keep people in detention in the town of Heilbron, rather than the camp. Water was in short supply so they had to carry supplies from a nearby dam, by train. To stop any ambush, the Brits tied Johan and the dominee (priest) to the front of the train."

I learned that Cornelia "didn't want to talk much about Gideon", though when she did, she would defend him. But she did once say to Marta, "It would have been nice if he'd been a nice person."

I'd hoped to learn more, but it seemed that Gideon was not popular in this branch of the family either, despite their matriarch having been Gideon's sister. Apparently "van Rooyen" was considered a bad name, a bad streak. They lived in Pretoria, as did Rosie, with Leo's support. But Marta and Elena didn't have much to say about Rosie and her family, and didn't have any further information about Gideon's role in Johan's downfall.

"Did you ever meet Gideon?" I asked Marta.

"Yes, once. He was very charming."

Of course he was. If only I could find a confirmed photograph of him.

No family relics had survived in this branch of the family. They were delighted to hear that I had a family tea service.

I did learn that Gideon and Cornelia had a younger brother who was shot and killed on his horse during the Boer War, when he was only fourteen. So Gideon, at age nineteen or twenty, somehow got out of serving and spent most of the war as a clerk, enjoying "the theatricals" in Bloemfontein, while his much younger brother signed up and was killed. How did that play in the family?

The divisions of war certainly gouged a chasm between the children of Leo and Cornelia's children, with five siblings identifying as English and three as Afrikaners.

"The Afrikaner side of the family called our great grandfather 'die verraier,'" (traitor) Elena told me. I didn't say anything, but this revelation pained me after everything I'd learned about Johan — his selfless years of service to the people of Heilbron, to the Republic of the Orange Free State and then the country of South Africa as a member of the Legislative Assembly working towards national self-government after the war.

I thought about Avis' comment. "Oh no, we were English," surprised at my question about our Afrikaner history. Growing up together in the British Protectorate of Basutoland, I assumed my mother had felt the same, despite her mother Grace's mixed lineage. They all spoke English. Oupa and the kids spoke fluent Sesotho, but Afrikaans was never heard.

Did this resolutely English upbringing cause my mother to lose touch with all the family except those who moved to the English city of Durban? It struck me again how the Boer War had affected our family, even me, though I'd had no awareness of these events and outcomes. I realised that my mother had already lost connection with her Afrikaner family before my father bewitched her, they married and moved to Cape Town. Perhaps her many aunts and uncles on the family chart were just names to her too. A small doubt crept in, as I wondered if she'd tried to find some of this information. Perhaps I'd been unreasonable to expect her to pursue it in a time before internet and email. It was hard enough now, with those tools.

It was astonishing to me how few descendants, just two generations down the tree, knew each other. Perhaps this was due to some potentially divisive issues along the way: *hensoppers* versus *bittereinders*, slave ancestors, prison sentences and the financial ruin of the family. There were daughters who married Jews through the generations but, thankfully, I found no evidence of anti-Semitism. Some of the stories would have provoked the Victorian morals that prevailed in the Cape for many decades, not to mention those of the Dutch Reformed Church that held sway over the Boer Republics, delivered with threats of eternal damnation by frothing ministers. Branches of the family might have elected to put some distance between themselves and these various sources of shame.

Divisions in families were ever thus. We lose much that can never be regained, and the rest of it requires an effort that few are willing or able to make. But every generation or two there comes a "Recording Angel", according to a friend from whom I stole that phrase. I feel a measure of alignment with this role, and it casts a more attractive light on my resentful scratchings on my mother's behalf into the past of her family.

The Recording Angels of their generation produced the impressive family tree that covered my living room wall and caused my mother such excitement that day, after which she folded it up, packed it away and rarely spoke of it again. Was I not excited enough? Did she need me to take that plunge with her? Would I have done so if she'd asked?

Even a good history book, unlike the grey sleeping-pill I had in high school, will naturally describe the battles, armies, economics, politicians and perhaps an occasional individual of note who had some major impact on the times. It falls to the family scribe to recount personal stories of the past, offering illumination of identity to descendants, and a window into social history, which continues to happen outside of a maelstrom such as war. There were ongoing political, military, domestic and social forces precipitating events of consequence in families. Real people with daily human concerns inhabited these events. Their lives were affected, their directions altered.

I had to acknowledge I'd now come to enjoy the pursuit of my mother's family, to the point where it was necessary to draw back from the many stories and refocus on the main game, the ants that were mine. Or rather, hers.

Twenty-four names, my mother's first cousins, fanned in a semi-circle on the family tree around the seven Luyt children. I now knew there were at least five more in this layer. Two of the names had turned into dear, familiar faces: Avis in New Zealand and Marta in Pretoria.

The next, much broader semi-circle surrounding them contained the names of the next generation, my thirty-five recorded second cousins. I'd met or made contact with seven of them, learned that two were dead, and that there were more to add. Impenetrable leaves in the genealogy jungle had parted to reveal fruits and flowers. I had no idea I would find them so full of flavour.

Pathways had opened to Rosie and Leo, two of the Luyt seven with descendants, and confirmed that Gideon van Rooyen had been the cause of misery and poverty for Rosie Luyt and their six children. But Helena, Cora and the youngest, Johan Jnr, remained untapped, and the two remaining son-in-law suspects continued to elude me, as did hard evidence on which to convict Gideon. The stories now led me to poor Cora, and the time of changing fortunes for the Luyt family.

THE FALL

"Careful," shouted Mary Ann as Gideon and Thomas, carrying a stretcher on which lay an inert figure, came through the front doorway.

"They are not going to drop her," snapped Johan.

Johan hovered over the end of the stretcher, from where he could best see their daughter Cora's pale features. Thomas Eckford, Cora's husband of less than a year, held his stretcher end tight, his face as pinched and drawn as Johan's. Two servants also hovered, trying to help, but causing the momentary crush at the front door. Thomas and Gideon could easily manage Cora's featherweight. Mary Ann, still in her travel coat, led them down the hallway to the bedroom reserved for guests, and supervised the transfer from the stretcher to the bed.

"Could someone else get everything from outside please?" asked Thomas. "I'd like to stay with her."

"Of course," said Mary Ann and drew Johan back into the hallway. "Johan, I'm sorry…"

"No, *I'm* sorry," he said, taking her hand. "We're none of us at our best," and as he squeezed her to him a loud wail came from outside.

"The baby!" shrieked Mary Ann. She ran outside, Johan following as quickly as he could with the cane he'd been forced to deploy lately. Their devoted Basotho servant, Puleng, had stayed outside waiting at the carriage. She'd already picked the baby up, but couldn't soothe the two-week-old infant.

"Bring her inside," instructed Johan, "and perhaps Cora can nurse her."

"Motsumi, please bring Mrs Luyt's and Miss Cora's cases inside. What's wrong Mary?"

"Within the first few days after I got to Kroonstad, Cora was too weak to nurse the baby very much. The coughing, then the fevers. We found a Xhosa nurse, and then …"

"Yes?"

"I know. You don't approve, but sometimes … I still nurse Fritz when he gets fussy, you know. So, well, I've helped Rosie with her babies. Don't look at me like that. It's the easiest thing sometimes."

Johan scowled at her. It was a look she seldom saw directed at her.

"The milk hasn't entirely subsided," Mary Ann continued, "and I was glad to be able to help. This baby needs feeding. Puleng, bring her inside before we all freeze out here. I'll just continue until Cora regains her strength. The doctor will be here soon and with God's help, and Lenie, Mary and Grace, we'll get Cora back to health."

"Here he comes now," said Johan. "Motsumi, come out here and make sure the doctor doesn't slip on the ice."

That July, of 1909, had been so cold in Heilbron that a report about it appeared in the *Bloemfontein Friend*. Every puddle of water froze into a treacherous sheet and stayed that way day and night.

"This way, doctor," said Mary Ann. He nodded a perfunctory hello and hurried into the guestroom. Johan, Mary Ann and their children huddled together outside the room and waited for him to emerge.

"I fear the difficult childbirth has made Cora vulnerable," he said to the distressed group shivering in the hallway as Cora lay struggling to breathe.

"She has surprisingly severe congestion in her lungs given the illness hasn't … well, it's not been long since she took ill. We have to try to get this fever down. Make sure she has plenty of fluids and inhales some steam. And do try to get her to eat. I'll be back tomorrow to check on her."

The year 1909 seemed to have started happily, with Cora's marriage in January to Thomas Eckford, an accountant at the National Bank of the Orange River Colony.

But the handwritten bank minutes from the forgotten cabinet at the back of the vault in Johannesburg revealed a murkier situation. My heart sank progressively lower over the ten days it took to transcribe the hundreds of images from the minutes of the Bank of the Orange River Colony that my Johannesburg researcher eventually sent me on a USB stick.

It emerged that Johan's enormous debt had not suddenly appeared in 1906, as I'd assumed from the files in the Bloemfontein Archives, but had built up over a long period. He had bought a number of farms around Vredefort and Parys having secured loans from the bank with the properties as surety. He already owed the bank a substantial sum, having borrowed money soon after the Boer War to restore the farm Zandfontein near Parys, for Leo to farm. Zandfontein was also signed over to the bank as surety.

A newspaper article from 1907 reported, "A rich copper reef has been discovered on the farm Anna's Rust, three miles from Parys, the property of Mr JG Luyt, MLA."

"It was the intensive exploitation of copper, followed by diamonds, gold and coal in the latter half of the nineteenth century, that ultimately catapulted South Africa's backward economy into the modern, industrialised era," says Jade Davenport in *Digging Deep*, a history of mining in South Africa.

Between 1884 and 1905, Johan steadily borrowed money and

bought property, eventually owning ten town properties, plus eight farms or shares therein. Two of the farms were mentioned in the report about copper.

I'd never heard much about mining activities outside of diamonds in Kimberley and gold in Johannesburg. But then I'd also never heard of the Vredefort Dome, the largest meteorite impact crater on earth, and home to the towns of Parys and Vredefort. The impact of this meteorite turned the earth inside out, raising its deep riches closer to the surface. Imagine. An asteroid bigger than Table Mountain heading for earth at twenty kilometres per second. Packing more punch than a thousand nuclear bombs, the hissing, ten-kilometre-wide fireball penetrated seventeen kilometres into the Earth.

On impact, it forced layers of molten rock outwards and downwards to form three crumpled rims and a three-hundred-kilometre-wide crater visible from outer space, and forced granite and gold to the surface, all in a matter of minutes. Pulverised rock powder rained down on the Earth for months, blotting out the sun. At 2-billion years old, Vredefort is far older and larger than Chixculub in Mexico, a mere 65-million years old, which is thought to be the site of the meteor impact that led to the extinction of the dinosaurs.

I took a geological tour to the Dome, to get a sense of the area, and wondered if Johan had bought all those farms in the hope of getting rich from mining. Prospecting started there in 1887, when he represented the area on the Volksraad.

The information from the slumbering bank records provided brilliant information about Johan's downward spiral, but there were concurrent events all through the years they covered. It was impossible to perceive the whole picture from viewing just one source at a time. I decided to develop a timeline drawn from all the sources I'd gathered.

The process of revisiting all the sources I'd found took weeks, and new heights in staying power. It included family records, bank minutes, archive files from Bloemfontein, Cape Town and Pretoria, old newspaper articles from the National Library of South Africa and many family sources.

But when I was done, the picture told a story that had been unseeable through the separate windows of each individual source.

In April 1907, exactly when the copper reef was discovered, Johan requested for his overdraft limit to be extended to £12,500. The value of that figure in modern terms, one source suggested, is indicated at something like 2 million US dollars. A financial term, "income value", suggested a much larger figure of around 7 million pounds sterling, as at 1970. I couldn't imagine what that translated into now. I settled for thinking of it as a huge stash of money, enough to buy properties totalling the landmass of a small country.

With Johan's loan already at £11,000 the bank was getting nervous. They approved a temporary extension of £1,000, and asked Johan to reduce it within six months. They were still waiting at the end of the year. But the matter remained a private one, that the gentlemen of the bank believed could be resolved.

On 1 November 1907, the *Heilbron Herald* published a set of letters whose expressions of public support belied the discussions going on behind closed doors. The first was signed by residents of Vredefort, and "similar requisitions were received from Heilbron and Parys". The hundreds of signatories included two town Mayors, various law agents and other notables from the three towns. It was an open letter to Johan, asking him to stand once more as a Member of Parliament. They praised his talents and experience as a legislator in the past, and expressed confidence in his ability to "foster a policy of racial conciliation and the avoidance of causes of distrust and division." They also recognised, should he be elected, "that you will be sacrificing your valuable time in attending the sittings of Parliament, and which to a man in your profession can ill be spared, still most of us remember how ungrudgingly your services were always placed at the disposal of the Public in the past."

Johan's humble public reply was printed below. He thanked the signatories and expressed, "my gratitude for your appreciation of my weak services in the Honourable Volksraad." And:

> "I had hoped that some other gentleman residing in one of the three towns could have been persuaded to come forward as a Candidate, as the indisputable fact mentioned by you remains that my absence from home and business must necessarily involve a sacrifice of time and means, but seeing that the almost unanimous choice of the voters has fallen on me, I consider it my duty to my country and fellow Citizens to put aside all personal interest and accede to your request.
>
> If elected I shall always endeavour to root out racial feeling, and unite those who have unfortunately drifted apart in consequence of the trying times in the past. There exists no reason why the old resident and the newcomer should not meet each other like brother inhabitants, bearing no ill will or mistrust to each other.
>
> My political ideas are so well known to the gentlemen who resided in the towns and districts concerned that I need not mention them here. You may rest assured that I shall ever labour for the welfare of the country in general and the three Northern Towns in particular."

Before November 1907 was out, Johan reported to the bank that he was unable to fulfil his promise to repay the £1,000, but was initiating the sale of three of his farms. They were satisfied, for the moment.

Days later, Britain declared self-government for the Orange River Colony (ORC). Johan was one of the thirty-eight members elected to the Legislative Assembly serving under his early mentor, Abraham Fischer, now Prime Minister. The cabinet consisted of:

> JBM Hertzog, the judge with whom Johan served in the criminal courts during the Boer War.

Christiaan de Wet, Johan's former Volksraad colleague, then detractor.

AEW Ramsbottom and CH Wessels. Both were also on the Board of the National Bank of the ORC, and present at meetings covering Johan's debt.

How did *that* work?

In January 1908, the bank became aware that Johan owed a substantial additional amount to Frederik Els, the great grandfather of Heilbron historian, Quarta Pretorius, who helped me with research in Heilbron from my first visit onwards. *Are there any threads that do not tie up?* Their levels of alarm rose.

That month Leo, by now living near Parys, had a freak accident while felling trees for sale on their farm, Zandfontein. It fractured his leg in four places.

"Lenie, you'll have to go to Parys to help," said Mary Ann. "Thank God, Leo is going to be alright, but Cornelia is finding Roma and Olive a handful without him at home."

"Well, Rosie has three," said Cora, "and another on the way, and *she* copes." Though loyal to her sisters, the next youngest to Lenie was secretly relieved not to have to miss the excitement of the forthcoming trip to Bloemfontein, where families of members were to attend the first sitting of parliament.

"Yes, but there's usually one of us for each child here," said Mary Ann. "It's very different living a couple of streets away from your family and living a day's journey away. I'm sorry you'll miss the trip, Lenie, but family comes first. Cora, I'm afraid you'll have to miss it as well. Don't look at me like that," she said as Cora's face fell. "We all know the dangers for Rosie in these final weeks of pregnancy, and one of us must be here to help if she needs it. The rest of the children are too young to leave behind."

February 1908: Johan ceded his life insurance policies to the bank and sold the farm, Merlewood, with proceeds going to the bank.

March 1908: Bank minutes raised a question over Thomas Eckford. The Heilbron Bank Manager recommended that he be transferred elsewhere "because of the company he keeps, and because he is engaged to Miss Luyt." Subsequent entries stated he was "too familiar with customers and members of the SA Constabulary," and that he couldn't keep his mouth shut about bank business.

Johan beat his overdraft down to below £10,000, but the first mention appeared in the minutes, of Johan's concern about "trust money, which he may be called upon to pay at any time."

Then the statement, in the minutes for 20 March: "Mr Luyt is laid up, having had a stroke of paralysis for the second time."

"No, no, no, not that one. The ones on the chair," Mary Ann yelled as her daughters and Puleng fumbled around trying to help. Puleng handed the two plump pillows to Mary Ann and ran to the other side of the bed to get Johan comfortable. "The doctor, he is here," she said.

Johan had collapsed in his office and, like his daughter Cora would be the following year, had been carried into the house on a stretcher. His already impaired health would henceforth deteriorate swiftly.

April 1908: Just three weeks later, on the day that Rosie and Gideon's next baby was born in Heilbron, the bank reported receiving a call from Johan promising to provide the balance sheet they had requested. During the six months before they actually received it, there were various irate exchanges and the first mention of "insolvent" by the bank.

November 1908: A speck of light appeared in the form of two contracts with the Weltevreden Prospecting Syndicate to prospect on Johan's farms Zandfontein and Anna's Rust.

The same month, the bank reassigned Thomas Eckford to Winburg. They had moved him to Kroonstad for the previous December, as relief accountant. On 12 January 1909, four days before his wedding to Cora, Thomas requested a permanent reassignment to Kroonstad.

I noticed a problem in the dates.

Even if Cora conceived on her wedding night, she would have been barely six months pregnant when the baby was born. It's unlikely that such a premature baby would have survived back then, and if it did, there would have been a story about it. I think Cora was pregnant when they got married, despite efforts, too late, to relocate Thomas. That could explain his enthusiasm for a long-term transfer to Kroonstad, where the specifics of their private life were, and could remain, unknown.

The wedding was a small, low-key affair at the Luyts' house, quite unlike Rosie's lavish wedding, and soon thereafter, the couple left for Kroonstad. Perhaps Johan had a hand in it. He was still Deputy Mayor, a man of influence and a longstanding, high profile customer of the bank. His financial trials were not yet in the public eye.

Entry in the minutes for 11 May 1909:

"The Manager, having reported that Mr Luyt's office is often closed, and that he does no business, nor do his farm properties bring him any return, also that interest on his debt to the Bank is steadily accumulating in the absence of any cash payment to account, resolved that Mr Luyt be written to, asking what he is prepared to do to liquidate or at least reduce his debt, which cannot be allowed to run on in the present unsatisfactory condition."

Johan made attempts to coax crumbs from outstanding bills and rents, but the fairy tale, his grand dream, was over. The timing couldn't have been worse.

25 June: The bank approved that Johan's outstandings be, "placed in the hands of Mr Deneys Reitz, Attorney, for recovery. It was also felt that Mr Luyt should instruct his Manager, Mr G.J. van Rooyen, who on Mr Luyt's account is believed to hold certain Promissory Notes, to hand them over to the bank."

How galling to be answerable to the son of his prior colleague on the Volksraad, Francis Reitz, a family friend, at that. Johan's health forced him to leave a lot to his trusted son-in-law Gideon. I wanted to call to Johan from across the century, "Look out, don't do it."

On 16 July 1909, days after the birth in Kroonstad of Cora's baby, there was a quarterly gathering in Heilbron of members of the Dutch Reformed Church. Attendance at services was reportedly huge. A preacher thundered against, "the mania for dancing, which seems to possess the young people, especially of this town, as a deadly peril to spiritual life."

Had he heard whispers of the curious time period from the latest wedding to the latest birth in the respected Luyt family?

By then Johan's situation was dire. He complained that he had been "deprived of the legal business of the Branch, which he had performed for several years." The bank minuted that, "he is said to be dilatory and unreliable, hence the reason for not employing him on behalf of the bank as before." Then the final hope was snuffed out: prospecting on his farms showed, in the sneer-edged words of one of the board members, that "traces of the supposed copper reef have disappeared."

I thought of a loose-pebbled, abandoned mineshaft we'd seen near Vredefort, and the prospectors who had drifted on to the next big thing.

A week prior, on 9 July, the board had decided that Johan must "assign or surrender his estate by the 17th instant, failing which the bank must take legal proceedings against him for recovery of his indebtedness."

The bank's letter from Bloemfontein arrived sandwiched between ever-darker news from Kroonstad about Cora.

"Johan, a letter from the bank has been sitting in the hall for a couple of days," said Mary Ann, as she waved to the servants to take her trunk out to the carriage.

"I know, but it'll have to wait until you get to Kroonstad. I need to get Rosie over here to help with the children. The girls and I can't do this with both you and Puleng away."

Some semblance of order was established by the next evening, and Thomas had wired with the news of Mary Ann's safe arrival. By then another three letters obscured the one from the bank, and Cora's health dominated Johan's mind. The news was bad and Mary Ann was making preparations to have Cora transferred to Heilbron.

The 17th instant came and went, as the pile of unopened letters grew in the hallway.

On July 20, the bank resolved to instruct their solicitors to send Johan a letter demanding payment and, "failing a satisfactory response, to have a summons issued for the amount." The letter could only have arrived from Bloemfontein on or after the day of Cora's dramatic arrival on July 22.

Mary Ann managed to reduce the letter pile once she was home, but could not induce Johan to sit down and do the same until a few days later.

"What is it?" she demanded, noticing his ashen face.

"Don't worry, I'll take care of it."

That evening Johan and Gideon talked for hours behind a closed parlour door. Mary Ann suspected something afoot with Johan's business, but had capacity for not much other than Cora and feeding the baby.

Tension hung so heavily in the house that it was hard to breathe. Grace crept into the room when no one was with Cora. She hated the smells of all the medicines and balms gathered on the dresser. And there was another, dark smell she didn't recognise. Mary Ann found her asleep leaning half-upright against the dresser, holding Cora's hand.

"Gracie," she murmured, eyes wet, "you should go to bed now."

The evening of the doctor's final visit, he emerged from the guest bedroom with an expression that lacerated Mary Ann. He said, "I think it's best that you call the dominee" (priest). Lenie caught her mother as Mary Ann's legs buckled.

Saturday 31 July: The death certificate stated "Galloping Consumption" as the cause of death. It was said to claim the lives of mostly children or young adults whose vitality had been reduced by previous illness or events. The term "Tuberculosis" hadn't arrived in the hinterland of South Africa by 1909, despite the eminent German scientist, Dr Robert Koch, having received the 1905 Nobel Prize for the discovery of the tubercle bacillus.

The bank's lawyers wrote to the bank on 31 July, the day of Cora's death, that no reply had been received from Johan and they had therefore issued a summons for the amount of his overdraft.

News travelled remarkably quickly between towns. It seems impossible that the Heilbron bank manager, who would have been aware of the tragedy unfolding in the home of the Deputy Mayor, would not have requested a compassionate halt in proceedings. The bank board members would have seen the notice in the *Bloemfontein Friend* on 29 July that, "Mrs Eckford, daughter of Mr JG Luyt MLA, arrived from Kroonstad, very seriously ill, on Thursday evening (22nd). I am sorry to say that grave doubts are entertained for her recovery."

It baffles me how, after waiting all that time, they could callously descend at this moment on a man of such reputation and stature, even if he did owe them a lot of money. But they did.

4 August 1909: The newspaper notice, respectfully inaccurate about the timing of the wedding, appeared in the *Bloemfontein Friend*:

> It is with deepest regret that I have to chronicle the death of Mrs TWF Eckford, which sad event occurred at her father's house on Saturday evening.
>
> Mrs Eckford was the third daughter of Mr JG Luyt, MLA, and Mrs Luyt, and was married a little less than a year ago to Mr TW Frackleton Eckford, of the National Bank, Kroonstad. Since the birth of her child last month, Mrs Eckford has been in very precarious health. She was pronounced to be in a galloping consumption and about a fortnight ago she was removed from Kroonstad and brought back to her father's house, alas to die.
>
> The funeral took place on Sunday afternoon and practically everyone in town attended. Numerous floral

tributes testified to the love and respect in which the deceased lady was held, and the deep sympathy which is felt for her sorrowing husband and parents. The last rites were conducted by the Rev. CW Lister, and before the mortal remains were carried out of the house a short service was held at which there were few dry eyes.

The late Mrs Eckford (known still and affectionately remembered by everybody as "Cora Luyt") was only 19 years of age, and the realisation that her bright young life has been thus abruptly terminated at an age when many girls have scarcely left school, has intensified the feeling of regret and sorrow which all in town experience.

Bent double with sorrow, Johan leaned on Gideon as they tried to manoeuvre out of the quicksand, even getting money owed to Johan paid into Gideon's account, to "hide" it and buy some time. But the bank was not convinced by the documents and assurances they supplied. The high court hearing was announced in the *Bloemfontein Friend*. Whispered rumour evolved into shocking fact.

September 1909: The National Bank of the Orange River Colony won the case. The newspaper announced that all Johan's properties were to be sold. A notice appeared in the *Heilbron Herald*, announcing an auction.

Mary Ann squared her shoulders as she walked past the courthouse, her head high and a pleasant smile pasted onto her face. The wife of an esteemed public figure, loved and respected in her own right; now her furniture, wash stands, their piano (*dear God*), pictures, carpets and anything else she had been unable to preserve would be on display for the public to purchase, along with her house. What might happen after that was unknowable. The uncertainty gnawed at her, despite her efforts to focus on the immediate challenges of the auction and preparing the family for a reduced quality of life.

The lovely house had seen the births of nearly all her children.

Mary Ann drew in a jagged breath. Grace had not taken the news well. Even the prospect of having to sell the home she had lived in all her life hadn't seemed to bother her. But the piano … Mary Ann tried to exhale evenly but it came out in shudders. This business with the bank; she knew it had been going on for some time. But how could they have been so cruel? Right then?

"Post Office and Court House, Heilbron, O. R. C."

Pain at the thought of Cora swept through her, taking the flimsy smile with it. My darling Cora, she thought. We are god-fearing people. Why? Why?

She felt a tingle in her nipples and realised she'd been walking longer than she'd intended. The baby, Iris Cora Mary Eckford, but always known as Cora, would be fussing by now.

My mother's cousin Avis always heard that Mary Ann took in baby Cora, breastfed her and raised her. I questioned how that was even possible, five years after Mary Ann's last child, but Avis was adamant. The Australian Breastfeeding Association confirmed that this would have been viable. It's even possible for someone who has never had a child to successfully breastfeed, for example, an adopted baby. And relactation? Absolutely. It does seem that Mary Ann always had a special bond with her granddaughter Cora, and spent close time with her in Durban.

Here they are together in 1935 on Cora's 26th birthday, then again in 1937, prior to Cora's marriage in 1938, at which my Granny Grace was a witness.

For the last few months of 1909 and into 1910 Gideon was active in court, on occasion winning cases against Deneys Reitz. There was no mention of Johan in the newspaper. Rosie gave birth to her fifth child and named her Grace.

I found no evidence either way, but perhaps even the cold-hearted bank officials could not insist that Johan include in the goods on auction the solid silver tea service bearing the inscription honouring him for his service to town and country. Its first moment of peril passed.

February 1910: the *Bloemfontein Friend* reported, "Property in Heilbron is not considered a gilt-edged security evidently, for there was no great rush to acquire it at the large sale of landed property on Friday week. Mr JG Luyt's very fine house was bought by Mr D. Craig for £1,625. It is an open secret that the erection of this house cost nearly £5,000."

A week later the *Heilbron Herald* reported that, "In a small village such as this, self-contained and isolated from the more stirring forces of progress in the large centres, from year to year few comings and few departures fall to be recorded. But some of our old families are going. Mr JG Luyt MLA and family, with whom every fibre of the life of this town is closely associated, is removing to Parys."

The week after that report, came, "Miss Lena Luyt, 2nd daughter of Mr JG Luyt, MLA, was given in marriage to Mr Henry Garner (known as "Chum") of Welgeluk. The ceremony took place in the Wesleyan Church and was witnessed by a large congregation. The bride was attended by her sister Mary as bridesmaid."

The reception was held at Mr Garner's house. The humiliating circumstances had stripped the Luyt house of the features that had provided the elegant venue Cora had enjoyed for her wedding, low key though it was. Nonetheless, "The usual toasts were proposed and the young couple, bearing with them the good wishes of a very large circle of friends, left by the evening train for Johannesburg."

Helena had been the most elusive of the Luyt children. The chart simply said, "Helena Luyt b. 1883 d. 1921 m. Garner of Heilbron", and listed one child, "Ernest Garner".

On my first visit to Heilbron, in 2011, I photographed a grave on which the stone read, "Hellena (Lenie) Garner, who died at Heilbron on the 16th January 1925, age 39 years". The dates of birth and death didn't tie up with the family tree, neither did the spelling, nor the nickname. I wasn't certain it was her.

The newspaper article put Helena's husband in the clear. It confirmed Helena's nickname. It also revealed, at last, which Garner she married, and unlocked the next branch of the seven surviving Luyt children. I now knew what to look for, and that the information about her on the chart was wrong. Better-informed searches delivered baptism, marriage and death records, and a colossal estate file that listed the six children of Chum Garner, whose father William Page Garner served for years with Johan, his attorney, on the Heilbron Municipal Council. Were they all Lenie's children? It wasn't clear. She died young, and there was a second wife.

I made contact with Danie and Dudley Garner, two more fellow great grandchildren of Johan and Mary Ann. A vista of new information opened up. All the children were Lenie's. She birthed nine from her marriage in 1910 to her early death in 1925, when her youngest child was three years old. The Garners sent me a photo of Lenie with her motherless niece,  Cora, in what looks like a christening dress. I could still picture Lenie in a sari.

I had found and followed the sorry trail of the downfall of the Luyt family. There was no evidence of my Granny Grace's version of the story, nor the similar version from Avis in New Zealand. It appeared to me to have been caused by a combination of over-investment by Johan, unlucky speculation and extravagant largesse to his family. Gideon was definitely dodgy, but by this point in their story, as they left Heilbron, I could see no clear connection between these events and Gideon's later crimes. Cora's husband, Thomas Eckford, though not without his shady moments, worked for the bank that lent Johan the money, and only arrived on the scene around 1908. Helena only married Chum Garner as the wagons bearing what was left of the Luyts' pride and possessions rolled out of Heilbron in 1910, headed for Parys.

What had I missed?

THE ROAD TO MASERU

"Can I offer you a cup of tea, Mr Smyth?"

"Yes please, Mrs Luyt, that would be much appreciated."

The furniture in the Luyts' parlour in Parys was of quality, but sparse, and had clearly weathered years and children.

John Smyth knew that the recent difficulties of this fine family had left them in need, but one didn't mention such things. Had he been less nervous, he might have registered the contrast between the humble surroundings and the gleaming teapot from which Mary Ann poured their tea. She lifted the ornate vessel from a heavy silver tray edged with delicate carvings and bearing an inscription. Beside it stood a matching milk jug and sugar bowl.

"Sugar?"

"Thank you, Ma'am."

Mary Ann sat down next to Johan, whose pleasant expression John couldn't read. He could feel the sweat on his back and hoped his damp face didn't betray his intense anxiety.

An anxiety no less intense gripped Grace and Mary Luyt, huddled together in their bedroom, four hands clasped, awaiting the outcome of the exchange in the parlour.

The sisters were just two years apart and had always been close, even before the older siblings married and left the family home. Grace and Mary often minded their two younger brothers, Johan and Frederick, as their parents became consumed by the demands of their very public demise in Heilbron. It had been over a year since their sad relocation to Parys. Mary had tried, without success, to break through the chill surrounding Grace. They still shared confidences, a bedroom, responsibilities in the house, with their brothers, and now in caring for their father. But Mary's sister had changed.

Grace was, however, living every minute of *this* day with Mary. John drew up in his horse and cart, and was ushered into the parlour. No one called for Mary, but her parents joined him. It could mean only one thing.

John Harold Smyth arrived from Dublin during the Boer War as an engineer. The Boer commandos were blowing up bridges as fast as the British could rebuild them. They kept on rebuilding, and for this they needed engineers. He stayed after the war, attracted by the space and opportunities. He worked for a merchant and travelled widely to distribute his goods.

The town of Parys was on his route.

Situated on the left bank of the Vaal River, Parys in 1910 was described in the *Braby Directory of the Orange River Colony* as being noted for its, "well developed trees, beautiful scenery and green lanes in the place of streets. Bathing in the Vaal River is recommended for certain rheumatic and nervous disorders".

Among the five hundred digital photographs that arrived in Sydney with me in 2012, on return from my first, rich week at the archives in Bloemfontein, at least thirty were images from a thick file containing the details of a legal case in Parys in 1911. I saw Johan's name in it, as "Tutor Dative". I assumed that he was functioning as a lawyer again. Nothing in this file attracted my attention, and I hadn't recognised the names in it. Not yet. I had 470 other images of unfamiliar content to view.

"Papa, does this mean we might be able to afford piano lessons again?" Grace asked her disabled father. "Can I help you with the paperwork?" Grace had achieved first place in English in Heilbron the previous year, which built her confidence. But Johan's pride prevailed.

"Thank you, Gracie, but with Gideon's help I can manage. I know you miss your piano lessons, and am working towards restoring these as soon as possible."

In the months that followed, John Smyth's employer wondered why trade in Parys outshone any other. John's route also took him to the mountainous area of nearby Basutoland. The small but genteel town of Maseru captivated him, striking a perfect balance between his British roots and the wilder offerings of Africa. John possessed a mystical gift: he was a water-diviner. It's a stretch to imagine such a job role in a modern government, but the colonial government of Basutoland would later hire him in this capacity.

He planned a perfect future with Mary in it. Hard work would in time yield enough to buy a garage to service the dazzling new technology of motorcars. In the meantime, his vision and resources had grown sufficiently to empower him to approach Mr and Mrs Luyt.

"It's not grand, Sir, but I have the means to offer your daughter a comfortable life in Maseru in a decent community not unreasonably far from here. Indeed, the whole country holds promise." Deep breath, sweat now in rivulets under his shirt.

"Mr and Mrs Luyt, I am ten years her senior, but this affords me the experience in life to take good care of Mary and perhaps provide guidance. I love her deeply and would be honoured to receive your permission to offer my hand in marriage."

He badly needed a sip of tea to moisten the desert in his mouth, but held Johan's gaze in stillness. It was a good strategy, and eliminated the minimal doubts remaining in Johan's mind.

"I've been watching you, Mr Smyth," he said, smiling, "and

wondering just how much more merchandise Mrs Luyt would be compelled to purchase before you found your way to your present situation."

John smiled weakly, his lips sticking to his teeth. "As it happens, my wife and I have discussed this very possibility, and what you have just provided is what we needed to hear. Mary will, I believe, receive your proposal of marriage favourably, and you have our blessing." Johan smiled at Mary Ann, also smiling as she passed their dripping future son-in-law a handkerchief and said, "Your ages are almost identical to Mr Luyt's and mine when we married."

Left *John and Mary Smyth, ready to depart on their honeymoon. They were the parents of my mother's cousin Avis, who grew up alongside my mother in Maseru in the 1930s.*

The *Parys Post* reported the nuptials. "A very pretty and attractive wedding took place in the Wesleyan Church in Parys on 18 July 1911. The bridal party entered the church to the strains of a bridal march and the service began with *The voice that breathed o'er Eden*."

The days of the Dutch Reformed Church seemed far behind. Grace, Mary's bridesmaid, wore "a very pretty dress of strawberry voile with a hat to match; the bouquet and gold brooch she wore were the gifts of the bridegroom."

As Rev Hepburn intoned the wedding ceremony, Grace clenched her teeth to hide the yawn that threatened to embarrass her. They had all risen very early and the waves of excitement delivered her now, at the crucial moment, onto a shore of fatigue, as the reality of her beloved sister's imminent departure from her daily life drew close and real.

Gideon and Rosie were there, and her brother Leo, with his wife Cornelia, Gideon's sister, five months pregnant. It was a fine family affair, on the surface. Gideon responded like a good son-in-law to the toast to Johan, who was unable to rise. Less than a year had passed since Johan endorsed Gideon's application to be examined as a Conveyancer and, in less than a year, Gideon would stand in the Heilbron court on his first charge of misconduct.

The bridal party left the church to Beethoven's "Wedding March". Grace's eyes were filled with tears; assumed, by those from whom she received broad smiles, to be an overflow of happiness for her sister. But the new Grace was, really, pained at having their cousin, Katie Francis, play the organ while her own fingers yearned so deeply for those keys.

Grace was a bright but distant, dreamy girl who cared little for the girlish concerns of her sisters. She was six years old when the cannons of the British Empire intruded on her world. Terrified, she sought solace at the piano, and rode her bicycle in the safe corridors of their gracious home. Incomprehensible events lurched around her, no one smiled and no one but her sister Mary and their nanny, Puleng, had time for her.

The British Command occupied outbuildings on their property, and pitched their tents on the croquet lawn and tennis courts. Her mother was pregnant again, then occupied with the new baby. Her brother and hero, Leo, was away on commando. Her older sisters Lenie and Cora, though barely old enough, helped Rosie run the house, taking over when she needed to sleep during the day. Grace, on her way to bed, would see her cloaked eldest sister slipping out into the darkness. Each night Puleng lay on the floor beside the bed, holding Grace's needy hand until it fell from hers. Even as an adult Grace needed a nightlight, and panicked if she woke up to darkness during the night.

Strange men gathered in their Heilbron parlour. The smaller children were banished as Rosie and Mary Ann carried refreshments in on a huge silver tray.

"Hush," they said, "it's important government business. That's President Steyn, you know."

Grace could taste the gravity in the air, but didn't understand anything. She turned to Mary, and her beloved cats, for comfort. Grace often had a mother cat and a litter of kittens sleeping on her bed. The cat-lover gene made it into every subsequent generation. The lengths to which my mother went to ensure the wellbeing of our cats infuriated my father, who lacked that gene.

After the war, Grace was a daughter somewhere in the middle of many siblings, going to school and pursuing her passion for playing the piano, helping to look after the younger children and watching anxiously as her father's health declined.

Grace was fifteen when she left her childhood behind. She felt her sister Cora's limp hand in hers as she sat beside her bed, willing her to recover, while Mary Ann obsessed over baby Cora, the grandchild she would raise as her own child.

The earth had barely settled on the older Cora's grave, when the writ arrived from the British Government to the Sherriff: "We command you that the goods and chattels of Johan Godfried Luyt, of Heilbron, Attorney-at-law, hereinafter styled as the Defendant, you cause to be made the sum of Ten Thousand Two Hundred and Thirty-Eight Pounds Eight Shillings and Two Pence …", etc.

Muffled, through two closed doors, Grace and Mary strained to hear.

"How can they do this to us, right now? You've been a trusted customer of the bank for more than twenty years."

"They have been patient with me, there is no doubt."

"Johan, we've just lost Cora," Mary Ann struggled to get past that statement, "and we've a new babe in our midst. The timing of this demand is a cruelty I cannot understand."

"I would also have expected a larger measure of understanding. If the mining prospects had come through …"

"I know. I signed those papers too. We're not the only ones whose hopes have been dashed."

"Perhaps all the more reason the bank is calling in debts now."

"I will be at your side in this matter, as in all others, but if there is anything you or Thomas can do to delay this anguish, I entreat you to do it."

One afternoon in September, with the chill of Heilbron still in the spring air, Mary Ann called the two girls into the parlour for their father to speak to them. Grace was sometimes invited to play the piano for guests, and spent hours at the piano when the parlour was not in use. But to be summoned by their father during the day was ominous.

"My dears," he said, "come and sit with us." His shoulders drooped and the purple pouches under his eyes shocked Grace.

"When I built this house in 1884, it was to be a home for our family for generations. You have both spent your entire lives here." He paused and drew a long, slow breath, held it for a moment and then let it out in a rush.

The girls held and released their breath with him. Their mother studied them anxiously.

"Fortune has not been kind to me, to us, lately. As if it were not enough to lose our Cora, the promise of our Vredefort farms has not come to fruition. I have had to borrow money from the bank and now find myself without the means to repay it. These past two years, I've spent a lot of time away on government business, and though Gideon has taken care of my business, there simply are not enough clients to secure an ongoing income. As you know, my ill health has not aided matters."

"It has become necessary to sell many things. The farms have to go. Also our properties in town. That includes this house." He looked back and forth between Mary and Grace. Their eyes widened as the information seeped in.

"Where will we go?" asked Mary.

"Leo has arranged for us to rent a house in Parys. It will not be what you're accustomed to, but we'll be together and we'll be safe." Johan emphasised the last point. Since the war, safety was always on Grace's mind.

"We're leaving Heilbron?" asked Grace, her voice very small.

"Yes. It's best that we make a fresh start."

Johan looked down at his hands, bracing himself.

"It is also necessary for us to sell much of our furniture. We can keep only what will fit into our new accommodation."

Looking up at them again. "Girls, next week there'll be a public auction here at the house, and we will have to say goodbye to many familiar things. The chairs we're sitting on, the dining room suite, that splendid sideboard over there, and … Grace, I'm sorry, but the piano will also be sold."

He reached out to take Grace's hand, but she leapt away from him.

"No," she shouted, uncharacteristically. "You can't let them take my piano!"

"My dear Grace," Johan murmured, and Mary Ann heard the pain she had heard so often of late. "You cannot know how much I would wish this necessity away. Every one of us will suffer in the coming months, and I am well aware of the suffering that the departure of our piano will cause you."

Grace burst into tears and ran. Their mother motioned for Mary to follow her and try to comfort her. But Grace, who'd flung herself on her bed and buried her head under the pillow, shrugged off any help. "Leave me alone," she sobbed. Mary, hurt and disconcerted by the new experience of her sister shutting her out, sat down on her own bed, and waited. After a while she lay down and dozed.

When she woke up, there was a new Grace sitting at one of the two chairs at the soon-to-be-sold table in their room. One of the cats sat on her lap and she stroked it absently, her face expressionless. "You can't trust people," she said when Mary sat down with her, "not even your family." She allowed Mary to put her arms around her, but didn't return the embrace. She would never again be quick to embrace another human, not even her own children.

On the day of the auction, when the servants carried the piano out to the waiting wagon, Mary Ann was embarrassed that the elegant piano stool with the mother-of-pearl inlays was nowhere to be found. She sent the servants all over the house to search, without success. "A lot of furniture was taken away today," she apologised. "I'll make enquiries to see if the stool was accidentally included with someone else's purchases."

"Please don't trouble yourself, Mrs Luyt. We are happy with the piano, sorry to acquire it under these circumstances, and very willing to find an alternate piano stool elsewhere."

The time drew near to leave for their new life in Parys and the small house with no space for a piano. Servants had brought Grace a chest in which to pack her personal belongings. They arrived to carry the filled chest from her room to the waiting wagons as she closed the lid over the last of her gowns, concealing a glint of mother-of-pearl below.

The Heilbron house began its mutations, first into a boarding house and later, engulfed by the expanding town but with the same garden wall as when it looked onto open land, a kindergarten school. It was the school we visited on my first, amateur jab at the past, where they had fairy floss, called "spook-asem" (ghost breath) on sale.

In Parys, it was easy for Grace to slip out to visit the piano stool, hidden in the back of the garden shed. It would never have escaped her mother's notice in earlier times, but now Mary Ann had so much to do, what with Johan's deteriorating health and only one servant. Grace would stroke the luminous swirls of purple, turquoise and aquamarine. Sometimes she played phantom keys as her mind's ear brought back the nurture of Chopin, Brahms and Schubert, the latter always a favourite because Uncle Piet's first wife, Elizabeth, was related to him.

"What have you been doing out there?" Mary Ann asked Grace one day, in the quiet following Mary's marriage and departure. The wedding had temporarily lifted the pall over the household, but that had settled again, compounded for Grace by loneliness.

"Nothing," she replied, flushing. "I just like looking at what's left from Heilbron. Maybe I can use some of those items if we can put Mary's bed in the shed instead."

"Of course. What a lovely idea."

When Mary Ann next entered Grace's bedroom, the rearrangements had already been made. The modest room felt more spacious with just one bed. Grace was seated at a small table she'd found in the shed; writing a letter to her sister.

"Oh, how nice" exclaimed Mary Ann, looking around. "You must be pleased. It even feels lighter somehow."

Grace looked at her mother, a strange defiance tempering the slight smile. She nodded. "Yes, I like it."

As Mary Ann turned to leave, Grace moved, the folds of her dress revealing the mother-of-pearl sheen of the piano stool. Mary Ann's eyes flew to Grace's, which were hard and unsmiling. Mary Ann could barely swallow as she left the room. There was nothing to be said.

Though shamefully uncaring about my mother's ancestors and their stories when I was young, I had an instinctive connection to a few of their relics. On those lilac afternoons hiding from my father during my brief adolescence, immersed in marijuana-powered biology, poetry and grammar, I sat at my grandfather's desk on the old wooden piano stool, mother-of-pearl inlays catching the late afternoon sun.

When Mark and I left South Africa, the small crate we shipped to Australia was largely filled by his vintage motorcycle. The only items I took, apart from some clothes, kitchen things and soft furnishings, were my grandfather's desk and the piano stool. You'd think I would have taken better care of it, having taken the trouble to ship it. But the piano stool suffered over the years, through moving house; careless storage in mouldy cellars; my not knowing its story. One entire side came adrift at some point, along with its inlay, and at least half the mother-of-pearl fell out of the remaining side. I didn't know. I didn't know.

Apart from the legal case suggesting that Johan had tried to resurrect a practice in Parys, and Gideon's tumultuous path, records on Grace and her family go quiet for a time after her father's lonely passing, so soon after his public accolades and election to the parliament of the Union of South Africa.

John and Mary Smyth's first child was born in Heilbron in 1912, their second in Maseru in 1914, after John accepted a post with the Basutoland Government, to, "keep three government cars in a state of repair". He received free housing, the house in question being vacated for the family by fellow employee Emil Heering, then single.

After 1918, Rosie and the children moved to Pretoria. I was incredulous, but presumed it was to be nearer Gideon in Pretoria Central Prison.

The earliest evidence of Grace in Maseru was a 1920 photo of her on horseback, in the leather-bound album of my Oupa, Emil Heering. I surmised they met through Emil knowing John, and Grace's visits to the tiny white community where her sister, Mary, lived. It seemed they married in 1921 but I found no marriage certificate, wedding photo or newspaper cutting. There were summer holiday photos in Cape Town in 1922. Was that their honeymoon?

It was another complex year for the Luyt family. Frederick Luyt died, aged eighteen, in Bloemfontein in September. His grave, beside his father at the Memoriam Cemetery, had just a small headstone inscribed: "FRED". Had Mary Ann's grief run dry? She'd already buried her husband and so many of her children. Or was she too distraught to manage more words than this? Fred was her last one, her baby. She was forty-one when he was born.

Left *Emil and Grace (date unknown) with their pet dog.*

My next piece of the chronology puzzle was the birth of their son, Ray, my uncle, in 1927 in Maseru. That's a long gap from 1921. My mother was born in 1932, another long haul. I believe, having visited the Lesotho Archives, that the remainder of my life would be too short to sift through the only slightly catalogued archives of the long defunct Basutoland Government. I doubt anyone would care enough about that history to digitise the records. I did find the government office for births and deaths, but encountered a local need for history to begin with the declaration of the Republic, years after the Heering family left for Durban. I accepted that I might never find out whether my Granny Grace also suffered from the genetic legacy of pre-eclampsia, and lost babies during those long gaps. Such losses were glossed over when my mother lost my sister Toni-Anne. Grace could have suffered even worse cheerfulness a generation earlier.

I imagined a conversation between Grace and her sister leading up to her decision to marry Emil.

"You could do worse." Mary tried to persuade Grace. "John and I have known Emil for years now. You'd struggle to find a better man, and he's smitten with you."

"I know," said Grace, "but he's not ... well, a picture, is he?"

"He has a fine physique. Look at all those athletics trophies. And he's a man of principle, with an excellent reputation here in Maseru."

"That's all true. It's just not the life I imagined."

"So much turned out differently to how we imagined."

"Remember the day in Parys when John came to ask for your hand? How excited you were? This doesn't feel anything like that. I wish Emil were more romantic, more dashing."

"I hadn't planned to remind you Gracie," said Mary, "but at twenty-seven you are no spring chicken. Don't you want to have a family of your own while you still can? Look around, there are so few men of Emil's calibre. And he's positively agitated to marry you."

"Did he put you up to this speech?"

"Of course not. I happen to think highly of him, and would love to see you settled down." Grace heard the implied, "at last." "He's already arranged for that good Basotho girl who works for his family to come and work for you in the house. It would be the best thing in the world to have you living here in Maseru."

"And there is …" added Mary, playing her final card, "the special wedding gift Emil has offered you."

The departure of Grace and Emil for Maseru was a quiet affair, as had been their wedding in Parys. She permitted an embrace with her mother and those of her siblings who were present, but her eyes were not glistening like theirs. There was no fond backward glance, though Emil turned to wave. He pushed aside a flicker of apprehension at his new wife's inscrutability, her lack of warmth for her family.

Grace's thoughts on the journey to Maseru centred on just one thing: the piano that awaited her.

MY NANNY, IDA

"Pulane," she pronounced when I was born.

"Bringer of rain?" my mother asked. "My mother had a nanny she loved called Puleng. Is that similar?"

"That means, In the Rain," said Ida. "The rain we needed arrived with this little one." And so I received my Sesotho name from our nanny.

Ida, the "good Basotho girl" who went with Emil Heering when he married Grace, was there when my mother was born in Basutoland, in 1932. "Mpho," she said on that occasion, and so Ida gave my mother June *her* Sesotho name, meaning, "A gift". An appropriate name, for it had been six years since her brother was born. And, for all her shortcomings, this was a perfect name for June.

She never did effect the transition from Ida's little girl to Ida's "madam".

"Go to bed," my mother begged her, after climbing the stairs for the third time one night. But nothing short of a nuclear explosion would have moved Ida from the doorway of the bedroom my brother, Mike, and I shared in our semi-detached house in Green Point, Cape Town.

"Your drunk friends will come and fall on the children." She yawned theatrically. The next morning Ida staggered into the kitchen, stiff with disapproval. This scene played out many times, as my father carved out his considerable reputation in the jazz clubs of Cape Town, and musicians continued their post-gig revelries in our living room.

I was oblivious to Ida's well-founded displeasure with my father, and the fact that she wouldn't communicate with him during their sixteen-year battle for sovereignty over his wife and children. She called him "Boy", the undignified term for grown black men working in the white gardens of South Africa.

"He thought his name meant 'wisdom' or some such attractive thing," my mother said. (My father spoke Zulu, but not Sesotho.) "And I never enlightened him. I tried to persuade Ida to be friendlier to him, but once she'd made up her mind, that was it."

One night she and June were in the kitchen preparing dinner. My mother was trimming fat off slabs of steak when another of their arguments over something silly broke out, Ida taking her usual obstinate position of the high moral ground. Even before impact, before the trail of blood started trickling down Ida's cheek, and before that prime piece of steak hit the ground, my sweet compliant mother knew she was wrong to have done it. She described the scene to me.

"Ida stood there looking at me like The Sphinx, making no move to wipe the blood off her cheek. Old witch that she was, she knew how instantly bad I felt, and how much worse I would feel if I had a good long look at the indignity I'd inflicted, before she bent down to pick up the steak. I don't generally hurl raw meat at people, but Ida knew how to press my buttons. I was always the child she'd raised in the absence of a normal mother."

Ida must have been about seventy when she left our employ, years later. She seemed older than that to me. I remember a bewildered sorrow, and shocking reality when a young Coloured woman, Miriam, arrived to look after us while my mother took Ida back to what was, by then, Lesotho. The two women spent the two-day train journey in their respective carriages, white and non-white. At each stop my mother jumped off and checked that all was well further down the train. In Maseru, an old family friend met them and helped her buy tinned foods, blankets and other supplies. He drove them to the Masite Mission.

It pains me that I don't know, can only imagine, how my mother felt waving goodbye to Ida on the grass verge outside the mission, after seeing her nearly every day for thirty-five years. June returned to Cape Town and stuffed Ida into her soul compartment for unspoken grief. The same compartment that held my sister, Toni-Anne.

My mother sent a letter and a parcel every month. With the parcel went money to pay for food and lodging at the mission, and at Christmas a wrapped gift for Ida and extra money for the nuns. Sometimes a letter from Ida arrived, that she had dictated to one of the nuns.

In 1969, three years after Ida left, and a few months before the diagnosis of my scoliosis, my mother and I drove across South Africa to Lesotho, to visit Ida. It took three days. The drive from Maseru to the Masite Mission was slow and bumpy, with few sealed roads and many potholes. Our Mercedes Benz built like a tank didn't help as much as one might have expected.

"You think I've got one foot?" the tiny woman demanded as she approached my mother, pulling a single sock from her apron pocket and shaking it at her. My mother explained this later, because I didn't understand a word of her scolding for one overlooked sock in a parcel bulging with clothing. She ignored me completely as she and Mpho tussled. Finally, they smiled, hugged and our group turned towards the mission house, my mother rolling her eyes at me.

"Is that her?" I asked, shocked on several levels. When she left I was nine. She'd always seemed huge to me, with a classic bosom that offered a child unassailable protection. Now I was twelve and trying with some success to look sixteen.

"Yes of course it's her."

"But … she's so small. And why won't she talk to me?"

"She's a lot thinner, but she was always short." She took my hand. "Judy, she won't believe that you are Pulane."

More shocks were to follow.

"Why won't she speak English?"

My mother looked at me incredulously. "She never spoke English."

"What?"

"She always spoke to you in Sesotho and you kids spoke to her in English."

I had no awareness of her ever having spoken a different language.

"Dumela," my mother said warmly to the sisters at the mission. They ushered us, and Ida, into their spartan dining room, clearly a rare treat for her, where they served us clear soup with bread for lunch. The four green beans in my bowl were four more than any of the sisters had in theirs.

"I don't remember a word," I said miserably to my mother as we bumped along dirt tracks through fields to see Ida's Chief. Ida hung out of the rear window, yelling to anyone we passed "Tsena ke sechaba sa ka o mosoeu!" ("These are my White People!!") All this, as well as the meeting with the Chief, my mother translated for me later. The meeting concerned Ida's funeral. Matters of burial are important in many parts of Africa. Ida was ensuring that the chief would, after this meeting, have in his possession the money for a decent coffin, a cow and other food for her funeral.

Such considerations may seem odd, but a 2009 study found that, despite loftier statements of intent, many people in drought-ravaged rural Lesotho attended funerals to procure a hefty meal including plenty of meat. Even with no family, and her long association with the Anglican mission, Ida wanted a traditional African burial. The rituals usher the departed to their place among the ancestors; without these, the soul wanders around the world of the living, causing trouble. The Sisters at Masite Mission had been in Africa long enough, had known

Ida long enough to take all precautions to ensure that this crabby old lady would find lasting peace in the hereafter, leaving the world of the living well alone.

"Give him something extra," Ida hissed at my mother after she'd handed over the cash to the Chief.

"Don't be ridiculous," she hissed back, embarrassed. The Chief, dressed in a suit and tie, smiled his understanding at my mother, reassuring her that he was not offended at Ida's ranting, and would take care of everything when her time came.

The two women bickered all the way back to the car.

"Ask her to sit in front so you can talk more easily," I suggested.

"She'd never accept."

British society had such protocols perfected long before anyone heard the word "apartheid". On the drive back to the mission, Ida and my mother continued bickering via the rear-view mirror.

We never visited again. Nine years later a letter arrived from the nuns to say that Ida had passed away and they had buried her according to her wishes. I felt regret, but not as much as I should have. I was busy avoiding mops and brooms with my lover in the back room of the computer department of Norwich Union.

May 2011.

Mark stayed at the hotel while Dean drove me to find the Masite Mission. "Masite" was listed under Anglican missions, but there was no website, phone number or address. Dean found a place on the map called Masite, thirty kilometres from Maseru, with a mission nearby. It was something.

Many of the tiny houses on the edges of town were made of drab, concrete blocks. Still, they were more substantial than the structures we'd seen in the townships on the way to Heilbron, constructed from corrugated iron, cardboard, tarpaulins and repurposed chunks of road signs that explained some of the difficulties we'd had with directions.

Near Maseru was a busy area along the major arterial road. It was a single lane in either direction, with no side streets and frequent, enormous speed humps. It cut through a chaotic mix of houses, roadside stalls, cars and minivans as informal taxis, no apparent road rules, people walking beside and on the road. Lowing cows, goats and sheep added a crazy element.

Then, suddenly, the swarm of activity gave way to pale yellow plains.

"Phew," said Dean.

Masite proved to be too much for the GPS. We abandoned it in favour of instinct, though nothing looked familiar.

A road sign caught my eye and I shrieked. "That sign says 'Masite Nek.'"

Dean veered onto the dirt road where we found another sign: Masite had scarce evidence of a town and just a primary school consisting of a few huts. In seconds, we were past it and onto open plains again. We asked some Basotho women on the roadside if they knew of the mission. We had just passed it.

We turned around, but in less than a minute, we found ourselves out on the other side of "town" again. On our third pass, Dean spotted a dirt track at the school. We tried it and, along the bumpy trail, saw another woman, with a baby in a blanket on her back.

"Excuse me, will this take us to Masite Mission?" I asked. She said it would. Up the hill we came to a gate. There was no signage but, at last, some faint stirring of memory.

The compound consisted of an old stone chapel, outlying buildings and huts, and a stone church further up the hill. We couldn't raise anyone at the main building, so walked up the hill to a house where a couple of women were hanging bright red church smocks out to dry.

One of them was the wife of Father Solomon Labona, recently arrived at the mission. She didn't look much like a minister's wife, with her shiny wig of long black ringlets, startling blue eye-shadow and high-heeled patent leather shoes. She led us inside to Father Labona's office.

"There's not much here," said the earnest young Minister. "But please take a look while I go ask around."

The meagre stack of tatty books contained details of births and deaths, but nothing far back enough. One of the nuns offered us a cup of tea.

"The only nun who might have remembered her died last year," she said.

They served two rounds of tea but there was still no sign of Father Labona. "Shouldn't we get going?" Dean asked. "We said we'd be back before dark."

The sun was low when the minister returned.

"There was an old man in one of the huts who said it might be his auntie. She died around the time you mentioned."

"She had no family of her own. It must be someone else he's thinking of. Thanks for trying."

I sadly consigned her story to permanent mystery. There was some satisfaction at having tried, having found the place of Ida's death. I was glad Dean shared the experience, it being unlikely that he'd ever find himself there again. He doesn't feel the connection I do, but he'll have visual images and an experience in his collection of personal memories.

There wasn't much moon to light up the drive back. We crawled through the busy part, dodging cooking fires, drinking parties and goats, vulnerable in our lone whiteness.

"Dad will be worried," Dean fretted. "Your door is locked, isn't it? Have we got reception yet? Try your phone again."

I was quiet with regret at how little I knew about the round woman who gave me a name and to whom I turned with every childhood hurt. Dim recollections included talk of her having some Indian blood. Would being an orphan from an indiscreet union have been sufficient reason for her to be at the Mission? She was still a teenager when she went to Oupa's. It was said she was married and her husband beat her with a hammer, leaving her mentally odd. Perhaps the nuns took her in to protect her. There was no question about her being odd.

"Oupa was very fond of her," my mother told me.

On one of my trawls through my mother's papers I discovered an undated item in her handwriting, about Ida. Another thread between my mother and I pulsed as I read an account she too had felt compelled to write "about a personality, a black lady who, after forty-eight years with three generations of my family, would not speak English unless it absolutely suited her, which was seldom."

"I can remember friction between her and my mother from the beginning," June wrote. "My mother laid herself open to be bullied by pursuing her social, sporting and piano teaching activities and leaving Ida to run the show. There were times when Ida's domineering ways made all the servants disappear in fright. Then Ida was cook, wash lady, inside maid and gardener — complaining all the time. This was perhaps her most infuriating fault. She talked to herself, and if one made the mistake of listening to her, you would hear her constant comparisons of her lot in life with biblical situations, and end up in an argument in which it would be impossible to reason with her."

The note verified Ida having moved to Emil's newlywed household in 1918, unexpectedly providing the best information so far on Grace and Emil's marriage, which was not in 1921 as I'd thought. That made it nine years before my Uncle Ray was born.

She continued, "To the end I was trying to convince her that we really appreciated her, but by then old age was taking its toll. In her prime, she competently axed off chickens' heads and prepared them for cooking, cultivated wonderful vegetable and flower gardens, tended the laying hens, chopped wood for the lounge, bedroom and kitchen fires, did the housework and cooking, and never failed to be at the school gate with my hot drink and snacks at break time."

"It was the custom in all families having more than one 'inside maid'," she wrote, "for one of them to go to school at break. We sat happily in their laps eating and joining in their chatter. How embarrassed my children would have been at such a suggestion. But those were times when we all spoke their language as fluently as our own, and are of a different era."

Below *June, age five, on her pony, Juppy, with Ida in the background.*

During my nine years with Ida, I never once entered her room situated at the back of our various homes. It never occurred to me to ask where she ate after she'd prepared our meal, or where she learned to make the fragrant medicine she administered when we were sick, batting aside my mother's half-hearted suggestions that we should have some "proper" medicine.

"No, not that one," Ida would snap, presumably in Sesotho, as we approached the wrong kind of eucalyptus tree. "There they are, over there." In this grove we'd find the right kind of blue gums, whose leaves we would stuff into a sack to take home for Ida to boil up into her famous "muti" and store in airtight jars to defend the family against the next germ assault.

On each of our birthdays, Ida would give me and Mike a number of pounds corresponding with our age, which would get deposited into our savings books. "Only for the future," she would say. "No withdrawals." I didn't know that these annual events were the only occasions on which Ida ever asked my mother for money.

"You mean she never received any pay?" I asked on the long drive back to Cape Town after that sad visit in 1969, during which my mother failed to convince Ida that I was Pulane.

"She said she didn't need money, except for birthdays. She never went out."

"But that's slavery."

"I suppose so, technically, but no one forced her to stay. She had nowhere else to go, no education, and no desire to do anything else. She couldn't remember anything before the mission."

Southern Africa was full of paradoxes.

And what a trail of odd mothering, I thought, as I tried to understand the forces that shaped the women of my family. Mary Ann, pregnant and apparently "delicate", then busy with a new baby, was not there for tiny Grace and her terrors through the Boer War. Later, through the tragedy of Cora's young death and Mary Ann's focus on the surviving baby-without-a-mother, Grace once again had to rely on older siblings and her dear Puleng for succour. Then she lost Puleng, along with so much else in the fall of the family.

I felt sure that the impact of her early life must have played a part in Grace's strangeness; her need to spend days at a time shut in her bedroom while Ida did the mothering, alongside tending the garden and chopping the heads off chickens. It sounded, to my untrained mind, like undiagnosed depression.

What impact, then, descended on little June? She would have had to play quietly so as not to disturb her cloistered mother. She loved Ida, the tiny woman who was part servant and part mother to her, and clearly struggled to find her way in that relationship in the face of societal expectations. When June had her own children, Ida was there to shoulder much of the load. I remembered Ida sitting on the floor in our loo, cheering me along the path of toilet-training. I doubt that my mother ever washed a nappy or cleaned up baby barf. She would never have had to find a babysitter. She had the freedom to do whatever she liked, because Ida was there and us kids were safe. Then June not only had to say goodbye to Ida, but to take responsibility for sending her away.

I began to see how June became 'my Ida' in Australia, in an era and society where that role did not exist. I did wash nappies, before and after June came to live with us. But once she was there, I too never had to find a babysitter, think about what we'd be having for dinner, or who would prepare it. She provided Dean with a third, loving parent. A gift, indeed, was Mpho.

I loved Ida too, and now, as I detected a small suggestion of daylight through the aggrieved layers around my heart, I saw how I had taken her for granted. Like my mother, I had been raised by her and couldn't remember a time when she wasn't there. Like my mother, I fell asleep safe from nocturnal perils each night in my early years with my hand firmly in Ida's as she lay on the floor beside my bed.

All I can say is, "I am sorry, Ida, for everything."

COUNTRY

Mark and I visited South Africa every few years after migrating to Australia. I celebrated with others at the rise of President Mandela and the joyous mixing of colours in the "Rainbow Nation", but my heart still lurched at the sight of shanties along the airport road, urchins begging in the streets, a young woman with a tiny baby living under a bridge in the middle of winter.

When I was growing up in Camps Bay we had low garden walls, if any, and open spaces where a white horse, Philly, roamed for years with his companion, a scraggly white donkey. We would run outside with apples and carrots when we saw the pair wander up the road, free spirits owned by no one, yet cared for by everyone. Over the years of visits to South Africa, the streets and houses of Camps Bay morphed into mansions protected by high walls topped with razor wire and signs of "24 Hour Surveillance & Armed Response". It saddened me.

Of course, the wrongs that underpinned the enchanted lifestyle we had enjoyed in white areas were undeniable; the ideology warped and unsustainable. I remembered Ida personally with love, but could never support the system of semi-slavery that made her relationship with my family possible. I was surprised and thrilled when the new regime arrived in South Africa. And yet, I've found it hard to adjust to all aspects of the new society.

The big cities have become cities of Africa, bringing a cheerful chaos ranging from exciting to confronting. Some expatriates resonate with the changes and feel called to return to their country of birth. Some expats view Australia as choked by rules and regulations that people observe like sheep, and prefer the edgier, colourful new South Africa. I have learned that I don't thrive in a chaotic environment, no matter how colourful. I don't mind the regulations of Australia. Some can be annoying, but I feel that they make systems underpinning daily life run relatively smoothly. Socialistic processes criticised by some do help to alleviate the suffering of many. On a personal level, I like being able to leave my unbarred doors and windows open all night to the fragrance of jasmine in spring. I like to devote my time to creative pursuits, and fostering arts in the community, with politics a sideshow, rather than something gnawing daily at my soul.

I read books about white South African heroes who devoted, and sometimes sacrificed, their lives to the "howling ambiguities" of South Africa, as author Rian Malan describes it. I admire their dedication and selflessness, but I lack the hero gene, and am not up to the task of living in what I experience as a tempest. Australia, while not above reproach, delivered a life that allowed me, after years of hard work, to pursue my dreams, and to make a difference as an individual in my community. I am grateful. In South Africa, I felt eternally helpless in the face of irresolvable injustice and boundless need. Even now, despite the hopeful changes of the 1990s, I feel a similar helplessness.

But, there was more to my embracing of Australia than escape from what I felt to be an intractable political system.

I could start over, and for the first time I felt visible, empowered. I built the primary threads of my life here, not there. I cannot claim it as my Country in the Aboriginal sense, but the connection is much stronger than merely country with a small "c". It is the birthplace of my son, the site of all my experience as a mother and as a Jew, a country where women could apply for home loans in the nineteen-eighties, the place in which I have found a community that has nurtured me as a musician and, now, a writer.

There was also more to the feeling of anxiety that continued to rise each time our flight approached Johannesburg. I could feel that it was not rational, but didn't know why.

As I perceived shapes emerging from what had been shadowy hints of the past, I started to wonder if in protecting myself I had shut out the good with the bad. I'd never before delved so deeply into the events of my early life, the time when I'd developed the protective thickening around my heart that somewhat shielded me from wounding. I had never been conscious of this layer, but now considered what other effects it might have had on me.

As the plane descended through the clouds on the most recent research trip, I saw that I was not only bracing myself against confronting, once again, the daily difficulties still suffered by so many people in my country of birth. I was experiencing a descent to unacknowledged memories of disempowerment, and a dark feeling of danger, not from physical violence, but from my past. This realisation and belated acknowledgement allowed my rational mind to at last take charge. The past was finally over, in the ways that had hampered me. Instead, I had made a new, unexpected connection to a more distant past. The discovery of my family's part in the earliest times in the Cape of Good Hope, the Boer War and its unfortunate aftermath, anchored me and placed me inside the beating heart of a rich and powerful story.

I'm not there anymore. "There" is not there anymore. The new South Africa pleases, perplexes and challenges me, as it continues to evolve from its fraught history. I fear that the stories of the white past will dwindle in importance as the neglected black past rightly takes the spotlight. But this white past — centuries of it — is part of my story. Defensible or not, it's what happened.

My protective shield helped me withstand the challenges of South Africa, but also blocked my connection to it without my realising it. I saw that it had also held me aloof from learning about the Indigenous people of my new country. I couldn't bear to open myself to another sorrowful reality. But now, as I experience this cautious softening, I want to learn about this history too, and find ways in which I might help to build bridges to it from my own community.

Though I've spent more than two-thirds of my life in Australia and it is home, I haven't, after all, left my crazy, vibrant country of origin behind. Instead, it informs and enriches me in a new, connected way. I care. Now I look forward to visiting South Africa, as I learn more about its complexities and compelling history that the prevailing order in the nineteen seventies did not include in our high school textbooks. It adds meaning to my life.

The Luyt family of the early Cape Colony sent its shoots out into the world, while countless branches still flourish in South Africa. Few of their stories have been recorded, and I noted a measure of 'bleaching', whether intentional or not, in the existing genealogical records. For half a century, my branch played a part in the course of the country's history. I can make a contribution here, by seeking and recording the stories, the leaves on this branch.

I'm seven years into the foliage, and knowing now what I do about research, I can't see how my mother would have accomplished this work of probing the past. June inherited her father's kindness and managed to survive her mother's strange detachment. Her tenacity shone in the face of repeated life-threatening illnesses that left her weaker each time, but she lacked the confidence to prevail in other areas. This handicap also left us, her children, at a loss. She was not someone I could turn to for support in the dark years of our family.

In shutting out painful aspects of the past, had I also played a part in blocking full connections to my family? It had become clear that business was not finished. A wound had festered beneath the love for my sweet mother, and I realised that I had never explored the forces that shaped Norina, the third player in my parents' ensemble.

DIFFERENT KINDS OF FAMILY

When my mother moved into the studio apartment above our garage in Sydney, my father rented out his beach bungalow in Cape Town and moved in with Norina.

The relationship with Norina and my father endured for thirty-five years alongside his marriage to my mother. But, though he often stayed at Norina's place, he had never before lived with her permanently. It must have been a shock for her.

"I've always been clear that I would never oust June as Colin's wife, nor have children of my own," Norina told me on many occasions. "This is … you are … my family." This is the truth, even if for a long time it glossed over her share in the damage that was done to two unsuspecting children by the trio of adults performing their untidy concerto.

Her own path, I discovered later, was not easy. Norina had been left as a baby in a shoebox on a doorstep on the fringe of Cape Town where the waters of race division mingled. The birth certificate tucked into the box suggested desperate circumstances: an Indian mother wooed by a passing Italian sailor during World War II. Her request that the baby keep its Italian first name at least suggested happy memories of the encounter. The white woman who found Norina on her doorstep was a tough single mother of a young boy, but took Norina in. As apartheid descended, the law forced Norina and her white brother to attend different schools.

Her foster mother had her own challenges in keeping the family afloat. She was not averse to using a leather belt to maintain discipline, gave her young children front door keys, and expected them to look after themselves each day after school. She rented out the best room in the modest house, and it was on the tiny veranda outside that room that Norina received a special gift; the kind that sustains people in life.

Norina looked forward each afternoon to when the kind, perceptive man renting the good room would return from work.

"Don't make a nuisance of yourself," her mother growled. "We need the money."

One warm, clear evening after dinner while her mother clattered in the kitchen, Norina sneaked upstairs. The room was dark and the streetlights in the lane were out, again. She hesitated, her mother's words ringing. As her eyes adjusted, she saw their tenant seated on a chair squeezed sideways on the veranda, gazing at the sky. He sensed her presence and beckoned her closer.

"Look up there," he said.

The Milky Way blazed across the darkness.

She gasped. She'd only noticed the stars distantly before, half-visible through streetlights.

"One of those is yours," he said. "Follow it, never give up on it, and one day you'll shine like this sky."

Norina never forgot that night.

She didn't tell me this story until recently. But before my family unravelled and the ice formed around my heart, she had, perhaps without even realising it, somehow shared this gift of faith in survival. It was something my parents couldn't give me, and, paradoxically, she helped me survive the storm of which she was a co-creator.

Norina did well enough at school to get into secretarial school. She graduated at eighteen and found a job at the sound and film studio in which my father would soon become a partner. Exciting work, travel and romance followed. The partners perjured themselves to secure the white ID card that would be produced many times during the apartheid years; that made it legal for her to live in a white area, and secure her entry to a bar or restaurant whenever her racial origins were questioned. Her lifetime commitment to my father, the business and to our family was sealed.

Norina pushed down a rising foreboding as Colin moved his mountain of belongings into what had been her pristine townhouse. June indulged in a small smirk, sitting in her pristine studio apartment across our driveway in Sydney. Norina valiantly converted her spare room into a music room for my father, and excavated an underground storeroom for the daunting overflow. Years of transcontinental travel followed, with times good and bad on both sides of the Indian Ocean.

Then, on one of his soul-searching trips into the bleakness of the Great Karoo, he encountered another Grace, a new woman in his life who would not tolerate other players on the stage, and whose powers of manipulation equalled his own. He was enraptured.

He soon moved into the separate apartment on the lower level of the bungalow on Glen Beach, ostensibly a single man once again.

"If this is what you want to pursue, then … well, do it," said Norina of the starry sky.

To the seething displeasure of the new arrival, Norina continued to run the remains of my father's business. No one else understood the convoluted legacies of its previous incarnations. He also maintained regular contact with my mother, who was summoning the remnants of her waning powers to fight worsening respiratory illness. But Colin's concern for June didn't impress Grace. Here, unbelievably, was a third woman in the picture — a wife, no less.

"It's me or them," she made quite clear.

My father was desperate for the favours dangled by this canny lady, rationed with skill to spark his fantasies.

And so — one year away from what would have been their fiftieth wedding anniversary — my father and mother divorced.

"It's just a formality," my mother said. "Our relationship could hardly be called a marriage." But I could feel her sadness. Or was it mine?

My father wrapped up the vestiges of his business and, theoretically, eliminated his reliance on Norina, though her specially built cellar still bulged with his belongings. As an irrefutable gesture of commitment to Grace, he bought a house in Bothasig, far from his familiar surroundings but close to hers, and they moved in together. For the first time in his life, he was constrained by convention. He delivered an engagement ring and took Grace on a lavish overseas trip. On their return, he worked as a pianist again, in a big band. In the increased togetherness of domestic life, he noticed oddities about Grace that troubled him slightly. He brushed them away, putting it down to her being a different kind of woman to June and Norina, more prone to jealousy and convention than the two women with whom he'd spent much of his life.

Eventually he lost hope for South Africa, and prepared to retire to Australia. He intended to marry Grace and bring her over once he'd gotten settled. But he had to convince her to make the move.

My father droned on for hours as we sat on the beach at Port Douglas, where I'd booked him as my pianist for the first week of my fancy Sheraton lounge gig. He seemed to need my approval, my confirmation that he was doing the right thing.

"June won't leave her life with your family. And I can't live in that little space permanently. I need my own place."

Thank goodness.

"I can understand that you want a partner," I said, "but the way this has run so far makes me uneasy. It's good that she's coming over for a trial run." This was a very mild version of what I really felt. I couldn't give him the approval he sought.

We also spoke about the few pieces of writing I'd nervously shared with him.

"For the first time, I feel that you've entered a creative realm where I can't follow," he said. "It's thrilling. This is yours. You must write more."

I was glad to have had this time with him, to talk and to share a musical connection. It was just one week out of a two-month engagement, before my regular pianist arrived. But by the end of the week I knew that I would never, ever do it again. I don't know how any of the women in his life did.

My mother was in hospital, again, and a few dear friends had joined the care roster that continued whether June was at home or in hospital. One was Donna, who recounted, as only Donna can, a memorable exchange with my mother.

"Hello June. How are you feeling today?"

"Not great. I didn't have a good night. Can you please pass me my water? And the mouth swab?"

She needed something at every moment, constantly striving for the physical comfort that so eluded her.

"Grace has come," she told Donna, whose eyes softened as she sat down at the bedside and took June's hand.

"Oh June …" said Donna.

My mother looked at her quizzically, then clucked.

"No, no. I mean Grace, Colin's new woman, has arrived in Australia."

They laughed about it all morning.

Grace's stay of a few months was precarious, until the whole mirage fell in tatters, largely due to the mental illness that she had managed to conceal up to that point.

"You didn't give her a chance," my father accused, still hurting.

"I tried, truly, but I don't like her and worse, I don't trust her. And you may not have noticed, but it's been tough around here with round-the-clock nursing."

I didn't much care what he felt, as he took up his noble position at my mother's hospital bedside. Mark and I were mind-body-spirit-exhausted from months of taking care of her, even with the help of friends. My father's absence on the care roster was maddeningly conspicuous.

Norina kept in touch, anxious and caring. Many were baffled by the friendship between my father's two long-term women. Norina grieved when my mother died, and she was gladder than I was that June had drawn her last breath holding my father's hand in the middle of the night.

My father's next venture, to bring Norina to Australia, didn't go well either. There were no dramatic scenes, unlike with the previous candidate, but she realised that she couldn't sacrifice the valued elements of her city life in Cape Town, and couldn't see how to replicate them in semi-rural Australia. I admired her clarity, and her decisiveness, so unlike my mother, and her willingness to consider this possibility after all that had happened. She had always been her own woman, and now more so than ever. I didn't begrudge her decision, as much as I wished for my father to have a partner.

Norina was the only family my brother, Mike, had in Cape Town. She recognised this, and supported him through challenging times.

Mike and I drew closer at those times, despite the separation of continents, and our disinclination to regular, newsy email. Our shared experiences of losing first our mother, then our father, also wove the threads of our lives together more tightly. Against all odds, we share a long history and deep connection with Norina. Though we each lived The Dark Years differently, those bonds too are there. I feel them all at last.

In 2016, both Mark and I were on the teaching faculty of the National Youth Jazz Festival in Grahamstown, South Africa.

"I chose this next piece for a few reasons," announced Dan Shout, conductor of the Schools Big Band. The concert was the culmination of an intense four-day program.

"I grew up in Namibia, and its awesome natural beauties are still dear to me. Also, my teacher, Mike Campbell, composed the piece. Though he's not here this year, he has been an integral part of the festival since its beginnings twenty-four years ago. It's called 'Etosha'."

The vistas of Namibia stirred our father's heart too, and unleashed a slew of visual and musical delights. One of his award-winning documentaries was, "The Etosha Pan", about the salt desert surrounded by harsh savannah that is home to a surprising array of wildlife, like elephants, lions, zebra and rhinos.

Many features of that stark landscape inspired him, like Mukurob, the "Finger of God", an ancient 450-ton rock formation twelve metres high and 4.5 metres wide, resting on a narrow base just 1.5 metres wide. It inspired centuries of tales and legends among the Nama people. Prone to theatrics and vanity, my dad started referring to himself in the third person as "Mukurob", with portentous wide-eyes. It wouldn't surprise me if he took it personally when Mukurob succumbed to the geological odds and fell down on the night of 7 December 1988. We didn't hear too much about it after that.

Just the mention of "Etosha" stirred these thoughts. Then the band started the introduction and an unexpected lump swelled in my throat as I heard my father in the music. But this was Mike's work. What's more, Mike actively avoided our dad's involvement in his work. Every time Mike had taken the risk of involving him in any project at the College of Music, it turned into a nightmare. That's how it went with our dad, though he didn't see it that way and felt wounded that Mike didn't turn to him more often in his professional life. But here he was in Mike's writing.

"Have you ever played that Etosha piece?" I asked one of Mike's past students, now a professional musician and the partner of Mike's talented daughter Amy, also a professional musician.

"Sure," he replied. "It sounds so much like your dad's pieces, hey?"

"How do you know what my dad's writing sounds like?"

"Oh, we did lots of your dad's stuff at the college."

I was amazed. Did my dad know that? It would have made him happy. Sadly, I suspect it would have made him even happier than the knowledge that his son had fostered a new, musically literate generation of jazz musicians in South Africa, and a new breed of jazz teachers who would go forth and perpetuate the artform. One of them was Dan Shout.

I was proud to be a small part of this festival, working with singers and continuing the Campbell family presence on the festival faculty.

WHO DONE IT?

My quest to explain Johan's ruin had unearthed pathways to the seven survivors of Johan and Mary Ann's children. I'd come to know a little about all but one of them.

Leo	Brave, jolly, popular, a real gentleman ("Die Engelse Boer").
Rosie	Talented pianist. Compassionate, brave, Boer War spy.
Lenie	The "Indian" child. Died at thirty-nine leaving six children.
Cora	Died at nineteen after her only child, Cora, was born.
Mary	Moved to Basutoland, later to Durban. Close to Grace.
Grace	Depressive, odd, detached. Talented pianist. Went to Maseru, then Durban.
Johan Jnr.	Who knows?

I assumed at first that there would be other descendants out on those branches who possessed relics, photographs and letters that would deliver the definitive truth. But it appeared that few such treasures had survived. Instead, clues fell out of side details in old documents, random photos and public records, and required patient attentiveness to weave together.

My newfound cousin, Daphne, in Sydney sent me a wonderful image of our great grandmother, attractive and elegant, perhaps in her forties. At her throat is a gold brooch that came to Daphne from her feisty grandmother, Rosie. The horseshoe surrounds a colossal diamond that Mary Ann eventually sold to support Rosie and her six destitute children, one of them Daphne's mother. Mary Ann was feisty herself, to hang onto that brooch through Johan's financial ruin. I wish they'd taken as much care with the portraits. I imagine one of the children trailing behind in the hallway as Mary Ann exited the imposing front door for the last time, vision blurred by sorrow.

MARY LUYT

"Mama, what about the pictures?" A shock wave passes through Mary Ann.

"Khabane, bring the paintings from the hallway, please," she calls to their remaining servant, blinking hard and trying not to think about leaving dear Motsumi and Puleng with their new masters.

"Yes Madam." But he pauses and considers the tower already lashed to the wagon. "Madam, I think you cannot take them."

Mary Ann follows his gaze. Everyone is now waiting, the sun already high, Parys many hours away and Johan, slumped, has a quizzical hand raised to her. "Just find a knife or something and cut them out of the frames," she tells Khabane. "Be careful. Roll them up and bring them to me." She checks the secret pouch under her bodice. The hard, rounded shape meets her trembling fingers.

"I still have the horseshoe," said Daphne when she visited, "but no diamond, you understand." And she opened a small jewellery case to reveal the gold brooch.

"This is the actual brooch?" I asked stupidly, holding it up to the light. Of course, it was, but this was my first look at another tangible piece of my history that came from somewhere other than my mother's possessions, and its empty centre told a story.

"The trouble in this picture," said Daphne, "is that it's upside down".

"I don't understand."

"You should never wear a horseshoe with the open end pointing downwards," she said. "All the luck falls out."

In the next chronological photo of Mary Ann, she's gaunt and hardly recognisable. I'm sad that this is the only photo of her with the silver tea service. It's painful to look at, as if she will never smile again.

She looks to be in her sixties, so the photo would be from the 1920s. Mary Ann had lost Johan, her daughter Rosie had suffered indignity upon indignity from her miscreant husband, Gideon, and now survived on the charity of her mother and brother Leo, himself not affluent. Helena had birthed nine children in Heilbron, three of whom had died. In this field of sorrow, Helena herself died, soon after her youngest brother, Fred.

With Johan's life insurance long lost to the bank, how did Mary Ann make her way? Did she consider selling the tea service? She could be forgiven for having thought, "You can't eat solid silver." Her remaining five children ranged from poor to working class. Leo was a clerk in Parys where, like his father, he served on the municipal council.

Rosie lived modestly in Pretoria, also supported by her adult children. Mary and her husband, a civil servant, raised their family in

Maseru, eventually alongside Grace and her Emil, also a civil servant. I couldn't find Johan Jnr, the youngest now that Fred was gone.

It appears, from photos, that Mary Ann travelled widely to attend births, baptisms, weddings and funerals. She was in Parys in 1936 for an important ceremony, as I rediscovered in another pass through Ma's old letters. They revealed a warm connection with Cissy, Daphne's mother. I didn't know who "Cissy" was when I first saw them, as the family tree showed her only as Edith Cora.

In one letter, Cissy transcribed an article from the *Parys Post* of 19 May 1936:

> "She (Mary Ann) handed to Mr Leo Luyt a medal which was awarded to her husband nearly 26 years ago. The accompanying letter, which is signed by Lord Gladstone, stated that King Edward VII desired to give to those South Africans who had worked and striven for Union a memento of the occasion, but he died before his wish could be carried out. Later in the year (1910) King George V carried out his father's desire. One of those medals was awarded to Mr J. G. Luyt …"

I felt proud. My research invigorated, I found brand new online records that confirmed the contents of the letter. I asked Leo's granddaughter, cousin Elena in Pretoria, if she knew anything. She told me that Leo had left the medal to his eldest son and that it was subsequently stolen, which broke Leo Junior's heart. It breaks mine too. The medal probably landed up in a garbage can.

Research also yielded darker truths.

When I was suffering through my grey history textbook at school, I had no real sense that it represented only the official government version. It was in a textbook and therefore fact, right? The milestones on the path to apartheid and the Republic of South Africa were presented gloriously, not as the birth of formalised injustice. Now, the insights of research as an adult had expanded not only my view of my family, but also my understanding of South Africa's complicated history. There was much more to it than I'd appreciated, and it stirred broader feelings of sadness about it than I'd previously experienced.

I'd learned that Johan's colleagues, Abraham Fischer and President Steyn, played important roles in the formation of the Union of South Africa. They were part of the National Convention that drafted the 1909 *South Africa Act*. Johan was a member of the Legislative Assembly that supported it, even as he battled to halt his downward financial slide.

But still the significance of the *South Africa Act* eluded me.

The 2015 Bram Fischer Memorial Lecture brought it home. A lecture is delivered every year at Oxford University, to celebrate the commitment to justice shown by Bram Fischer, grandson of "Oom Abraham". Constitutional Court Judge Edwin Cameron explained how Bram's grandfather had played "a profound part in the dispossession of Africans from the land, and in the destruction of their safety and security and prospective prosperity."

Those who drafted the Act were all white men. Black South Africans condemned it, and representatives met in a parallel, unofficial convention, the South African Native National Congress, which became the African National Congress (ANC).

My textbook pages hadn't indicated that these events impacted the darker-skinned people of South Africa immediately, or that the struggle against it commenced instantly. Nelson Mandela and the African National Congress were names I heard in the conversations of adults; nothing to do with me.

But there was more. The Act was sent to London, where it passed without a single amendment through both Houses of Parliament. King Edward VII ratified it. I'd always been critical of Afrikaner policies, but now felt that Britain could not duck having played its part, with similar racial attitudes, and the same arrogance with which Lords and Generals disastrously carved up the Middle East after World War I. British history reeks of the mess its agents left in their wake around the globe.

Today, it's easy to forget that these attitudes were shared by leaders on all sides. I'd never considered that they were typical of white men in colonial times everywhere, when punishments such as flogging were still common. It didn't make it more palatable, but I could now discern the historical pathways that led to it. The South African statesmen involved included several legendary lawyers who mentored and influenced Johan. They were educated, visionary men of the world. Though Johan never travelled internationally as they did, he held his place among them on the local political scene.

I also hadn't considered how miraculous it was that they could form the Union of South Africa so soon after the damage of the Boer War, just eight years after the surrender. And how ironic it was that they did so via the kind of political channels recommended by the reviled *hensoppers*. I'd felt disappointed when I learned that Johan was a *hensopper*, as if he'd failed morally. With what I'd now learned, I questioned the waste and misery of the final two years of war, spearheaded by the *bittereinders*. It's as a pragmatist, as well as the great granddaughter of a *hensopper* that I feel the worst of the destruction and loss of life might have been avoided.

I'd also like to think that, with his compassion and sense of honour, Johan would have been appalled at the excesses later reached by the system he helped to foster.

The avalanche of information I'd gathered about Johan and Mary Ann created a mosaic stretching to her death in 1949. I'd recreated the trail of Johan's financial ruin, but still hadn't determined why descendants from multiple strands of the family believed that Gideon was responsible. I made another attempt to map Johan's final descent, returning to the documents from the period following the move to Parys.

In late 1910, only six months after the departure of the Luyts from Heilbron, the *Bloemfontein Friend* reported that the Heilbron Circuit Court heard several cases with Advocate Percy Fischer, Abraham's son, as Crown Prosecutor, and "Advocate Luyt defending in each instance". On Day Two of the proceedings, another attorney was, "acting on behalf of Advocate Luyt by special permission of the Bench, because of Mr Luyt's indisposition."

Johan had, by then, been replaced on the Heilbron School Committee, and by Deneys Reitz on the committee of the Heilbron Public Library. The sale of almost everything the family owned didn't cover Johan's debt and he was declared insolvent. These records demonstrated that Johan was both ill and broke by late 1910, and he was still trying to work. The legal case of 1911, I'd found early in my searching had suggested he was succeeding, from Parys. Surely that must have generated some income? It had by now been several years since I'd viewed the thirty images from that thick file, and I'd amassed much more material since then. It took a while to find it. When I did, the last of the puzzle pieces fell into place.

Johan was not a lawyer working on the case at all. "Tutor dative", I learned, meant he was a representative for the minor children of a Mr Otto, deceased, like an unpaid legal guardian who commits to look after their interests and assets if their parents die. Mr Otto must have known Johan well, to have trusted him with the welfare of his children.

Mr Otto left properties to his children, but they moved away and the properties fell into disrepair. The Heilbron council wrote to Gideon, who represented the owners, giving notice of legal action if the arrear rates were not paid. "Tutor dative" Johan weighed in, with the required petition to the Supreme Court for he and Gideon to sell the properties on behalf of the children.

The sales took place in the week following Mary's July 1911 wedding to John Smyth, where Gideon had been sufficiently esteemed to be the respondent to the toast to the bride's father on behalf of the disabled Johan. The following month, speculators Lotzof & Cohen bought one of the Heilbron properties and paid £84 10/ to Gideon to pay the family. Lotzof & Cohen? This hadn't meant anything to me six years previously, but now it triggered a memory. I went back through Gideon's criminal charges.

Oh, no. Gideon had sold the Heilbron properties as requested, but the money never reached the Master of the High Court, let alone the family. The charge laid by Lotzof & Cohen, the agents in the sale of the Otto property, was the case that got Gideon disbarred for misconduct. I had found the missing link, hiding in plain sight. A memory had stirred when I first read the misconduct case, but I still lacked familiarity with the players, and wasn't able to see the vital connection.

In my subsequent searching, there'd been no evidence that Gideon caused Johan's financial ruin, which was all over by 1910. I'd found plenty of evidence of Gideon's crimes, but the court cases only started in 1912, after the fall of the family, which I'd assumed was also the ruin that was said to have precipitated Johan's death within six months. The Otto case took many months to proceed from Mr Otto's death in 1911 to Gideon's confession in 1912. The evidence proved that Johan had trusted Gideon up until that point.

June 1912. Mary Ann found Johan in the parlour with his head in his hands, a letter in his lap.

"Johan, I've been calling you. What …?" she ran over to him. "Johan, are you alright?"

The face that looked up shocked her. His skin was grey and his lips trembled.

"I've been so stupid. I've failed Otto, like I've failed you all."

"What news came?"

"Gideon confessed to the charges. The Magistrate spoke of other wrongdoings and disbarred him forever. There were signs, Mary, but I pushed them away. I couldn't … wouldn't … believe it." The agony in his eyes was unbearable. "I can't trust myself anymore and neither should anyone else."

Mary Ann pulled him towards her and held him close as his wrenching sobs drenched her apron. She had never in all their shared life seen him like this.

Mary Ann had been brave before, learned social graces to host great men, endured the loss of four children, and public humiliation. But as she and Johan wept and clung to each other, the premonition of a new era filled her, one that would require strengths she wasn't sure she possessed.

Family mythology maintained he died of shame, six months after his ruin. I thought it unlikely that financial collapse could fell someone so strong, even a public figure, plus the timing was off.

But this was the felling of an honourable soul, the ruin of a good heart. I believe this was the basis of the story that went forth along all the branches of the Luyt family of Heilbron. And for this, Gideon was responsible. Johan's death six months after his ruin was true, but it was not the ruin that everyone had assumed.

After burying Johan in 1913, Mary Ann would attend the funerals of her children Fred and Lenie in 1921, Rosie in 1940, and Leo, her eldest, in 1948. She died in Durban in 1949. She was buried in the grave where my sister would join her three years later. Only two of her eleven children, my Granny Grace and Johan Jnr, remained.

Johan Jnr, born while British soldiers camped on their tennis court in Heilbron, died ten years before Grace, leaving June no living uncles and aunts from her mother's enormous family by the time I was born. That further explained our lack of wider family. But what about all those cousins?

There were at least thirty, no match for Mark, but still a significant number of close relatives. I only ever heard of Cora and Avis, though there is evidence that Ma had contact with more cousins than those two. Why didn't we know them?

I'm sorry, Oupa. I wish I'd spent every one of those afternoons at Hillcrest at your side, writing down all you could tell me about your life in late-nineteenth century Basutoland, about your strange wife and the family stories she must have told you.

I took another trip through Ma's papers. They never failed me. I found the original photo of Mary Ann wearing the gold horseshoe brooch. It had been there all the time. I must have seen it when I first went through them, but wouldn't have recognised Mary Ann back then.

I decided to have another try with Johan Junior, the last of the Luyt seven. In the humble telephone directory, I found a Cape Town number for a Francois Luyt. One of Johan Junior's sons was named Francois Frederich, and perhaps he named *his* son Francois, though the family tree didn't indicate any children. I left a voicemail trying to briefly explain myself, and left my email address. Two days later I received an email. "Yes, I am the one you seek, the son of Francois Frederich (Fritz)."

He said there were some "broken links", and even less connection to the past than for the other Luyt children, but I was excited to find this final branch.

Francois tells me he is an attorney, just like our shared great-grandfather, and that he has no relics, letters or photographs from that generation. His grandfather, Johan Junior, was the personal chauffeur of the Prince of Wales during his visit to Cape Town during the 1920s. There is a pocket watch with the Prince's acknowledgement somewhere in the family. I hope to see it one day, and learn how Johan Jnr came to be in Cape Town.

I finally found public recognition of my great grandfather in the *Anglo-African Who's Who* of 1910, honouring him for his decades of public service. The content would mercifully have been gathered the previous year, before the sky fell in.

Then I found a transcription, in Ma's handwriting, of an obituary from the *Heilbron Herald*, 6 June 1913, acknowledging Johan's many noble contributions.

I was glad to see him publicly acknowledged after all. He'd earned it. I saw his failings: over-extravagant largesse to family members, his speculative naiveté and lack of judgement regarding Gideon. But his inauspicious end after decades of civic duty and dedication to others saddened me. I wished he could have had rewards, satisfaction and old age, not ill health, bad luck, and skulking away to an early death with a pauper's burial, ashamed of his protégé son-in-law in prison, and recognising the desperate circumstances to which he would leave his wife, their children, and grandchildren.

The once-baffling family tree has come into focus, the names on many of the leaves now representing people I know and care about. These are my people, my "ants" continuing their trails, their descendants scattered across the world. I claim them unequivocally. They were for the most part well-intentioned people for whom all the luck fell out, and who did the best they could within complex social and political systems that were not of their making. I lament the contribution their beliefs, their lack of questioning and even their direct influence might have made to the suffering of racial groups other than their own in South Africa, but I now better understand the forces that shaped them. I will do my best to straighten out the twisted sections of the tree for those I imagine out there on the branches yet to come.

FINAL CHORDS

The old dirt track runs alongside the highway from Heilbron to Frankfort. The undulations in the terrain are mild. To make this trip by ox-wagon would have been comfortable enough, but would have taken a full day. The nineteenth century postal services in the Orange Free State were impressive, but my great-grandparents and their relatives nonetheless made this trip repeatedly to visit one another in person, feeling the passing of the ground beneath them. These families made journeys between Parys and Heilbron too, for weddings and funerals, times of illness, joy and disaster, many of them pregnant, with swarms of children, in all weather.

Perhaps technology will one day bring the feeling of physical presence closer. God bless technology, but it ain't the same thing as being in a room with someone.

My father spent the final days of his life in a room at a hospice in Newcastle, Australia. Nine months prior, the oncologist had told him he had three to five years. My brother was able to make two trips to Australia during those months and made the best peace he could with his dad.

I made my own peace a few years before, largely thanks to my dad's late-life partner Doris, another angel, from whom he finally learned the art of happiness. His manipulations had little effect on this woman of no pretensions from the Australian soil. His dramatic outbursts elicited little more than an eye roll before she returned to the crossword puzzle.

In his last few years he jettisoned not all, but many of the demons that had plagued him for most of his life. I could see how much he and Doris loved one another.

This magical time also illumined his relationship with Dean, by then studying film at university. My multiple award-winning filmmaker father understood nothing of modern techniques. But the way light falls into a room doesn't change, whatever camera you point at it, and he understood these things. Dean was spellbound and "Pa", melted in the glow of his admiration.

I saw again in my father the maker of creative games. It manifested in long conversations over red wine about language, storytelling and sound. Now he wouldn't miss a single choral concert or jazz gig, and wanted to discuss every detail afterwards. I felt the disappointments of all those missed school prize-giving events and performances recede.

"Write," he said in some of his last words from his hospice bed. "Promise me you'll write."

"I will," I said without flinching, but with no expectation of fulfilling this undertaking. It wasn't the first time I'd lied to him in the latter stages of his illness. It was just easier that way.

He bled where the drip entered his hand. The next day he bled from his nose.

"His platelets are so low that he could bleed from anywhere, internally or externally, possibly quite copiously," said one of the blessed hospice nurses, handing us red towels so it wouldn't distress us quite so much.

They allowed us to wheel my father to the grand piano in the lounge area, and there to hold a gentle party, with wine sipped from plastic pill cups. We propped him up in his techno-bed-seat-on-wheels. Mike played the bass lines at the bottom end of the piano and our dad played the chords further up the keyboard while I sang "Summertime," both the first and last song I sang with him. Gershwin smiled down on us. My dad could barely hold his hands up to play, but the old bastard could still swing.

They installed a small refrigerator in his room for food, and even alcohol, to sustain our vigil. We brought in a sound system so music would light his journey. He was terrified to be alone, so through each night one of us dozed in his room on a rickety, portable bed. One morning, Mark reported a special hour of listening to music together in the middle of the night.

He had a last challenge for me, beyond those you'd expect while walking the final path with a parent. It was my turn on the portable bed, and keeping him company in the early hours of the morning. He started speaking about love. Coherent speech had left him by then, scrambled by illness and weeks of morphine. But enough still remained for him to communicate, with his drug-dry mouth, that he was grateful for all the special moments of love he felt he'd had in his life. His fading mind had conveniently edited out all the bad parts, but I was glad that good memories were the ones to accompany him now.

"An' some grea' kisses," he said, squeezing my hand, "like in hall a' Hillcres' dat day."

He turned his head toward me and opened his eyes, wide and intense. I'd pushed the teenage memory of the awful kiss in the hallway at Hillcrest far, far down and away, but here it was again. I froze, appalled that he'd included this incident in his reminiscences of great romantic moments of his life. His eyes closed again and his grip slackened, leaving me alone to process this revelation. Had he always remembered it in spite of being so drunk, realised it wasn't okay and made a conscious choice to behave as if it never happened? Or had his failing brain now short-circuited and unearthed items that had been buried for decades? Either way, there was not, and had never been, any kind of apology or recognition of wrongdoing. I'd known since adolescence that dark seams ran through my father's character, but had believed that his final years had brought a deep change.

My tangled thoughts and I sat in the softly humming darkness of the hospice night. After a long time, I released his hand and returned to the lumpy wakefulness of the portable bed.

The following day he could no longer sit up. His speech departed entirely the day after that, along with eating. Doris spent the night. "I wouldn't have given ya tuppence for 'im this morning," she said when Dean and I arrived to find him somewhat participating in the building of a model boat. This was one of those Mark ideas I questioned at first, but then I saw that it gave everyone something to do other than sit around and have conversations in which Pa was unable to participate. He couldn't keep his eyes open for more than a couple of minutes at a time, but seemed aware that there was a mission going on. Drills hummed and Mike sloshed tiny metal parts in black paint. When Pa's dinner arrived, we brought out the Shabbat candles, the wine and challah I had brought from home, sang the blessings and wished each other Shabbat Shalom. It was a poignant moment, knowing it would almost certainly be Pa's last Shabbat.

I sat at his bedside as we listened to Oscar Petersen and "The Singers Unlimited", the lanterns now far behind us on our path back to one another. Once again, we listened to "The Shadow of Your Smile". Once again, no words passed between us. But this time our eyes brimmed as the voices closed the circle from that night of the major chord, three-and-a-half decades earlier.

Mark, Mike, Doris and I were at his side at one am on New Year's morning when the rattle of his last breath subsided. The shadow of his smile would indeed colour my dreams and light my dawns, the gifts of his last years having vanquished his earlier selfishness and misdeeds.

I've been more resilient in my interactions with the world as a result of the unplanned survival training I had in my early family life. That resilience has helped me. I am grateful for the lessons in creativity too, along with the lessons in kindness from my mother, and strength from my father. And though she could well have done with more strength and he more kindness, I had both models.

The combination of upbringing and my DNA has, I fear, tilted me toward obsession. But what else would maintain the dogged pursuit of history lost, and scattered shards of self?

My choices in life have ranged from remarkably good to appallingly bad. June's strengths have guided me in some of the better ones. Yet no therapy or soulful wand waving will eradicate the consequences of her failings. I still hurt from her complicity in my wounding.

It helps me to recognise these things, and the forces that delivered her so wretchedly ill-equipped to the challenges of a life with my fascinating but rogue father.

Here they are at their wedding on 4 August 1951. She is nineteen; he is twenty-one. She is three months pregnant with my sister, Toni-Anne.

I encounter a sleeping file in her papers, a parting gift awaiting its moment. It contains three pieces of her writing that I don't recall seeing before, as if a poltergeist had slipped them in since I last looked.

The first is a copy of a typed letter that accompanied videotapes of short documentaries my dad's studio made. There is no indication of the recipient, but she feels the need to describe some of the background.

"Until quite recently, there was a family of elephants still wild in one of the forests. When we made this film, I was on the location and we drove up and down in the elephant trails trying to find them. I was driving the van with Colin out of the roof with his camera and the assistant out of the window with another. My heart was thumping but we never saw them."

It's hard to connect the spunky protagonist of this and many other adventures with the fearful woman who left me such a legacy of disempowerment.

She seemed to not keep copies of her correspondence, but perhaps she kept a copy of this because she liked it, even, perhaps, felt proud of it. Others have kept her letters, saying how they loved her entertaining correspondence.

The second is an "Account of Percy Sledge Documentary — 1991".

"SWAZILAND

Introduction

At the beginning it was to make money. It soon became the most massive ego trip of all time in our studio's life, which wasn't to be for too much longer.

The event was the making of a documentary film of the South African tour of the soul singer, Percy Sledge. It was the idea of an ex-partner of our studio — a brilliant sound engineer, entrepreneur and destined alcoholic. In good faith, he saw the venture as a black and white, half hour music interest film of the tour and more specifically, of the concert in Swaziland where the audience would be 99%

black. AKA Studios was ready for …"

That's all there is — the scant beginnings of a story she also thought worth telling, but abandoned before the end of the second paragraph. The "destined alcoholic" was an early adventure in my mother's own rich, extra marital life that I later discovered. Later, when living in Paris, he had a brief, but intense relationship with Norina as well, to my father's deep consternation, and she relocated for a time to his houseboat on the Seine.

Never simple, my family.

The third piece is handwritten in pencil on three pages of a lined A4 writing pad. It's the beginnings of a story called "The Luyt Brothers".

She clearly lacked most of the information I've now gathered, though her notes on the final two pages, added in pen, show that she'd started digging. She knew that Johan's Uncle Petrus was hanged for murder, and which of his ancestors were blacksmiths, grocers, farmers, tailors and carpenters. She must have written this piece on the basis of the few stories she'd heard, but had to invent most of it. The identities and background of Johan's brothers, and the original migration are far from accurate. But I love it, and ache, that she wrote something, anything, and that she wrote it as a story.

If I'd shown more interest in the family history, devouring less of the time she offered up, and here I feel my father's blood in my veins, might she have shown me these pieces? Or shared her early explorations of the family tree? Could we have reached, together, the knowledge that all versions of Johan's story were in some way true, that history was as much to blame as any one individual, and that our ancestor was someone we could be proud of?

I am sorry, Ma. In these pages I have left behind the sunny memories of your sweetness and entered underground caverns to explore my own need to tell this story. I've found you there, quivering with fear, and beside you a scowling shadow of myself, one hand holding a burden of grudge, the other still trying to protect you from the beasts deeper in the cavern.

I am sorry, Ma, for the ways in which I have added to the litany of loss that has stalked our family. I would love to have shared with you the journey of reclamation, and to climb together back into the sun, our respective burdens left behind. Instead, I make that journey alone, holding out an olive branch and comforting myself with the fantasy of you doing the same, lit by a shaft of Africa, and freed from your darkness to a path beyond my reach.

None of us is so simple or straightforward; neither wholly good nor bad, strong nor weak, wise nor foolish. In each generation we can choose to make sense of who we are and where we came from, to make peace not only with our ancestors, but with ourselves.

I once told Dean, then a teenager, that my adolescence had been lost.

"So, you're having it now," he said with a clarity unburdened by the complications I carry.

"I suppose you're right," I replied as I packed another shimmery dress into the suitcase that would accompany me to my next Port Douglas residency, leaving the family and household in my mother's capable hands. Now, seventeen years after her death, I see the arc of her taking from me, and then giving, giving, giving back.

In a mirage where olive branches touch, her sacrifices meet mine and embrace. Her failings and mine sit down together and share a laugh. Her story is my story, and her not writing it was the greatest gift of all to me.

EPILOGUE

I light candles and pour a glass of wine. Even wearing my strongest glasses, I have to squint at the tiny print on the can of Silvo. Then I pull on the special gloves for handling fine silver.

It is my turn to polish the tea service. It must be forty years since it felt the caress of caring hands.

I am astonished at the gleaming results and gaze at my reflection in the tray; there's a glimpse of my five-year-old grandmother licking her sticky fingers, and another of my mother's resigned face. I feel the ghost breath of the women who have polished these pieces around tables by candlelight, smiling as I work with a soft cloth into the grooves of the intricate handles of the tray.

This tray has been privy to the discussions of government during the Boer War; one of the most challenging wars the British Empire fought prior to the twentieth century, and the conflict that birthed the modern Afrikaner people. The milk jug has delivered a portion of its contents to the teacup of the revered President Steyn. Prime Minister Abraham Fischer, grandfather of Nelson Mandela's legendary lawyer

Bram Fischer, has dipped his teaspoon into this sugar bowl. Incredibly, among the many descendants of Johan Godfried Luyt, I am the custodian history has chosen for this shining relic. It passed from Mary Ann to her odd daughter Grace, then to my mother June, and now to me. Its future will be a matter for others to decide.

For now, it is safe, and its story told.

Acknowledgements

They say it takes a village to raise a child. It's probably been said before, but it's a bit the same with a book.

Teacher and mentor Joanne Fedler opened up the path of actual writing for me, and has walked it beside me these past five years. The combination of her skill, wisdom and plain speaking has been pivotal to my process. Thank you, Jo, for your gifts, and your faith.

Shelley Kenigsberg, editor extraordinaire, thank you for your work on the manuscript, and for teaching me to be much, much more mindful.

I am grateful to the descendants of the Luyt family, who have spent time with me, sharing their relics and their stories. The first was Pam Welch in New Zealand, and her mother Avis Mace, my mother's cousin. Then Daphne Hollis and Margaret Jaco (nee Luyt) in Sydney, Australia. In South Africa: Elena Perel, Marta Luyt, Marietjie Luyt, Paddy Bevan and the Garners. Also, in South Africa, the kindness of Vivienne van der Merwe allowed me, a virtual stranger, to borrow and copy the precious book that accompanied the family tree chart. She shared the voluminous scrapbook of her Uncle Gabriel Luyt, including newspaper cuttings about his illustrious brother, Johan, in Heilbron.

It was not always possible for me to stay in South Africa for long enough to follow some avenues of research. At these times, I received vital assistance from researchers Petrie le Roux in Cape Town, and Derick Griesel in Pretoria.

Once the writing has reached a certain point, the value of feedback from early readers cannot be underestimated. Thank you, Marcia Abboud, for review and feedback on the first full draft to be seen by anyone besides me. And my thanks to readers of a later draft: Mark Ginsburg, Margaret Grove, Glen Heneck, and Xanti Bootcov. A special call out to Xanti, who provided incredibly useful input in a most insightful, helpful manner, even if it did precipitate an eleventh hour restructure. You were right. She then read the whole book for a second time. I'm so grateful, Xanti.

And to all in our writing sisterhood, who continue to provide loving encouragement.

On a practical note, I would not have reached this point without the support of Pauline Lazarus, who for several years protected my "writing Tuesdays" like a lioness.

For the visual aspects, I thank Dean Ginsburg for the lovely images of the silver tea service, and Nailia Minnebaeva for crafting them into the book cover concept.

My thanks to the impressive team at *the kind press*, led by Natasha Gilmour, for pulling it all together, and shepherding me through the publication process for the first time. Your company is well named. Not only is the production process dazzlingly efficient, but your kindness in all our interactions was a comfort as a new author.

Finally, I'm forever grateful to my family for respecting my new need for long stretches of undisturbed time. Especially to Mark. Your love and support, including for my repeated disappearances to far flung parts of the world to write or research, have been essential pillars during these past several years. You are a blessing.

For the historically inclined, or the genealogically interested, these appendices aim to provide background to the lives of the family, and expand on some of the characters in the generations of Luyts leading to Johan, my great grandfather, whose ruin created the mystery I set out to solve.

Following genealogical trails is an endless mission. Those included below are the ones I researched. They exclude many of the spouses' and siblings' trails.

APPENDIX 1: CHRONICLES OF THE EARLY LUYT FAMILY

The Early Days at The Cape

Like many endeavours that sound adventurous and romantic, life in the early Cape of Good Hope was hard. The settlement was vulnerable, but the new fruit and vegetable gardens were soon productive, despite irrigation and other challenges the harsh environment posed. The gardens are still there today, preserved as a calm public space, inhabited by furred and feathered creatures, amid the city bustle.

The ways of the nomadic Khoi and Gorachoqua were mysterious to the Dutch East India Company (VOC), who paid no attention to the seasonal trails and lands used by indigenous people to move and graze their herds. Despite conflicts with the Khoi, the increase of farms of the released VOC employee "free burghers" continued, with areas of the Cape Peninsula starting to look German, rather than African.

The early immigrants described as Germans (though Germany as such did not yet exist), stuck together and often found marriage partners from within their community, with the French Huguenot community also a good source of wives. A group arrived in 1688. They were Calvinist Protestants, driven from France as a result of Louis XIV revoking the near century-old Edict of Nantes, which had granted them substantial rights in the essentially Catholic country. This triggered an exodus from France, including the men, women, and children, who came to the Cape. Within two generations the French language was forgotten, and the descendants of these refugees merged with the Dutch community on every level. But they left an astonishing range of French names littered through generations of early families, including mine.

The arrival of each boatload of new families would have elicited great excitement from the young men, craning their necks along the wharf to catch sight of rustling young skirts and bonnets gratefully disembarking after the long voyage. Who would be the first to offer a gracious arm to the prettiest one?

Anna Groothenning van Bengale

This is the furthest back in history I have reached.

Anna was a Bengali slave, who was shipped from Batavia in her early twenties. It would be four generations before her descendant, Magdalena Johanna Vos, would intersect with one of the Luyts. Anna, I discovered, was shipped to the Cape of Good Hope before 1698. Hans Gerringer, the business partner of one of Johan's ancestors, Christiaan Bok, bought her to serve in their bakery and home. By 1702, she was Christiaan's concubine and had borne their first child, Michiel. They married after several years and children, her baptism and emancipation. In the early Dutch colony, the colour of one's skin was less important than the allegiances of one's soul. My best efforts failed to uncover the origins of the "Groothenning" part of her name.

Friederich Leitt (Luijt, Luit, Luyt)

Friederich sailed to the Cape in 1735, on the Petronella Alida. He was from the Baltic seaport of Königsberg in East Prussia, nestled between Poland and Lithuania, where his father was a distiller. Königsberg later became "Kaliningrad" in Russia.

Friederich was a free burgher in Stellenbosch by the time he married his first wife, Rachel le Roux, in 1741, six years after his arrival at the Cape in the employ of the VOC. The VOC had granted her father, Jean le Roux of Normandy, the farm "Langverwacht" near Stellenbosch in 1721. For many years it belonged to others but is now back in the Le Roux family, and an upmarket guesthouse on the wine route. Friederich and Rachel divorced, and she remarried. I wondered what extreme conditions caused this, given the shortage of females in their society. Perhaps Friederich was a brute. Rachel could surely pick and choose. They had one daughter, Maria.

In 1748, Friederich married the German-Dutch Hendrina Steenbrugge who, at eighteen, was already a widow, though childless. She gave birth to seven children. Their joint will of 1755 states that Friederich was "sickly and bedridden", perhaps the motivation to create the will at that time. The birth of three more children after that suggests he was capable of more in that bed than illness. His end came six years later, in 1761. Small wonder that Hendrina found the protection of a new husband in the unseemly haste of a few months after Friederich's death. She had the clear and present requirement to feed seven children, too young to put out to work, and no education to respectably earn her a living. At only thirty-one years of age, why not benefit from being a rare commodity in a predominantly male community? Johan Michael Steyn, Hendrina's third German husband, also from Königsberg, took on the children. Perhaps he already knew the Luyts through his shared background with Friederich.

Coenraad Luijt (or Luit, or Luyt), b. 1753

Coenraad was eight years old when his father Friederich died. He became a blacksmith, and left his birthplace of Stellenbosch to set up his furnace and tools in the growing settlement at the Cape. He married Johanna Elizabeth Braune, in Cape Town, April 1777. He was twenty-four, she not quite sixteen.

Johanna's shoemaker father, Daniel Coenraad Braune from Saxony-Anhalt in Germany, initiated the torrent of Daniel Coenraads across the length and breadth of the Luyt family tree. Braune was said to be a cruel man who, due to his ill treatment of them, was prohibited from keeping slaves. Ironic that Johanna's father should ill-treat slaves. His own wife had two relatively recent slave ancestors. Her great, great grandfather was Nicolaas Kemp, a mulatto — one white and one dark parent — from Batavia. Nicolaas' wife, Cecilia, was the daughter of Lourens Swerisse, from Holland, and a slave, Dorothe van Angola. In one of history's fun ironies, their daughter married Jacob Kruger, from Germany, giving one of Afrikanerdom's most revered icons, President Paul Kruger, mixed ancestry. It also makes President Kruger my fourth cousin, four times removed. Distant, certainly, but still a shock to have a link.

The pressure must have been immense on Coenraad, the only boy among Friederich's children, to propagate the Luyt name. Could this explain why Coenraad sired eighteen children? Or was he just a horny bastard?

Johanna gave birth to their first child within ten months of marriage. Over the ensuing quarter century, she churned them out at the rate of nearly one per year. Exhausted, no doubt, she died at fifty. Their youngest child was only nine, the first Johan Godfried in a similar stream of like-named Luyts, and the one after whom my great grandfather was named. This earlier Johan and his wife signed as witnesses half-a-century later at the baptism of my great grandfather.

Daniel Coenraad Luyt, b. 1784

Johan's grandfather was the fourth of Coenraad and Johanna's eighteen children. Their first child, also named Daniel Coenraad, perished soon after his first birthday. Their second child, a girl, didn't make it even that far. It's hard to imagine, from the modern perspective, with its high expectations of the reproductive process, how a young couple would keep going after such a tragic start. But they kept going, and going, and going. Eighteen times.

Daniel-Coenraad-who-survived grew up alongside his many brothers and sisters under the grandeur of Table Mountain, to a soundtrack of clanking metal and the hiss of his father Coenraad's furnace. The girls married young, and the boys continued their father's tradition as tradesmen serving the burgeoning city of Cape Town — coopers like Daniel Coenraad making and repairing casks and barrels; tinsmiths and blacksmiths, with one brother branching out to become a general dealer.

It was the time of tall ships in the bay and the imposing "Chavonnes Battery" jutting out into the water, the ruins now a basement museum

at the tourist magnet of "The Waterfront". It had been a prime fortification since its completion by the VOC in 1725, assisting nature's provision of rough seas and wild winds in the seaside defence of the Cape. Half of the modern city, built on reclaimed land, was still ocean, the Castle was still on the shorefront and there was still a Woodstock beach. There were a couple of fine churches, a hospital, the Slave Lodge adjacent, a large, windowless fortress that housed the many VOC slaves. The spaces between blocks were unpaved, turning to mud in winter and dust bowls in summer. Complaints about offal and refuse in the streets, common.

Daniel "married well" at nineteen. His eighteen-year-old wife, Magdalena Johanna Vos was of French and German descent, her wealthy soldier-farmer family dating back to the early days of the settlement. Her father, Johan Hendrik Vos, was the great grandson of the slave, Anna of Bengal.

Johan and Magdalena had eight children, only one of whom died. That left Johan's father Gabriel Jacobus, one girl named Elizabeth, and Johan's five uncles.

The Siblings of Gabriel Jacobus Luyt, Johan's father

Their stories are tantalising, with the promise of many descendants. There is the Jewish strand, Elizabeth having married Charles Benjamin Solomon, son of an early Jewish settler, Benjamin Solomon. She produced ten little Solomons. According to *A History of the Jews in South Africa*, "Benjamin was the forefather of many South Africans, and most of his children married into "Dutch" families."

With no consideration for future genealogists, each of the Luyt boys in Gabriel's family named one of their sons Daniel Coenraad, with a middle name of "Johan" or "Adriaan" sometimes inserted. Imagine family gatherings where five cousins shared the same name.

"Oh Danie, pass the salt, will you?"

But genealogical restraint is indicated, and I will take but one side trip, to acknowledge Johan's ill-fated uncle who left no descendants.

Uncle Petrus

Johan's Uncle Petrus was executed at nineteen years of age. In the legalese of the time, replete with spurious capital letters, here's what happened. *Read aloud for maximum effect.*

"The Jurors for our Lady the Queen, upon their oaths, present:
> That Petrus Johannes Luyt, now or lately a Wagonmaker, and now or lately residing in Castle Street in Cape Town, is guilty of the crime of MURDER:- in that, upon the Thirtieth Day of January, in the Year of our Lord One Thousand Eight Hundred and Thirty eight, and at a certain place, situate on the Sea Beach, near the Castle, and about the distance of eighteen yards from the Wreck of the Vessel called the Antelope, and in Cape Town aforesaid, the said

Petrus Johannes Luyt did wrongfully, unlawfully, and maliciously assault Jan Jansen, the Younger, Son of Jan Jansen, the Elder, a Sawyer, and lately residing in a Lane, called Opperkant, in Cape Town aforesaid, and did then and there, with a Razor, or with some other Instrument to the Prosecutor unknown, cut and mortally wound the said Jan Jansen, the Younger, upon his Neck, and other parts of his Body; of which said cutting and mortally wounding, the said Jan Jansen, the Younger, did languish, and languishing did live from the said Thirtieth Day of January, to the Thirteenth Day of February, in the said Year of our Lord; on which said Thirteenth Day of February, and at the House of the said Jan Jansen, the Elder, situate in the Lane, called Opperkant aforesaid, in Cape Town aforesaid, the said Jan Jansen, the Younger, of the said cutting and mortally wounding, did die, and thus the said Jan Jansen, the Younger, was killed and murdered by the said Petrus Johannes Luyt, of his malice aforethought."

I think that means that Petrus attacked Jan with a lethal pointy thing and Jan later died from his wounds. A stupid, wasteful encounter between over-stimulated young men, possibly aggravated by alcohol. Petrus was hanged on 1 June 1838, leaving his sister, five brothers and their grieving parents to console one another.

Gabriel Jacobus Luyt, b. 1814

Johan's father Gabriel Jacobus Luyt was the seventh child of Daniel-Coenraad-who-survived, and Magdalena Johanna Vos, descendant of Anna of Bengal. Gabriel was named after his maternal French great grandfather who married his French first cousin, Elizabeth. They did that in those days. He followed in his grandfather Coenraad's footsteps and became a blacksmith. There was no evidence of Gabriel having attended school, but his signature on the death certificate of his wife, Helena Gertruida Barendina Berning, was strong and attractive.

Helena was the one with noble French heritage, generations of Spanish royalty before that, and a line through ancient Rome and Judean kings all the way back to King David of Israel, says Geni.com. Did the Luyts know she had added all that royalty to their DNA? Johan and all his siblings carried her royal bloodline forward from that genealogical point.

Gabriel and Helena named their firstborn Daniel Coenraad, naturally. This new Daniel was the first of the siblings to marry; his bride, Dorothea, was another descendant of French nobility. I imagine Johan as a six-year-old pageboy, saying, "Let *me* stand in front with them … no, me, me!" Daniel was the first in this line of Luyts to move away from the trades, he became an accountant.

He was also the first to die, a week after his thirty-fourth birthday. It is hard to imagine the preciousness of those seven days, during which he signed his will and welcomed his daughter Dorothea to the world. His death notice didn't state the cause of death, but the timing of the will suggests he knew he was dying. His widow Dorothea, aged twenty-nine, was left with six children at their home in Long Street, Cape Town, including a newborn.

It's not surprising that she sent the three boys to live with three different uncles, hard as it must have been to split up the family. One was named — yes — Daniel Coenraad. He went to live with his Uncle Johan, my great grandfather, in Heilbron. This Daniel Coenraad was known as "Coenie". He was the one who married Mary Ann's sister, Winnie, becoming Johan's brother-in-law and nephew, he was imprisoned for two years in Bermuda during the Boer War.

Out of Johan's six siblings, one other — his older brother Pieter Christiaan Berning Luyt — also migrated to the young Republic of the Orange Free State. Pieter had eighteen children. Records show many linkages between his and Johan's families.

The branches, and stories, of this generation beckon and tantalise, as did the one before. Perhaps I will live long enough to take excursions into more of them.

Johan Godfried Luyt, b. 1852

The pages of this book have told much of his story. The full wordings of some public letters and statements can be found attached to his record on Geni.com, along with further images. I hope this resource will grow over time, and that more descendants will feel motivated to add additional content about Johan and Mary Ann and their descendants, only some of whose stories have so far been recorded.

APPENDIX 2: THE PRESIDENTS WHO ENTERED THE BOER WAR

Afrikaner nationalist, Marthinus Theunis Steyn, was born on a farm in the Republic of the Orange Free State (OFS) in 1857, and had little systematic education before he was sent to Grey College in Bloemfontein, aged twelve. The brilliant young man was called to the Bar in 1882 at the Inner Temple in London, returning to South Africa to built a flourishing law practice in Bloemfontein. Steyn became Attorney General, and was appointed to  the High Court in 1889. He held himself aloof from politics, however, until in 1895 President Reitz resigned, and the charismatic Steyn offered himself as a candidate. Steyn's platform was to pursue a policy of "economic independence and protection of the Dutch language against English-speaking immigrant influences". The OFS population had a good sprinkling of Scots, Germans, and Englishmen among the greater population of Dutch people.

In one of many such paradoxes, his opponent, who favoured alignment with the British, was the uncle of Steyn's Scottish wife, Tibbie Fraser, whose family of ministers had aligned early with the Dutch Reformed Church. Despite her background, she considered herself a Boer, later known as "mother of the nation".

Leadership in the other young Boer Republic, the Transvaal, had been less successful than in the OFS.

The discovery of gold, and the hordes of gold-searchers who arrived from around the world, raised a ragtag tent-and-tin city that became the metropolis of Johannesburg. Living conditions were makeshift and challenging, the men created families with local black women and white women brave enough to follow them. Their numbers mushroomed into communities with needs. General dealers, blacksmiths and other tradesmen followed, barely able to keep up with the demand. Mining claims, disputes, deals and chopping up of farms called for lawyers.

The sprint soon pushed the country into chaos, with burghers refusing to pay taxes, government debts mounting, no money for schools, roads or services, the Volksraad arguing and accomplishing little.

Enter the revered Boer leader, Paul Kruger.

Kruger was a child of the Great Trek. He was the strictest of Calvinists, interpreting the *Bible* so literally that he once assured Captain Slocum, the American circumnavigator, that the world was flat. Despite his quick mind and reputation for astuteness, Kruger was barely literate. He was said to read nothing other than the Bible. Even the act of signing his name required a great effort. I couldn't help think how far this image was from the near-divine personage I had encountered in my history studies, such as they were. I learned only much later, he and I shared some ancestors — and that they were dark-skinned — no shortage of irony in South African history.

Kruger rose early each day, held a religious service for his sixteen children, then held court from the "stoep" (outside veranda) of his modest house in Pretoria, drinking copious cups of coffee and smoking his pipe. A huge man with a large head and less-than-handsome face, he apparently spoke as if sermonising, the great jaws and cheeks heaving. He impressed with his sheer strength of will, even though he was perceived to be uncouth and surly.

The British, after losing the first Boer War, had retreated somewhat sourly, having concluded that the useless lands of the Boer Republics were not worth all this trouble. But then came the discovery of gold in the largest quantities on Earth. Not only was the wealth irresistible, it also provided Britain with a pretext for getting involved.

To maintain control of the wealth, the Transvaal government had decreed that "Uitlanders" — foreigners — only got voting rights after having lived in the country for fourteen years. This didn't bother most prospectors, who were there purely to make their fortunes. But the British government leapt to the "moral cause" of their subjects and all others thus disenfranchised.

In these efforts, the British Government was represented by the cold and arrogant Lord Milner, the new High Commissioner. He believed that Englishmen must not be ruled by others. With support from Colonial Secretary Chamberlain, and with more than a little interest in the treasures beneath the rolling hills, he led Britain down a path of provocation.

In 1899, President Steyn led a conference between President Kruger, and Lord Milner, in a desperate attempt to avert war. He did everything in his power, but Milner had asked for conditions that he knew Kruger would refuse. The latter obliged, famously and correctly saying, "It is my country that you want," leaving the conference with tears running down his pouchy face.

Despite continued efforts from the leaders of the two Boer republics, Britain's desire for war was clear. "Peace feelers and compromising mediation were ignored or brushed aside for fear not that they would fail, but that they might succeed."[10]

Neither president would lead their republics to the end of the war.

APPENDIX 3: THE CURIOUS TALE OF 'CAPTAIN' WEILERT

My great grandmother was Mary Ann Christina Weilert. Family stories indicated that her father, Christiaan Frederich Weilert, was a sea captain, born in 1835 in the tiny mining town of Wildemann, the Kingdom of Hanover, later a part of the central heart of Germany. Christiaan, apparently of noble birth, met and married Rosina Marie Clements in Colchester, England. At some unknown date, they left for South Africa, and settled in Heilbron around 1853.

But my attempts to confirm this story only raised questions.

There was no town of Heilbron in the OFS in 1853. It seemed odd, too, that a sea captain would be drawn to a hamlet nearly 500 kilometres from the sea in a wild area not yet declared a country. How, too, could someone be a sea captain at age eighteen?

A little online digging revealed the following.

- The British German Legion was a group of German soldiers recruited to fight for Britain in the Crimean War. The recruitment process of 1855 was dubious, conducted in taverns,

and targeting inebriated young men. In 1856, members of the legion were reported to be billeted at Barrack field in Colchester Garrison. They didn't make it onto a battlefield before the war ended, but many had by then married local women. The Legion was disbanded near the end of that year and most members were resettled in South Africa.
- Christiaan's insolvency papers from 1881 say he is a "butcher". His 1893 death notice records his profession as that of a "general dealer".
- The name "Weilert" was first found in Upper Swabia more than a millennium ago. It was close to Heilbronn in Hanover, which would later become a part of Germany.
- In the British census of 1861, Rosina Clement's father was listed as a "Mariner".

Here's my version:

Christiaan Weilert, a footloose young man of modest nobility and privilege, and no profession, had visited a tavern one night, and could only vaguely remember the generous stranger who plied him with drinks.

A few days later, he found himself in uniform, with some compatriots on a ship to England. He was not unhappy; he could see nothing more exciting than training to be a soldier on his present horizon.

He trained with the British German Legion at their barracks in Colchester, Essex. The Crimean War ended before the Legion saw any military action, but there was plenty of action at the barracks.

Rosina Clements, the daughter of a British sea captain, was one of the adventurous young women of Colchester. Many local women were said to have made their interest in the soldiers known. She and Christiaan married, and were among the many couples who took up the military's offer to start a new life abroad. They arrived in South Africa in the late 1850s and travelled to the interior, having heard about the lands of opportunity. The couple supplied farmers and townsfolk with meat and other provisions for years before Heilbron's official naming in 1873, already establishing their family, four daughters. They'd always called their tiny community "Heilbron" ("Spring of Bliss") — perfect, really, given Christiaan's heritage and the ceaseless bubbling of the pristine stream from the earth near the centre of the town.

Fanciful? Perhaps. But the pieces fitted, and eliminated the holes in the story.

This photograph of Christiaan, Rosina and their youngest daughter, Winnie, is from 1882, the year Mary Ann and Johan's first child was born. It intrigued me. What sort of stars were those on Christiaan's waistcoat? And what sort of hat was that?

Christiaan Weilert died in March 1893, just over a year before the birth of my grandmother Grace. He was buried in the cemetery in Heilbron. His headstone reads, "After life's struggles may his rest be sweet".

About the author

Author Photo by Mark Zworestine

Judy Campbell is an author, composer and lyricist. Her work has featured on recordings, in a new musical, and she has written many music related articles.

Judy was born in Cape Town, South Africa, to a family of musicians. Despite early musical promise — and contrary to family tradition — she began working as a computer programmer by the age of 17. She spent the next 25 years working in Information Technology, all whilst writing lyrics and singing in bands. Judy and her husband migrated to Australia in 1982.

In 1999, she left IT and turned her full attention to music, taking up the job of Choir Director at North Shore Temple Emanuel in Sydney.

In 2003, she founded the world jazz group MOSAIC, with whom she went on to compose three albums of original music and perform on six national and international tours spanning seven years. She is the founding director of the Australian Jewish Choral Festival, inaugurated in 2012.

In what began as a record of the rise and mysterious ruin of her great grandfather, *The Silver Tea Service* grew into a personal memoir about the ironies of history, the unexpected personal outcomes of her quest and the stories it uncovered.

Judy is currently working on her next book, based on the story of a Bengali slave in the early days of the Cape Colony and how it unexpectedly found expression in the politics of the 20th century in South Africa.

Bibliography

Churchill, Winston 1990, *The Boer War*, W. W. Norton Publishers, New York.

Davenport, J 2013, *Digging Deep*, Jonathan Ball Publishers, South Africa.

Farwell, Byron 2009, *The Great Boer War*, Pen and Sword Military; Republished edition, South Yorkshire.

Harrison, David 1983, *The White Tribe of Africa*, University of California Press, California.

Nasson, B 2010, *The War for South Africa*, an imprint of NB Publishers Tafelberg, South Africa.

Rayne Kruger 1996, *Goodbye Dolly Gray: The Story of the Boer War*, Pimlico, United Kingdom.

Van Heyningen, E 2013, *Concentration Camps of the Anglo-Boer War, A Social History*, Jacana Media, South Africa.

Worden, van Heyningen, Bickford-Smith 1998, *The Making of a City: An Illustrated Social History*, David Philip Publishers, South Africa.

References

Braby Directory of the Orange River Colony. Selected years from 1898-1910.

For Queen and Empire, a Boer War Chronicle, New South Wales Military History Society. (75th ed.)

Herrman, L 1935, *A History of the Jews in South Africa,* Cape Town.

Philip Pienaar of the Transvaal Telegraphic Service Methuen & Co 1902, *With Steyn and De Wet,* Project Gutenberg.

The Cape Odyssey 101, Historical Media, South Africa.

The Project Gutenberg eBook of The Peace Negotiations, a gathering from 1908 of the actual minutes and correspondence documenting in ferocious detail the processes, meetings and emotions of the Peace of Vereeniging.

Archives

Archives of the First National Bank of South Africa.

National Archives of South Africa, Bloemfontein, Cape Town and Pretoria.

National Library of South Africa, Cape Town repository. (NLSA)

Rabone, A (ed.) 1966, Records of a Pioneer Family, Cape Town.

Newspapers

Excerpts from *The Bloemfontein Friend,* from 1907-1910. (NLSA)

Articles

"Kindergarten School Built in 1884", by Quarta Pretorius of Heilbron. Translated from Afrikaans by Petrie Le Roux.

Websites

familysearch.org
geni.com
myheritage.com
stamouers.com

Family documents

"Some Reminiscences of the Boer War" by Edith Cora Wilson (born van Rooyen). Provided by her nephew-in-law, Rory Kroon.

"Memoirs of Rosie Luyt" by Edith Cora Wilson. Provided by her daughter, Daphne Hollis.

Notes

[1] "Boer" is Afrikaans for "farmer". Its popular meaning has changed over time, but the term is generally used as a description of an Afrikaans speaking South African of European descent.

[2] *Braby Directory of the Orange River Colony*, 1907.

[3] Heilbron, Northern Free State, 2012. showme.co.za.

[4] *Heilbron Herald*, June 1899.

[5] *Heilbron Herald*, 25 January 1907. Source: Vivienne van der Merwe, Cape Town.

[6] *Los Angeles Times*. http://articles.latimes.com/1985-03-05/news/mn-12467_1_controversial-book.

[7] Wikipedia. https://en.wikipedia.org/wiki/White_South_Africans.

[8] *The Boer War*, by Winston Churchill.

[9] Much of this section draws on *The Project Gutenberg eBook of The Peace Negotiations*. A gathering from 1908 of the actual minutes and correspondence documenting, in ferocious detail, the processes, meetings and emotions of the Peace of Vereeniging.

[10] Bill Nasson 2010, *The War for South Africa*, Tafelberg, an imprint of NB Publishers, Cape Town.

www.ingramcontent.com/pod-product-compliance
Lightning Source LLC
Chambersburg PA
CBHW062056290426
44110CB00022B/2613